The BRICS Legal Cooperation and Perspectives

Tao Du • Xiuyan Fei
Editors

The BRICS Legal Cooperation and Perspectives

Springer

Editors
Tao Du
International Law School
East China University of Political Science and Law
Shanghai, China

Xiuyan Fei
International Law School
East China University of Political Science and Law
Shanghai, China

ISBN 978-981-95-4355-7 ISBN 978-981-95-4356-4 (eBook)
https://doi.org/10.1007/978-981-95-4356-4

This Springer imprint is published by the registered company Springer Nature Singapore Pte Ltd.
The registered company address is: 152 Beach Road, #21-01/04 Gateway East, Singapore 189721, Singapore

Contents

Part I
The BRICS Legal Approach to Regional Cooperation

Chapter 1
The Role of BRICS in the Formation of Regional Monetary Unions

Mekhti Mekhtiev

Abstract The article analyses current trends in international monetary law. Though the international monetary and financial system is amenable to never-ending changes, its international legal regulation evolves over time in a slower pace. To reveal the nature of these trends, it is necessary to employ comparative methods for studying new treaties and existing universal one. New treaties not only enrich current international law but also demonstrate how the meaning of provisions in existing treaties evolves over time. Comparative international law is supplemented by the synthesis of regional treaties and treaties adopted by BRICS countries. The article concludes that regionalisation itself contributes to universal regulation but the process of transformation of universal monetary law is driven not only by the International Monetary Fund (IMF) but also by BRICS countries.

Keywords International monetary law · Regional monetary unions · BRICS monetary regulation · Universal monetary regulation · Fragmentation of international law

1 Introduction

International monetary law is known to be one of the most dynamic branches of international economic law. The regionalisation, fragmentation and the emergence of alternative reserve currencies accelerate the evolution of international monetary law. On top of it, anti-Russian sanctions of 2022 undermine the trust to a Western financial infrastructure, which is practically an exclusive, monopolistic (in global

M. Mekhtiev (✉)
Laboratory of legal research on new forms of intergovernmental cooperation and integration, Institute of Legislation and Comparative Law under the Government of the Russian Federation, Moscow, Russian Federation

T. Du, X. Fei (eds.), *The BRICS Legal Cooperation and Perspectives*,
https://doi.org/10.1007/978-981-95-4356-4_1

level) payment system. But the lack of the trustful financial system disturbs the functioning of the global economy and its international legal regulation. Thus, it might be assumed that creating an alternative international monetary and financial system is not only the geopolitical or economic task but also a necessity to restore the smooth functioning of international monetary law.

The fragmentation mentioned above is one of the most important challenges. It has multi-layered characteristics. The first level concerns international economic law itself, since its sub-branches may regulate trade, investment and monetary affairs independently.[1] Another level concerns regional treaties, which establish regional legal mechanisms to regulate local (regional) markets.[2] These treaties may detail universally recognised norms of international law differently and cause fragmentation.[3] But the most challenging fragmentation is a divide in the global level, what the International Monetary Fund (IMF) calls the "geoeconomic fragmentation".[4] This challenge needs to be evaluated based on the BRICS+ concept, as it is the only alternative to existing model of regulation and has the capacity to develop coordination mechanisms for regional organisations. This divide also touches the concepts of inter-regional regulation. Therefore, the assumption in this article is that the regulation of inter-regional relations based on BRICS+ forum might be a way to restore international legal unity. At the same time, this work focuses only on the regulation of interstate currency relations as BRICS itself is focused on this sphere.[5] For this purpose the paper also provides by means of comparative international law the evaluation of regional legal systems, where Russia, China and India participate.[6]

[1] The fragmentation is caused by "the emergence of specialized and (relatively) autonomous rules or rule-complexes, legal institutions and spheres of legal practice", as it is stated in the first sentence of the para. 6 of the Report of the Study Group of the International Law Commission "Fragmentation of International Law: Difficulties Arising from the Diversification and Expansion of International Law", Fifty-eighth session. A/CN.4/L.702. 18 July 2006; see also: Abubakar Isa Umar. The Fragmentation/Bifurcation of International Economic Law: The Doctrine of Legal Convergence to the Rescue. International Journal of Law, Humanities & Social Science. Volume 2, Issue 4 (March 2018), P. 25–26.

[2] For example, Regional Comprehensive Economic Partnership Agreement (RCEP); Treaty on the Eurasian Economic Union, Treaty on the Functioning of the European Union; etc.

[3] These issues will be discussed in following chapters.

[4] Aiyar, Shekhar, Ilyina, Anna, et. al. (2023). Geoeconomic Fragmentation and the Future of Multilateralism. Staff Discussion Note SDN/2023/001. International Monetary Fund, Washington, DC.

[5] Unlike monetary affairs BRICS has not adopted any trade treaty, while there are the Treaty for the Establishment of a BRICS Contingent Reserve Arrangement and the Agreement on the New Development Bank (both adopted in July 15, 2014, Fortaleza, Brazil).

[6] The choice of these regional legal systems is based on the fact that BRICS originally started with the meeting of the ministers of foreign affairs of Russia, India and China in 2002, (last visited Feb. 6, 2024) https://www.nkibrics.ru/posts/show/5cfa52836272692ee0170000.

2 Modern International Monetary Law and Its Foundations

The modern global financial architecture and its international regulation start with the abolition of the gold parity in 1971.[7] Until 1971 there was a par value, i.e. currency exchange rates of developed countries were fixed to the US dollar, and the US dollar exchange rate to gold prices.[8] But the gold prices were also formed by market forces. This deduction can be drawn from the fact that Western countries' central banks attempted to keep the gold prices at a certain level, what M. Bordo, E. Monnet and A. Naef called an unprecedented cooperation.[9] It also means that central banks' roles and mandates in international law have evolved, as well as international monetary law itself.

On the other hand, Lowenffeld characterises this transformation not as the evolution but as a revolution, when he says about the IMF that "*the institution was preserved—that is, the skeleton; but the fundamental rule was replaced by a non-rule, and the mission gradually changed*".[10]

One can agree with this conclusion but only if one does not lean on the principles of the IMF's constituent act. Even if the mission of the IMF has changed, still it is not a fundamental transformation, and hence it is not a revolution. This is evidenced by the fact that there was a change in the international monetary system by the transition from a fixed exchange rate to free floating and other regimes according to the new wordings of the IMF's founding treaty:

> Under an international monetary system of the kind prevailing on January 1, 1976, exchange arrangements may include (i) the maintenance by a member of a value for its currency in terms of the special drawing right or another denominator, other than gold, selected by the member, or (ii) cooperative arrangements by which members maintain the value of their currencies in relation to the value of the currency or currencies of other members, or (iii) other exchange arrangements of a member's choice.[11]

This new provisions mean that if before the amendment of the IMF Articles of Agreement all Western currencies exchange rates were pegged to the US dollar and the US dollar to gold, while gold prices were formed by market forces, then after this amendment (of the IMF Articles of Agreement) the Western currencies'

---

[7] It led to amending of the IMF Articles of Agreement; see FRS. The Smithsonian Agreement. Federal Reserve History, (last visited Feb. 6, 2024) https://www.federalreservehistory.org/essays/smithsonian-agreement.

[8] *Ibid.*

[9] Bordo, Michael D. and Monnet, Eric and Naef, Alain, The Gold Pool (1961–1968) and the Fall of the Bretton Woods System. Lessons for Central Bank Cooperation (November 2017). NBER Working Paper No. w24016, Available at SSRN (last visited Feb. 6, 2024): https://ssrn.com/abstract=3070040. P. 2.

[10] See the reference: Lowenfeld, Andreas F., "The International Monetary System: A Look Back Over Seven Decades," Journal of International Economic Law 13(3), p. 582; in: Thorstensen V., Müller C., How Does International Trade Regulation Addresses Exchange Rates Measures? Revista Direito GV, São Paulo. 10(2), 2014. P. 382.

[11] Articles of Agreement of the International Monetary Fund, Art. IV, Section 2(b).

exchange rates are formed directly by market forces, i.e. gold and the US dollar were abolished as mediators. The basic principle of market based exchange rates is preserved; thus it is not a revolution.

Moreover, the states' obligations on exchange arrangements are part of the broader international legal framework. The General Agreement on Tariffs and Trade states, that:

> Any contracting party which is not a member of the Fund [the IMF; added by the author] shall, within a time to be determined by the CONTRACTING PARTIES after consultation with the Fund, become a member of the Fund, or, failing that, enter into a special exchange agreement with the CONTRACTING PARTIES. A contracting party which ceases to be a member of the Fund shall forthwith enter into a special exchange agreement with the CONTRACTING PARTIES. Any special exchange agreement entered into by a contracting party under this paragraph shall thereupon become part of its obligations under this Agreement.[12]

The above-mentioned provisions refer to the IMF Articles of Agreement, which member-states are obliged "*to avoid competitive exchange depreciation*".[13] Though the competition in international economic relations is regulated by the GATT in broader sense,[14] still the monopoly of the IMF's founding agreement concerning exchange rate arrangements on universal level is recognised in the GATT, as the latter states that:

> The terms of any such agreement [on exchange rate arrangement; added by the author] shall not impose obligations on the contracting party in exchange matters generally more restrictive than those imposed by the Articles of Agreement of the International Monetary Fund on members of the Fund.[15]

Therefore, it should be stated that one of the core principles of the international monetary law is to pursue orderly exchange rate system, its stability based on the rate that is in conformity with market prices.[16] It is the competition that forms market prices, and exchange rates of currencies must comply with it. In other words international monetary law regulates not the competition itself but relations concerning exchange rate, which also should lead to "*reasonable price stability*"[17] in global markets.

The price stability is also an object of national legislations. *Prima facie*, there are signs of a clear separation between international and national legal regulation on this matter. International law achieves price stability mainly by regulating exchange rates of currencies as primary aim, while national laws usually (though not always and exclusively) rely on stabilisation of prices in national markets as primary aim of

---

[12] General Agreement on Tariffs and Trade (GATT 1947), Art. XV, para. 6.

[13] Articles of Agreement of the International Monetary Fund, Art. I (iii).

[14] Article I of the General Agreement on Tariffs and Trade requires equal conditions for international trade.

[15] General Agreement on Tariffs and Trade (GATT 1947), Art. XV, para. 7 (b).

[16] Articles of Agreement of the International Monetary Fund, Articles I (iii) and IV (i).

[17] *Id.* Article IV.

central banks. The central banks are mandated to use their key rate, exchange rate interventions, etc.[18] As a result, this interaction (of international law and national law) is not trouble-free.

It can be illustrated by analysing BRICS states national monetary laws. Brazilian Constitution assigns to the central bank the exclusive competence to issue currency.[19] Its legislation also establishes the National Monetary Council[20] and empowers it to conduct monetary policy "*in such a way as to further regular operation of the exchange market, exchange rate stability and balance of payments equilibrium*".[21]

The Russian Constitution states similar provision on the Bank of Russia.[22] It then requires that "[p]*rotecting and ensuring the stability of the rouble shall be the principal function of the Central Bank of the Russian Federation...*"[23] Indian law on its Reserve Bank also establishes that "*the primary objective of the monetary policy is to maintain price stability...*"[24]

Unlike previous countries, the Chinese legislation establishes the currency regime itself, as it declares that the "*unitary and well-managed floating exchange rate system that is based on market supply and demand will be carried out to the exchange rates of Renminbi.*"[25] And finally, the South African law defines national central bank's exclusive mandate as "*protecting and maintaining financial stability...*"[26]

Central banks' exclusive powers and their independence from other executive authorities do not mean that they are private persons.[27] Neither it means an absolute independence but only a functional independence[28] to conduct monetary policy and

[18] Except treaties that establish integrated organisations, e.g. the Treaty on the Functioning of the European Union in its Article 127 (para. 1) empowers the European Central Bank to maintain price stability.

[19] Constitution of the Federal Republic of Brazil, Art. 164.

[20] Law 4.595, dated 12/31/1964—National Financial System, Art. 2., (last visited Feb. 6, 2024) https://www.bcb.gov.br/content/about/legislation_norms_docs/Law%204.595%2C%20dated%2012_31_1964%20-%20National%20Financial%20System.pdf.

[21] *Id.* The first sentence of Article 11 (III).

[22] Constitution of the Russian Federation, Art. 75, part 1, (last visited Feb. 6, 2024) https://rm.coe.int/constitution-of-the-russian-federation-en/1680a1a237.

[23] *Id.* Part 2.

[24] The third sentence of the Preamble of the Reserve Bank of India Act, 1934, (last visited Feb. 6, 2024) https://www.indiacode.nic.in/bitstream/123456789/2398/1/a1934-2.pdf.

[25] Regulations of the People's Republic of China on Foreign Exchange Control, Art. 33, (last visited Feb. 6, 2024) http://www.asianlii.org/cn/legis/cen/laws/rotprocofec630/.

[26] South African Reserve Bank Act, para. 3, URL: https://www.gov.za/documents/south-africanreserve-bank-act-24-mar-2015-1516.

[27] Though some are established as legal persons, e.g. Federal Law No. 86-FZ of 10.07.2002 (as amended on 24.07.2023) "On the Central Bank of the Russian Federation (Bank of Russia)" (with amendments and additions, intro. effective from 12.09.2023), Art. 1.

[28] As an example see Judgment ECLI:EU:C:2003:395 Commission of the European Communities v European Central Bank, para. 126 (last visited Feb. 6, 2024) https://curia.europa.eu/juris/liste.jsf?language=en&jur=C,T,F&num=C-11/00&td=ALL.

promote exchange rate stability without unfair political interference into the market economy.[29] Finally, central banks—empowered by legislation—may act in international level as state bodies, though not all legislations assume that central banks can conclude an intergovernmental agreement.[30] One can conclude that national laws can define the value of its own currency, while international law regulates exchange rates to limit states policies on exchange rate of their national currencies.

This interaction of international law and national law causes dilemma for central banks, because in some cases they must choose between stabilising prices through exchange rate arrangements under international law in international markets and stabilising prices in national markets under national laws. It causes a compelled gap in international law, because the IMF Articles of Agreement can state only recommendations on monetary policy coordination and not the obligation to coordinate them.[31] It thus might be assumed that states will consider such a coordination obligation as a vital reduction of their monetary sovereignty, because it might mean for them the stabilisation of the international financial system at the cost of the national financial stability.

There are different ideas how to eliminate this dilemma. One is to assign to the Financial Safety Board powers to determine the standards of monetary regulation, while the IMF would assess the compliance of domestic regulation of countries with such standards.[32] Another one is to strengthen the role of special drawing rights (SDR) of the IMF in international settlements.[33] This, in fact, would turn the IMF into a global regulator, i.e. the central bank of the central banks. It would also mean that the IMF would be authorised to emit and absorb SDR as it was a universal currency even with a limited turnover. Thus, international reserves of states with a surplus of the balance of payments would become an instrument for financing other countries with deficit balance of payments, which would empower the IMF to conduct foreign exchange interventions.[34] However, there may be a difficulty, which can be expressed in the rhetorical question: how likely do states agree to transfer such authority of central banks (exchange rate interventions) to an international organisation?

---

[29] See First Lamfalussy Lecture by Mario Draghi, President of the ECB, at the Banque Nationale de Belgique, Brussels, October 26, 2018, (last visited Feb. 6, 2024) https://www.ecb.europa.eu/press/key/date/2018/html/ecb.sp181026.en.html.

[30] For example, the Russian legislation, where the Bank of Russia only recommends concluding a treaty: Federal Law No. 101-FZ of July 15, 1995, (as amended on Dec. 8, 2020) "On International Treaties of the Russian Federation", Art. 8, para. 1.

[31] Articles of Agreement of the International Monetary Law, Art. IV.

[32] Eichengreen B., Out of the Box Thoughts about the International Financial Architecture, IMF Working Papers. WP/09/116. 2009, (last visited Feb. 6, 2024) https://www.imf.org/external/pubs/ft/wp/2009/wp09116.pdf. P. 18.

[33] *Id*. P. 9–10.

[34] See Modern concept of Interaction between International and Domestic Law: monograph, editor-in-chief A. Y. Kapustin, Moscow, The Institute of Legislation and Comparative Law under the Government of the Russian Federation: Norma: INFRA-M, 2023. Pp. 317–318.

But it is not a full picture of the subject matter. Article 4 of the IMF Articles of Agreement starts with the following wordings:

> Recognizing that the essential purpose of the international monetary system is to provide a framework that facilitates the exchange of goods, services, and capital among countries, and that sustains sound economic growth, and that a principal objective is the continuing development of the orderly underlying conditions that are necessary for financial and economic stability.[35]

In other words, it means that neither the IMF member-states nor the IMF itself is responsible for the (1) trans-boundary movement of goods, services and capital, for (2) sound economic growth or (3) economic stability, as these both are the purposes of the international monetary system. Moreover, the principal task of this system (not the IMF and its member-states) is "*the continuing development of the orderly underlying conditions*",[36] which means that the stability of the global monetary system may be achieved only if exchange rate arrangements reflect these conditions.[37]

Nevertheless, there are another hidden issue within the same Article 4, which concerns the provisions on national social and economic policies. It is not clear whether different economic and social systems and policies of states—which must be respected by the IMF[38]—are in conformity with the task to promote "*the orderly underlying conditions*"[39] by international monetary system mentioned above. It is also not clear whether a choice of exchange rate arrangements by a member-state[40] may affect negatively other countries' economic interests and cause the amendment of their exchange rate regulation. This provision also does not necessarily create conditions for achieving stability of the international monetary system. It might cause a fundamental contradiction since member-states leave the regulation on international affairs concerning the movement of capital, its stability and economic growth to the international monetary system, while their obligations do not necessarily maintain such a system.

---

[35] Articles of Agreement of the International Monetary Fund, the first sentence of Art. IV.

[36] *Ibid.*

[37] IMF, "Article IV of the Fund's Articles of Agreement: an Overview of the Legal Framework", IMF Legal Department, June 28, 2006. P. 2, (last visited Feb. 6, 2024) https://www.imf.org/en/Publications/Policy-Papers/Issues/2016/12/31/Article-IV-of-the-Fund-s-Articles-of-Agreement-An-Overview-of-the-Legal-Framework-PP3883.

[38] *Id.* Section 3(b).

[39] Articles of Agreement of the International Monetary Fund, the first sentence of Art. IV.

[40] *Id.* Section 2(b).

3 Regional Treaties and Currency Relations

Ironically, despite the founders' recognition in the IMF's constituent act that the international monetary and financial system itself chases its own stability (as its mentioned above), the globalisation led to various shocks since late 1990s,[41] which stimulate the regionalisation. These regional agreements (unlike the universal one) expand the powers of central banks to coordinate their policies with other central banks in order to both (1) stabilise the regional financial systems of the regions and (2) ensure the integration.[42]

The interaction of universal agreements with regional agreements in international economic law is a distinct issue. While the GATT in its Article XXIV establishes provisions on regional agreements, the IMF Articles of Agreement deals with member-states only.[43]

3.1 *Eurasian Economic Union*

One of the examples of the central bank cooperation for exchange rate regulation is Article 64 of the Treaty on the Eurasian Economic Union (EAEU). It directly and clearly enshrines the obligations of the member-states to promote mutual convertibility of their currencies and conduct coordinated monetary policies by central banks based on the following principles:

1) gradual implementation of harmonization and convergence of approaches to the formation and conduction of the currency policy to the extent where it corresponds the current macroeconomic integration cooperation demand;

[41] The most significant crises were the Asian currency crisis of 1997, see IMF, The Asian Crisis: Causes and Cures, June 1998, Volume 2, (last visited Feb. 6, 2024) https://www.imf.org/external/pubs/ft/fandd/1998/06/imfstaff.htm; the Global Economic crisis of 2008, see Federal Reserve History, The Great Recession and Its Aftermath, November 22, 2013 (last visited Feb. 6, 2024) https://www.federalreservehistory.org/essays/great-recession-and-its-aftermath; the Eurozone debt crisis of 2010, see Britannica, The euro-zone debt crisis, (last visited Feb. 6, 2024) https://www.britannica.com/topic/European-Union/The-euro-zone-debt-crisis; currency crisis since 2012 till modern days: Harvard Business School, Global Crises Data by Country, (last visited Feb. 6, 2024) https://www.hbs.edu/behavioral-finance-and-financial-stability/data/Pages/global.aspx.

[42] Though almost all regions of the world have regional financial mechanisms to regulate exchange rate, or provide foreign liquidity, still this paper evaluates only some of them, as it is hardly possible to cover them all in a single article.

[43] See the discussion of dilemmas concerning monitoring of member states' monetary policies by the IMF, which does not cover monetary policies of monetary unions, like the Eurozone: Ling Hui Tan, "IMF Engagement with the Euro Area Versus Other Currency Unions", (last visited Feb. 6, 2024) https://ieo.imf.org/-/media/IEO/Files/Publications/Books/background-papers-for-eac-crisis/eac-background-papers-chapter-3.ashx.

2) creation the necessary organizational and legal conditions at national and intergovernmental levels for the integration processes development in the monetary field, coordination and correlation of monetary policy.[44]

These provisions demonstrate the crucial difference from the IMF's Articles of Agreements. While the latter empowers the Fund only to advise member-states on exchange rate arrangements and national monetary policy principles,[45] the EAEU Treaty turns this mechanism into mandatory international legal norms. Even though the provisions do not guarantee achieving most of the principles in Article 64, still they (principles of Article 64) obligate member-states to act accordingly.

The above Article 64 of the EAEU Treaty is not inclusive on macroeconomic integration and coordination matters. While the IMF Articles of Agreement state the orderly economic growth with the reasonable price stability, the EAEU Treaty clarifies and promotes monetary cooperation also through the establishment of the following main directions of the coordinated macroeconomic policy:[46]

1) ensuring sustainable economic development … and competitive advantages of each member State;
2) creation of common principles of functioning of the economy of the member States and their effective interaction;
3) providing for the … internal stability of the economy of the member States, including macroeconomic stability, as well as resistance to external effects;
4) development of common principles and guidelines for social and economic development of the member States.[47]

These provisions increase the role of the EAEU's intergovernmental organs in the functioning of the regional markets since they coordinate member-states' economic policies by adjusting and clarifying the common goal of the EUEU Treaty. It is this mechanism, which is absent in the IMF's Articles of Agreement (as mentioned earlier concerning the first sentence of its Article 4). Therefore, the principles established in the EAEU Treaty can be considered either as a filling the gap in the Fund's Articles of Agreement by the subsequent practice or are contrary to the universal agreement. The latter can be a case if one supposes that the gaps in the IMF Article of Agreement are not a result of the non-willingness of states to coordinate monetary and macroeconomic policies due to their national interests but the belief that the international monetary and financial system would tend to stabilize by itself

[44] Treaty on the Eurasian Economic Union, Art. 64 (1), (last visited Feb. 6, 2024) https://www.wto.org/english/thewto_e/acc_e/kaz_e/wtacckaz85_leg_1.pdf.

[45] Section 3(b) of Article 4 of the Articles of Agreement of the International Monetary Fund is a basis for the Article 4 consolations, e.g. with Kiribati on September 15, 2023, with the Republic of Latvia on September 12, 2023, or Bosnia and Herzegovina on September 7, 2023, (last visited Feb. 6, 2024) https://www.imf.org/en/News/SPROLLs/PRSurveillance134#sort=%40imfdate%20descending.

[46] Treaty on the Eurasian Economic Union, Art. 62(1), (last visited Feb. 6, 2024) https://www.wto.org/english/thewto_e/acc_e/kaz_e/wtacckaz85_leg_1.pdf.

[47] *Id.* Article 62(3).

(without or with minimal involvement of national or intergovernmental organs into the global market functioning). Nevertheless, the formal wording in the IMF's constituent act demonstrates the nature of principles enshrined in the universal agreement, which can be described as a general provisions.

Finally, the EAEU Treaty aims both at "*comprehensive modernization, cooperation and competitiveness of national economies within the global economy*"[48] and "*development of the EAEU as efficient and competitive organization within the global economy*."[49] The latter aim is supported by the Treaty on the EAEU Trademarks of 2021 and reserves for the EAEU the role of a subject in the multipolar world.

Since interstate and supranational institutions are subjects of international law—as they are based on treaties—their subjectivity in international monetary system is rather a "radical evolution" then a revolution, since the meaning of the principles in the universal agreements (such as those in Article 4 of the IMF founding agreement) evolve over time and are not substituted by regional agreements.

3.2 Regional Monetary Integration in Eastern and South-Eastern Asia

Similar trends are observed in other regions of the world. Their constituent acts—like the Treaty on the EAEU—still remain within the framework of the IMF Articles of Agreement.

A very illustrative example here is East and South-East Asia, where integration is one of the most dynamic one in the world.[50] The adoption of the Regional Comprehensive Economic Partnership (RCEP) Agreement seems to be the peak of this region's integration law to modern days. As in other regional treaties, this one provides higher degree of liberalisation within regional markets than universal agreements for global markets, while the former details the provisions of the latter.

However, the RCEP Agreement does not regulate exchange rate arrangements but defines the term "freely usable currency" referring to the IMF definitions.[51] It once again means that the monopoly for most of the interstate currency relations' legal regulation remains within the Fund's Articles of Agreement. The RCEP Agreement also includes provisions on financial services, but its scope is limited by

[48] *Id.*: the third sentence of Article 4.

[49] *Id.*: Article 33 (1).

[50] Pasha L. H.,. New Asian Regionalism in International Economic Law, Cambridge University Press & Assessment, July 2023. P. 2.

[51] Regional Comprehensive Economic Partnership (RCEP) Agreement, para. 10.1(b).

liberalisation of monetary affairs through changes in national legislations to allow entities across the RCEP member-states to engage in foreign investment relations.[52]

What might be within the IMF Articles of Agreement in terms of financial integration are the stabilisation mechanisms of financial system. This matter is avoided by the RCEP Agreement. In particular, the prudential policies are out of the scope of the IMF Articles of Agreement, as these policies mainly concern banking regulation and not monetary one. However, the measures to promote financial stability are partly included into the IMF's founding treaty in its Article 4 mentioned earlier but in a different dimension.[53] The RCEP Agreement, in turn, has a dual approach:

> Notwithstanding any other provision of this Agreement, a Party shall not be prevented from adopting or maintaining measures for prudential reasons, including for the protection of investors, depositors, policyholders, or persons to whom a fiduciary duty is owed by a financial service supplier, or to ensure the integrity and stability of the financial system. Where such measures do not conform with the provisions of this Agreement, they shall not be used as a means of avoiding the Party's commitments or obligations under this Agreement.[54]

The last sentence seems to limit the capacity of national laws to impose protectionist measures. The same principle is seen in Article 11, which covers payment and clearing settlement but only to foster regional investment.

Measures outside of necessary limitations for financial stability is enshrined also in Article 17:15 of the RCEP Agreement on safeguarding the balance of payment.[55] It relates to the exchange rate arrangements adopted in the IMF Articles of Agreement[56] (like the above mentioned provisions of Article XV of GATT do). This approach once again recognises the supremacy of universal provisions.

It might be appropriate to return to the founding treaty of the EAEU, which Annex 15 also regulates measures for the balance of payment stability. These approaches in the RCEP Agreement and EAEU Treaty duplicate the GATT provisions in its Article 12. However, the question here is whether regional trade agreements are sufficient enough if there is no regional fund and exchange rate arrangement regulation by the same treaty or treaty that includes states of the same region. On the universal level the GATT refers to the IMF Articles of Agreement that establishes the Fund and regulates the currency relations. The EAEU Treaty in its Article 64 (mentioned above) regulates currency relations, and most of its

---

[52] *Id.* Article 3 of Annex 8A. This legal mechanism can be found also in the Annex on Financial Services of the GATT 1994.

[53] International investment and capital movement might be interrelated. In the author's opinion foreign investment is a part of a trans-boundary capital movement, and hence international monetary law and international investment law should not be considered independently. However, the link between them is mainly in economic dimension and not necessarily legal one.

[54] *Id.* Article 4 of Annex 8A.

[55] *Id.* Art. 17:15, para. 1(b).

[56] *Id.* Para. 3(b).

member-states adopted another treaty—the Treaty on the Establishment of the Eurasian Fund for Stabilization and Development.[57]

Nevertheless, monetary and financial stability of the Eastern and South-Eastern Asian region mostly remains outside of the RCEP Agreement's regulation.[58] Like other regional organisations, countries of this region (Eastern and South-Eastern Asia) established financial mechanisms to overcome the balance of payment deficit. The logic behind this tendency was the East Asian currency crisis and inability of the IMF as a creditor to curb or localise the crisis that started in Thailand.[59] In 2001, ASEAN+3[60] presented a report on the prospects for further deepening of monetary and financial relations, or more precisely, on financial integration based on two principles: the creation of a reserve fund and the regulation of the exchange rate arrangements of national currencies.[61]

This reserve fund would have to be found together with the formation of supervisory and monitoring bodies concerning the exchange rates of the member-states' national currencies in this region. It was not supposed directly to replace the IMF as a creditor but to supplement this (the IMF) intergovernmental organisation, which (the Fund) empowered to supervise the exchange rate regimes of member-states on the basis of Article 4 of the Articles of Agreement of the IMF.[62]

In view of this, one might say that—like Article 64 of the EAEU Treaty and Article 4 of the IMF Articles of Agreement—ASEAN+3 aims to establish the principles for regulation and conducting central banks' monetary policies, even though

---

[57] Originally the treaty was called "Treaty on the Establishment of the Anti-Crisis Fund of the Eurasian Economic Community of 2009", as the regional economic organisation was established by the Treaty on the Eurasian Economic Community. After the adoption of the Treaty on the Eurasian Economic Union in 2014, most of its member-states adopted the Protocol amending the Treaty on the Establishment of the Anti-Crisis Fund of the Eurasian Economic Community dated June 9, 2009, to replace its name with "Eurasian Fund for Stabilization and Development". See Article 1.1 of the Protocol amending the Treaty on the Establishment of the Anti-Crisis Fund of the Eurasian Economic Community dated June 9, 2009.

[58] International agreements on these matters co-exist with the RCEP Agreement, and they might function as a complex mechanism for international economic regulation in this region.

[59] Sussangkarn, C., The Chiang Mai Initiative Multilateralization: Origin, Development and Outlook, ADBI Working Paper 230, 2010, Tokyo: Asian Development Bank Institute, (last visited Feb. 6, 2024) http://www.adbi.org/working-paper/2010/07/13/3938.chiang.mai.initiative.multilateralisation/. Para. 2.1.

[60] The ASEAN+3 international legal framework consists of joint statements and declarations. It should be noted that they do not have the nature of international agreements, which establish the goals and objectives of cooperation mechanisms and monitoring activities. At the same time, ASEAN and South Korea, China and Japan (with each state) have concluded mutual trade agreements. Thus, the international legal framework for the activities of ASEAN + 3 is of a mixed nature, combining soft law, informal regulations and international legal norms.

[61] East Asia Vision Group Report "Towards an East Asian Community" 2001, para. 44, (last visited Feb. 6, 2024) https://aseanplusthree.asean.org/wp-content/uploads/2020/01/east_asia_vision.pdf.

[62] *Id*. Para. 47–48.

the theoretical literature does not concentrate on this matter as much as on international trade law.[63]

Apart from monetary authorities' policy coordination, East and South-East Asian countries established the financial mechanism to protect the balance of payment stability by adopting the Chiang Mai Initiative Multilateralisation (CMIM) Agreement. The CMIM Agreement involves central banks (or monetary authorities) to conclude currency swap agreements to overcome the balance of payments deficit.[64] It is worth noting that the regulation of the exchange rate at the national level differs in the countries included in ASEAN+3, but given the intention of the member-states to ensure regional integration, international legal regulation of exchange rates has become a condition for ensuring this integration, which is based on the following statement:

> …. A coordinated exchange rate mechanism becomes important with the growing interdependence among East Asian countries that have different exchange rate systems. Policy dialogue, which is a part of regional financial cooperation, is an ongoing activity performed through the ASEAN+3 Finance Ministers Process. Efforts are also being made to strengthen coordination through a bilateral and voluntary exchange of data on short-term capital flows. As a mechanism to be formally established in the long-term, an East Asian regional surveillance process will help enhance the financial stability in the region.[65]

Though this mechanism is not based on purely international legal norms, still it establishes the international mechanism to overcome the short-term balance of payment deficit, while the IMF Articles of Agreement provides long-term financing through agreements between the IMF and its member-states' monetary or fiscal agencies.[66]

The link between these two funds—the IMF and the multilateral swap lines of the CMIM Agreement—is found in the latter's most recent wording:

> To increase the IMF De-linked Portion from 30% to 40% of each member's maximum arrangement amount.[67]

---

[63] International monetary policy regulation as an international legal institute within international monetary law covers principles of conducting monetary policy and other norms in international agreements. It also has its hierarchy: basic universal principles of conducting monetary policy may be found in the IMF Articles of Agreement. At the same time intergovernmental financial institutions and their soft law norms and standards might not be necessarily considered as international legal regulation.

[64] See: Chiang Mai Initiative Multilateralisation (CMIM) Agreement.

[65] Para. 30 of the Final Report of the East Asia Study Group. ASEAN+3 Summit, November 4, 2002. Phnom Penh, Cambodia, (last visited Feb. 6, 2024) https://aseanplusthree.asean.org/wp-content/uploads/2020/01/easg.pdf.

[66] "*Each member shall deal with the Fund only through its Treasury, central bank, stabilization fund, or other similar fiscal agency, and the Fund shall deal only with or through the same agencies*", see Section 1 of Article 5 of the Articles of Agreement of the International Monetary Fund.

[67] Amended Chiang Mai Initiative Multilateralisation (CMIM), the first sentence of para. 1, March 31, 2021, (last visited Feb. 6, 2024) https://www.boj.or.jp/en/intl_finance/cooperate/rel210331a.pdf.

Concurrently, the CMIM Agreement breaks through the IMF's monopoly as a financing institution, because in case the CMIM member-state does match to the IMF's credit lines,[68] then CMIM's currency swap lines fill the gap in the IMF's founding agreement concerning the short-term financing.[69] But what is more important, the last version of the CMIM Agreement promotes also the local currencies for financing the balance of payment deficit of its member-states,[70] and academicians today try to predict the future of currency relations in this region.[71] Finally, the latest Report 2023 of the CMIM also demonstrates that the stronger global financial shocks lead to tighter relations between CMIM states.[72]

Another complimentary statement (for CMIM Agreement's adoption) in the above-mentioned Report 2023 is its recognition of the CMIM's importance for the region by considering it (the CMIM Agreement) as the part of the national reserve arrangements.[73]

The CMIM Agreement and the currency swap lines operated by central banks are not comparable to the nature of the EAEU Treaty as international legal mechanisms, since the former is based on the memorandum of understanding.[74] One cannot state undoubtedly that the central banks' cooperation (including their monetary policies) is institutionalised in terms of public international law.

---

[68] *Id.* Para. 1 of the Attachment.

[69] IMF's short-term financing has a number of limitations, as it is considered by the Fund as a supplementary financing mechanism for countries with sound economic conditions. See The Short-term Liquidity Line (SLL), (last visited Feb. 6, 2024) https://www.imf.org/en/About/Factsheets/Sheets/2023/Short-Term-Liquidity-Line-SLL.

[70] *Id.* Para. 2 of the Attachment.

[71] Whether Chinese yuan is a future axis of the alternative US dollar financial system; see, e.g. in the conclusion in Marcus, Noland "Asia's push for monetary alternatives". East-West Center. Munich Personal RePEc Archive. 2022, P. 8–9, (last visited Feb. 6, 2024) https://mpra.ub.uni-muenchen.de/115527/1/MPRA_paper_115527.pdf.

[72] In addition to replacing the IMF and use of local currency in the CMIM, the swap agreements between central banks of states in this region illuminate the shift of the exchange rate arrangement regulation to the local level. See the statistics in Asian Economic Integration Report 2023 "Trade, Investment, and Climate Change in Asia and the Pacific" of the Asian Development Bank, February 2023, p. 94, (last visited Feb. 6, 2024) https://aric.adb.org/pdf/aeir/AEIR2023_complete.pdf.

[73] *Id.* P. 103.

[74] Except the Philippines, who considered the Memorandum as a treaty. See Hoffner B., "ASEAN Swap Arrangement, 1977–2021," Journal of Financial Crises: Vol. 5: Iss. 1. 2023, p. 117.

3.3 South Asian Monetary Integration

Regional financial mechanisms for providing foreign liquidity also exist in South Asia. This region remains the least integrated on the continent, despite the signing of the Charter on South Asian Association for Regional Cooperation (further, SAARC) at the end of the twentieth century.[75]

The SAARC Charter not only admits the supremacy of the United Nations Charter.[76] It requires that member-states' cooperation should be based on "*the principles of sovereign equality, territorial integrity, political independence, non-interference in the internal affairs of other States*"[77] and places this cooperation to the secondary (substitutionary) position in relation to "*bilateral and multilateral obligations*".[78] At the same time, the platform established by the SAARC Charter led to the adoption of the on SAARC Preferential Trading Arrangement (SAPTA) in 1993,[79] which was later superseded by the Agreement on South Asian Free Trade Area (further, SAFTA) in 2006.[80]

The SAFTA Agreement goes beyond the GATT when it liberalises trade except quantitative restrictions "*permitted under GATT 1994*"[81] while reaffirming its obligations on internal taxation and regulation under GATT.[82] At the same time the SAFTA Agreement's member-states may agree on trade facilitation including "*exceptions to their foreign exchange restrictions, if any, relating to payments for products under the SAFTA scheme, as well as repatriation of such payments without prejudice to their rights under Article XVIII of the General Agreement on Tariffs and Trade (GATT) and the relevant provisions of Articles of Treaty of the International Monetary Fund (IMF)*".[83] These principles of regional trade and partly exchange rate regulation are concurrent with the regional treaties in the Eurasian region and Eastern and South-Eastern Asian area mentioned earlier.

---

[75] In 1985, seven states (Bangladesh, Bhutan, Maldives, Nepal, Pakistan, India and Sri Lanka) founded the South Asian Association for Regional Cooperation (further, SAARS). In 2007 Afghanistan joined the economic and political union. See Official website of the SAARC (last visited Feb. 6, 2024) https://www.saarc-sec.org/index.php/about-saarc/about-saarc.

[76] See Charter of the South Asian Association for Regional Cooperation 1985, para. 1 of the Preamble.

[77] *Id.* Art. 2, para. 1.

[78] *Id.* Para. 3.

[79] SAARC Preferential Trading Arrangement 1993, Art. 25, (last visited Feb. 6, 2024) https://www.saarc-sec.org/index.php/resources/agreements-conventions/35-agreement-on-saarc-preferential--trading-arrangement-sapta/file.

[80] Agreement on South Asian Free Trade Area 2006, Art. 22, (last visited Feb. 6, 2024) https://www.saarc-sec.org/index.php/resources/agreements-conventions/36-agreement-on-south-asian-free-trade-area-safta/file.

[81] *Id.* Art. 7, para. 5.

[82] The Agreement on South Asian Free Trade Area refers to Art. III of GATT 1994. See *id.* Article 5.

[83] *Id.* Art. 8, para. (1).

Concerning the exchange rate arrangements and monetary affairs, the key event for the SAARC was the creation of the "Network of central Bank Governors and Finance Ministers of the SAARC" (further, SAARSFINANCE) in 1998 for a dialogue on the macroeconomic policy and financial stability.[84] Then, in 2002 SAARCFINANCE turned into a permanent and officially recognised body of the SAARC at the 11th Summit,[85] where the member-states decided to establish the international financial mechanism for providing foreign liquidity, as it is the case in other similar regional associations. Ever since, SAARCFINANCE regulates regional monetary policy by means of soft law.

The main goal of SAARCFINANCE is the exchange of experience on macroeconomic policy issues. Nevertheless, other objectives of SAARCFINANCE are (1) to develop and submit proposals for the harmonisation of banking legislation and practice in the region; (2) to contribute to the formation of a more effective payment system within the framework of the SAARC and closer cooperation in the field of finance; (3) to monitor changes and reforms in the international monetary and financial system and to achieve consensus among the SAARC member-states regarding the ongoing reforms; and (4) to develop practical joint strategies, plans and a unified approach in the international arena based on mutual benefit, especially in the field of financial services liberalisation.[86]

While the ASEAN+3 member-states provide foreign liquidity by means of multilateral currency swap agreements jointly,[87] the SAARC member-states conclude bilateral swap agreements with the Central Bank of India.[88] However, both regional mechanisms mentioned above (ASEAN+3 and SAARSFINANCE) are based on soft law norms, which is contrary to the EAEU, because the latter is established by treaty. It should also be mentioned that the IMF Articles of Agreement (unlike Asian regional mechanisms concerned but like the EAEU) regulate both exchange rate arrangements and find the Fund for providing liquidity in case if there is a fundamental "*disequilibrium in the international balances of payments of members*".[89] But this kind of international legal mechanisms (for financing international balances of payments of countries) exist also on global (but not universal) level, i.e. the BRICS Contingent Reserve Arrangement (CRA) Agreement 2014. Its adaption complicates the global financial architecture.

[84] The 10th SAARC Summit, Colombo, July 31, 1998; Declaration of the Tenth SAARC Summit, Colombo, July 31, 1998, para. 15.

[85] The 11th SAARC Summit, Kathmandu, Nepal, January 4–6, 2002.

[86] Terms of Reference of SAARCFINANCE 2002, Section B.

[87] Sussangkarn, C., The Chiang Mai Initiative Multilateralization: Origin, Development and Outlook. ADBI Working Paper 230. Tokyo: Asian Development Bank Institute, 2010, (last visited Feb. 6, 2024) http://www.adbi.org/working-paper/2010/07/13/3938.chiang.mai.initiative.multilateralisation/. P. 6.

[88] SAARC Currency Swap Framework, (last visited Feb. 6, 2024) https://www.drishtiias.com/daily-updates/daily-news-analysis/saarc-currency-swap-framework.

[89] Articles of Agreement of the International Monetary Fund, Art. I(vi).

4 The BRICS Concept of Monetary Regulation

This complication started in the 2000s. After the first gathering of Russia, India and China in Saint-Petersburg (2006)[90] in 2009, Russia hosted the first meeting of the BRIC heads of state.[91] In fact, that year demonstrated a split in the world over what regionalisation model would follow up: the one based on G7, G20 or the BRICS one.

In the G20 London Summit Leaders' Statement, the participants reaffirmed their willingness to act in line with Article 1 of the IMF Articles of Agreement (concerning competitive devaluation)[92] and the path towards liberalisation of international economy.[93] Yet the GATT and the IMF Articles of Agreement rather imply non-discrimination rules than prohibition to establish any barriers by a member-state against all other countries and not particular countries, if such measures are based on the principle of reciprocity and competition.[94] Therefore, the path towards liberalisation is the free will of sovereign states defined in, for example, joint statements (like the above-mentioned G20 one). The liberalisation also can be seen in treaties (e.g. regional treaties analysed earlier in this paper), while the WTO and IMF treaties mostly state market principles of global economy.[95] This approach is attracted also in the London Summit Leaders' Statement that the IMF should be preserved as the universal independent surveillance interstate organisation on monetary and financial matters.[96]

As a result the G20 London Summit adopted the Charter of the Financial Stability Board (further, FSB),[97] which mandates FSB to coordinate with international financial organisation for promoting stability of the global financial system.[98] Its mandates to assess vulnerabilities, exchange of information and provide consultations

[90] Gorbacheva V., Russia-India-China: RIC Format Receives New Impetus, (last visited Feb. 6, 2024) https://www.nkibrics.ru/posts/show/5cfa52836272692ee0170000.

[91] See: Previous BRICS Summits, (last visited Feb. 6, 2024) http://en.brics2015.ru/russia_and_brics/20150301/19545.html.

[92] London Summit—Leaders' Statement on April 2, 2009, para. 12, (last visited Feb. 6, 2024) https://www.imf.org/external/np/sec/pr/2009/pdf/g20_040209.pdf.

[93] *Id.* Para. 4.

[94] Avoidance of discriminatory currency practices in para. 3 of Article VIII of the Articles of Agreement of the International Monetary Fund and Articles I and XIII of the General Agreement on Tariffs and Trade.

[95] The IMF Articles of Agreement empowers the Fund to "**assist** in the … elimination of foreign exchange restrictions which hamper the growth of world trade", which does not mean the obligation of states to liberalise interstate financial and trade relations. See Articles of Agreement of the International Monetary Fund, Art. I (iv).

[96] London Summit—Leaders' Statement of 2 April 2009, para. 12, (last visited Feb. 6, 2024) https://www.imf.org/external/np/sec/pr/2009/pdf/g20_040209.pdf.

[97] *Id.* Para. 15.

[98] Financial Stability Board Charter, Art. 1, (last visited Feb. 6, 2024) https://www.fsb.org/wp-content/uploads/r_090925d.pdf?page_moved=1.

can be compared to the IMF's constituent treaty[99] and the Terms of Reference of SAARCFINANCE.[100]

The first BRIC Summit's Joint Statement of the BRIC Countries' Leaders recognised the central role that G20 played for overcoming the consequences of the 2008 World Economic Crisis.[101] However, it also called for "*the reform of international finàncial institutions, so as to reflect changes in the world economy*".[102] This difference between the BRICS and G20 statements of the same year marked the conceptual contradictions of the further development of international monetary law.

In 2010 the 15th General Review of Quotas of the IMF became a subject of the Fund's Report,[103] which was not implemented till today.[104]

In 2011, the Republic of South Africa joined the BRICS forum.[105] Then like the Bretton Woods Conference that established the constituent acts of the International Reserve Fund (the IMF) and the International Development Bank (International Bank for Reconstruction and Development) in 1947,[106] in 2014 at the Brazilian summit the Treaty for the establishment of the BRICS Contingent Reserve Arrangement (CRA)[107] and the Agreement establishing the New Development Bank (NDB)[108] were adopted. This Declaration also mentions their (leaders of BRICS states) disappointment "*with the ... non-implementation of the 2010 International Monetary Fund (IMF) reforms, which negatively impacts on the IMF's legitimacy, credibility and effectiveness*".[109] This split of the BRICS with the Western countries

[99] Articles of Agreement of the International Monetary Fund, Art. I(i).

[100] In particular, Articles 1 and 2 of the Financial Stability Board Charter and Section B of the Terms of Reference of SAARCFINANCE state provisions, which are of advisory (non-legal) nature and partly similar meanings.

[101] Joint Statement of the BRIC Countries Leaders. June 16, 2009, Yekaterinburg, Russia, para. 1, (last visited Feb. 6, 2024) https://brics-ysf.org/sites/default/files/2nd_Summit.pdf.

[102] *Id.* First sentence of para. 3.

[103] 2010 Reforms and Fifteenth General Review of Quotas—Report of the Executive Board to the Board of Governors, (last visited Feb. 6, 2024) https://www.imf.org/external/np/pp/eng/2015/012815.pdf.

[104] G20 Leaders' Communiqué Brisbane Summit, November 15–16, 2014, para. 15, (last visited Feb. 6, 2024) https://www.consilium.europa.eu/media/23866/g20-leaders-communiqu%C3%A9-brisbane-summit-15-16-november-2014.pdf; later it was a concern of the G20 Summit in 2014, see G20 Leaders' Communiqué in Brisbane Summit, November 15–16, 2014, para. 15, (last visited Feb. 6, 2024) https://www.consilium.europa.eu/media/23866/g20-leaders-communiqu%C3%A9-brisbane-summit-15-16-november-2014.pdf.

[105] III BRICS Summit Sanya Declaration, para. 2, (last visited Feb. 6, 2024) http://brics2022.mfa.gov.cn/eng/hywj/ODS/202203/t20220308_10649517.html.

[106] Annex A (Articles of Agreement of the International Monetary Fund) and Annex B (Articles of Agreement of the International Bank for Reconstruction and Development (World Bank Group at present days)) of the Final Act of the United Nations Monetary and Financial Conference, (last visited Feb. 6, 2024) https://fraser.stlouisfed.org/files/docs/historical/eccles/036_17_0004.pdf.

[107] See the 6th BRICS Summit: Fortaleza Declaration July 15, 2014, para. 13, (last visited Feb. 6, 2024) http://www.brics.utoronto.ca/docs/140715-leaders.html.

[108] *Id.* Para. 11.

[109] *Id.* First sentence of para. 18.

turned into fragmentation. The logic behind this split was that both the G20 and BRICS aimed at coordination of economic potentials, while BRICS countries contributed to the global economic growth more than developed countries.[110]

The IMF reforms supposed that the member-states' quota in the IMF—which defines voting power, access to financing and the share of a member-states in IMF's reserves—must reflect the rise of the BRICS countries and other developing countries. But what is more important, since none of other treaties place itself higher than the IMF Articles of Agreement in terms of exchange rate arrangements, the voting quotas to amend this arrangement are defined as follows:

> To accord with the development of the international monetary system, the Fund, by an eighty-five percent majority of the total voting power, may make provision for general exchange arrangements without limiting the right of members to have exchange arrangements of their choice consistent with the purposes of the Fund and the obligations under Section 1 of this Article.[111]

The 85% of quota means that the member-state with more than 85%—in particular, the USA[112]—is able to veto any such decision. This share can also be an obstacle to reform the international monetary system itself, as 85% of votes is necessary to adopt a par value as a single benchmark for exchange rates of IMF member-states' currencies.[113] Thus, it is an essential contradiction of the reality (the share of BRICS in the modern global economy[114]) and its international legal regulation.

In this regard the CRA Treaty of BRICS has a fundamentally different approach. It establishes the Governing Council,[115] which "*shall take decisions by consensus and shall be responsible for high level and strategic decisions of the CRA*".[116] At the same time the CRA Treaty does not regulate exchange rate arrangements, but it is responsible for the short-term balance of payment financing.

However, the counterargument against the CRA Agreement (when it is compared to the IMF's Articles of Agreement) can be the provisions on the weighted voting: "*(i) 5 percent of total voting power shall be equally distributed among the Parties; and (ii) the remainder shall be distributed among the Parties according to the*

---

[110] *Id.* Paras. 8–9.

[111] Articles of Agreement of the International Monetary Fund, Art. IV(2c).

[112] The International Monetary Fund: 15th General Review of Quotas, European Parliament Briefing, (last visited Feb. 6, 2024) https://www.europarl.europa.eu/RegData/etudes/BRIE/2019/631059/IPOL_BRI(2019)631059_EN.pdf.

[113] *Id.* Section 4.

[114] See Statista. BRICS and G7 countries' share of the world's total gross domestic product (GDP) in purchasing power parity (PPP) from 2000 to 2023, (last visited Feb. 6, 2024) https://www.statista.com/statistics/1412425/gdp-ppp-share-world-gdp-g7-brics/#:~:text=By%202023%2C%20the%20difference%20had,held%20by%20the%20G7%20countries.

[115] "*The Governing Council shall comprise one Governor and one Alternate Governor appointed by each Party. Governors must be a Finance Minister, Central Bank Governor, or hold an equivalent post*". See Treaty for the Establishment of a BRICS Contingent Reserve Arrangement 2014, Art. 3, para. B.

[116] *Ibid.*

relative size of individual commitments".[117] Concerning the second subparagraph, it is worth to note that China's contribution is the largest (41% of total reserves).[118] But even in this case (in contrary to the IMF's 85% of voting quota), China possesses less than 40%.[119] Moreover, this kind of voting is referred to the Standing Committee[120] and still requires the majority vote[121] and only in relation to "*ii. Approve requests for support through the liquidity or precautionary instruments; iii. Approve requests for renewals of support through the liquidity or precautionary instruments*".[122] Finally, the latter's powers are considered as secondary to the Governing Council,[123] where (as it is already been mentioned) consensus is required.

The IMF Articles of Agreements, in turn, mention 85% of voting quota more than 20 times.[124] It means that most decisions of the Fund can be accepted only in case if the country with more than 15% of voting quota authorises them.

Finally, till the end of 2023 BRICS countries in aggregate had 14.15% of votes in the IMF, while new members possess 3.76%, and in total BRICS+ has 17.91% of votes.[125] Therefore, possessing more than 15% of voting quota in the IMF means that the monopoly for vetoing by the USA the Fund's decisions is overcome (in case if BRICS countries adhere to similar positions).

This issue is of special consideration for BRICS countries. International reserves of states, currency swap agreements, regional reserve funds (like the EAEU, Chiang Mai Multilateralisation Initiative and SAARCFINANCE evaluated above), global reserve funds (BRICS CRA) and the universal fund (the IMF) itself comprise the Global Financial Safety Net (GFSN or Net).[126] This Net should also be regulated, and even not necessarily by international agreement, still IMF decisions can be the instrument for this. BRICS joint declarations mention this problem, and when say that BRICS "*support a robust Global Financial Safety Net with a quota-based and adequately resourced International Monetary Fund (IMF) at its centre*".[127] At the

[117] *Id.* Art. 3, para. E.

[118] *Id.* Art. 2, para. A.

[119] Due to the distribution of 5% equally among all BRICS states, China's 41% decreases to 35.75%.

[120] *Id.* Art. 3, para. D.

[121] *Ibid.*

[122] *Id.* Art. 3, paras. Cii and Ciii.

[123] *Id.* Art. 3, para C.

[124] Section 2(c) of Article III, Section 2(c) and Section 4 of Article IV, Section 7(c) and (d), Section 12 (b), (f) and (g) of Article V, Section 1 and Section 3 (c) of Article XII, Section 2 of Article XV, Section 3 of Article XVII, Section 4(d) of Article XVIII, Section 7(b) of Article XX, Section 1 and Section 2(e) of Article XXIII, Section 2(c) of Article XXVI, Section 1(a) and (b) of Article XXVII, Section A of Article XXVIII, Section B of Article XXIX, Section C(iii) of Article XXX of the Articles of Agreement of the International Monetary Fund.

[125] IMF Members' Quotas and Voting Power and IMF Board of Governors, (last visited Feb. 6, 2024) https://www.imf.org/en/About/executive-board/members-quotas.

[126] UNCTAD, The Global Financial Safety Net (GFSN) Tracker, (last visited Feb. 6, 2024) https://mobilizingdevfinance.org/tool/global-financial-safety-net-gfsn-tracker.

[127] Para. 10 of the Johannesburg II Declaration. BRICS and Africa: Partnership for Mutually Accelerated Growth, Sustainable Development and Inclusive Multilateralism, Sandton, Gauteng,

same time it adds that it can be done so only if the IMF voting system is reformed,[128] so that there is no bias in the Fund's policies. This also can answer the question on how BRICS is going to build a fair world if not all countries participate there (e.g. Western countries).

5 Conclusion

International monetary law is primarily based on the IMF's constituent act. The latter monopolises the exchange rate regulation on universal level and is indispensable for regulation of international trade on the same universal level. But as it is well known, the IMF's Articles of Agreement and GATT 1994 establish broad and vague wordings, so that most of countries of the world can accept them without vital reduction of their economic sovereignty.

The interaction of national law and international law is a permanent issue as international legal norms are vague. But on top of it today it is also complicated by regional treaties. It is therefore worth to note that regionalisation may lead to researches on interaction of universal, regional and national law. It is illustrated in this article on the example of the wordings about the price stability and monetary policy coordination of the Articles of Agreement, the treaty on the EAEU and constitutional provisions of Russia.

It can also be stated that universal norms are detailed to adapt them to regional needs and to promote regional integration. But similarities among regional economic organisations also exist. Firstly, it is a combination of monetary and trade integration, even if it is not based on a single regional agreement. Secondly, they all require the creation of regional reserve funds. At the same time a number of issues are not necessarily regulated by international legal norms but by policies or informal agreements.

Regionalisation, however, demonstrates also the third consensus—their constituent acts are based on the IMF's Articles of Agreement and the GATT 1994. But one cannot argue that IMF's policies are widely accepted. However, at the moment it is policies, which are considered as instruments to coordinate regional reserve funds, which are created for regional integration and not for globalisation purposes. This issue causes the fragmentation, where BRICS plays a crucial role.

In the global financial architecture, it is hard to define a clear role and place of BRICS+. However, its CRA Agreement demonstrates that there is a model to overcome such a fragmentation. In case decisions of the IMF do not match the interests of all countries, and if such decisions are concerned of national and regional monetary and financial systems' stabilities, the CRA Agreement provides alternative financial instruments to achieve those aims of states, which cannot be achieved by the IMF.

South Africa, August 23, 2023, (last visited Feb. 6, 2024) https://mid.ru/en/foreign_policy/news/1901504/.

[128] *Ibid.*

Chapter 2
New Formats of BRICS Cooperation in Economics, Science, and Technology ('BRICS+', 'BRICS-outreach') in Light of Basic Principles of International Law and Jus Cogens

Ludmila P. Anufrieva

Abstract The current stage of the BRICS countries' cooperation opened a new page of interaction between the parties thereto, which encompasses various spheres and vectors of geographic, political, economic, social, and other sides of life of the above grouping with eventually aimed at more integrational targets and communitarian trends in the interstate links. Certain new formats of BRICS relationships in economics, science, technology, and innovations ('BRICS+', 'BRICS-outreach") that have recently emerged reflect the future path of the alliance and even to some extent the world development. Realization of modern tracks of cooperation requires the deployment of platforms for dialogue as well as for multilaterality, accompanied by creation and/or adjustment of legal mechanisms of interaction, especially in the fields of newest technologies and innovations, inevitably obtaining nowadays the extraordinary significance.

BRICS serves nowadays to act as an evident center of influence within the relevant regions (Russia—through the Eurasian Economic Union (EAEU) and the Shanghai Cooperation Organization (SCO) in Eurasian subregion; China—in the South-East Asia as the leader of the Association of South East Asian Nations (ASEAN); India—in the South Asian Association for Regional Cooperation (SAARC) and 'Bay of Bengal Initiative for Multi-Sectoral Technical and Economic Cooperation (BIMSTEC); Brazil—in Latin America and Caribbean region through the Southern Common Market (MERCOSUR—span.: Mercado Común del Sur, port.: Mercado Comum do Sul) alongwith the Community of Latin American and Caribbean States

The paper is prepared within the commitments of the author under the "Program of the Strategic academic Leadership Priority-2030."

L. P. Anufrieva (✉)
International Law Department, Kutafin Moscow State University of Law (MSAL), Moscow, Russian Federation
e-mail: lyu-anufrieva@yandex.ru; lpanufrieva@msal.ru

T. Du, X. Fei (eds.), *The BRICS Legal Cooperation and Perspectives*,
https://doi.org/10.1007/978-981-95-4356-4_2

(CELAC—span.: Comunidad de Estados Latinoamericanos y Caribeños); the Republic of South Africa—within the African Union and the South African Development Community (SADC), etc.). The said circumstances suppose impressive extension of the alliance and respective availability of various combinations of mutual influence between basic and special principles within the regulatory system. Thus, the chapter discloses the impact of basic principles of international law along with the specific peremptory norms of general international law (jus cogens) upon the part of legal ground which is formed by the sectoral (special) guiding—or saying in other words—prevailing—rules of law jointly agreed by all members of the alliance.

Keywords BRICS · BRICS+ · BRICS outreach · PartNIR · Legal grounds · International law · Principles of international law · Basic principles · Jus cogens · Co-operation in science · Technology · Innovation · International regulatory system · World legal order · International institutions and organizations · Para-organizations · Integration associations.

1 Introduction

According to one of the official acts classified as guide for the Russian national policy in the international affairs, viz., "The Concept of Russia's participation in BRICS" approved by the President of the Russian Federation yet in 2013, the BRICS group is to be considered to serve as a tool for strengthening the "Big Twenty" which was the main forum for international economic cooperation of the countries participating therein at the time of drafting the document. Nowadays, BRICS, due to current geopolitical "*realignment*" and restructuring the world order, widely strengthens its performance being one of tangible components within the global scope of bilateral and multilateral economic cooperation between nations in multiplicity of areas. In the economic sphere, the certain tasks are to be solved, in particular, of creating more favorable conditions for development of mutual trade and increased investment links, joint operation with non-BRICS countries within the frameworks of international organizations to promote common interests in the international trade.. Since the economic interaction tends certainly to be the key vector in BRICS development, all states of nonformal association are strongly interested in formulating a common strategy for economic cooperation and generally relevant acceptable legal ground in the form of common principles of partnership.

2 Past Experience, Emerging Problems, and Prospects

At present it is highly unlikely someone would refute the BRICS group is functioning being an integral component of the geopolitical and manifesting constructive interaction based not merely on a combination of strategic interests of the participants but rather on essentially deepening accounting thereof. Due to the effects of external challenges generated by miscellaneous global turbulences, radical changes are taking place following the multiplicity of directions: the global structure, legal order prevailing in international relationships, natural phenomena, extraordinary political events influencing the life of the international community, etc., which push various states toward rapprochement, forcing them, in particular, to transform models of international cooperation for the purposes of better choice of the forthcoming future.

The current period in the development of BRICS grouping opened a new page of interaction between its participants, demonstrating the need for dialogue on the matters of design, deployment, and adjustment of legal mechanism of cooperation, especially in the fields of trade, economics, science, and technology in the newest areas of the innovation spectrum between countries serving to act as major centers of influence within the relevant regions (Russia, in Eurasia, through the Eurasian Economic Union (EAEU) and the Shanghai Cooperation Organization (SCO); China, in Southeast Asia as the leader of the ASEAN; and Brazil, in Latin America and the Caribbean region with regard to Mercado Común del Sur (MERCOSUR) and Comunidad de Estados Latinoamericanos y Caribeños/the Community of Latin American and Caribbean States (CELAC)). This is a response to the needs of restructuring the world with the growing intensity of integration processes, the rejection of the hegemony of the only one or a small group of states, and the desire for regionalism, transparency, openness, flexibility in coercion with mutual respect, and equality in international relationship.

The fact that actually a considerable number of countries representing developing economies (or, according to current and becoming very popular terminology, "Global South") have expressed their wills either to join the BRICS group or become the partners thereof is self-evident for the point that BRICS is currently one of the most claimed and highly appreciated international groupings throughout the world.[1]

In addition, the latest formats "BRICS+" and "BRICS outreach" were considered as very productive for the purposes of implementing a "multi-vector" policy: firstly,

[1] Following the applications to join the BRICS formats by Iran and Argentina in 2022, another country expressed desire to cooperate with BRICS: Bolivia in 2023 became the next candidate. The relevant intention of the President of the country, Luis Arce, has been intimated on his Twitter page, as it was communicated by the Foreign Minister of this South American state, Rogelio Maita. The leaders of Ethiopia, Bangladesh, Egypt, the UAE, and Indonesia also shared similar regards to join the BRICS grouping earlier. President Cyril Ramaphosa of South Africa, who chaired the BRICS alliance at that time, noted that the alliance "would fully accommodate about 50 countries", available at: https://tsargrad.tv/news/bolivija-poprosilas-v-briks-stremimsja-k-razvitiju_836681. August 1, 2023 (accessed Feb. 08, 2023).

by cooperation between individual states within the "five"; secondly, by means of ties between the "five" itself as the grouping of participating countries and other states outside the BRICS; and thirdly, by way of interaction between the regional associations, including the most authoritative ones as the African Union (AU), EAEU, SCO, APEC, ASEAN, MERCOSUR, Caribbean Community (CARICOM), CELAC, etc. The target should be achieved by strengthening the vectors of polycentricity and regionalism against the background of globalism. Thus, the formation of the list of candidates-recipients of an invitation for joining the new format provides an explicitly regional approach to the model construed for the BRICS+ platform. The wording shall be as follows: "The extended BRICS+ meeting at the level of foreign ministers held in June 2023 in South Africa in addition to the 'original' BRICS countries, has been attended by the representatives of 15 states from Africa (Egypt, Nigeria, Senegal), Latin America (Argentina), as well as of Indonesia, Kazakhstan, Saudi Arabia, the UAE, Thailand and others.[2]

In light of the circumstances mentioned above, the efforts of the BRICS countries clearly demonstrate that the group is able to successfully adapt and respond immediately to emerging global challenges, such as, for example, in cases of controlling the production and supply of food and energy, creation of innovations, new technologies and information research, as well as in general intimation of a common course for sustainable development. When drawing attention toward the evolution of BRICS grouping of the latest decades aimed at the efficiency in its development, it needs to mention the initiative suggested by Russia which was supported by in the Declaration of Brasilia (2019) where the leaders of "the five" expressed the necessity to encourage, in particular, the platform of energy research. In this connection, it is worth emphasizing again following the above theses the effective role of "partnership" as a form of cooperation. It deserves to specifically note the positive experience in this respect of the EU countries broadly widening the spheres of application thereof, especially for the purposes of resolving the various funding problems, as external projections, competitiveness, research and innovation, as well as migration and helping to address major global challenges such as energy security, climate change, and environmental protection.[3]

Due to exposed deliberations, "the 'waiting list' for economic and technological integration within the new BRICS+ structures, as it was pointed out in special literature, already covers Algeria, Egypt, Indonesia, Kazakhstan, Cambodia, Senegal, Thailand, Uzbekistan, Fiji, Ethiopia and even Turkey".[4]

It is worth admitting the afore-referred situation conditioned by expanding is not utterly devoid of a certain spectrum of problems for the grouping in its initial configuration. The fact is there are diversities of positions that Russia, India, and Brazil

---

[2] The Indian Express, June 2, 2023.

[3] See Europe 2020 Strategy, *The Partnership Instrument, advancing the EU's core interests*, available at: https://ec.europa.eu/fpi/what-we-do/partnership-instrument-advancing-eus-core-interests_en.

[4] Dinic L., *Will the "BRICS-Plus" Keep Growing?*, China-US Focus, https://www.chinausfocus.com/finance-economy/will-the-brics-plus-keep-growing (Mar.10, 2022).

are having on this issue. However, despite this, any difficulties can always be removed through negotiations.

The current development of international relationships as it turns out provides certain patterns of ways and/or tools normally used in the global practice to promote the overall realignment of forces operating in the international arena. In this respect, one of them is the positive role played by the new actors, including the alliances of states, having emerged at the turn of the twentieth and twenty-first centuries, to which prima facie belongs the BRICS group. Besides, the transformation process which encompasses all subjects and spheres of international relations makes to raise the question of a necessity to approach in a more concentrated manner to the legal basis of cooperation between the members of so called "traditional" and "nontraditional" entities. Concerning the means to respond to this challenge, the main guideline should consist in juxtaposing the system of international law principles in whole with those particular ones pertaining to the integration communities or other institutions/para-organizations while construing the contemporary international legal order.

In so far as it is witnessed by reality, the mere fact of BRICS existence creates new opportunities for mutual prospective development of economic and innovative cooperation effected by the grouping. At the same time, it is needed to emphasize one major detail: the situation aggravated when BRICS became to be treated as a powerful grouping in the international arena, "which members, for various reasons, were not satisfied with the old world order and with the international institutions created in the framework of the prevailing dominance of the Anglo-Saxon geopolitical actors".[5] Thus, as for the BRICS parties, the external vector reflects their resistance to the Western countries' efforts to uphold the previous hegemony thereof within the unipolar world order. Alongside this, from the point of view of domestic political and economic impulses, the cooperation within the framework of BRICS group for each of its participants acquires a specific peculiarity, i.e., the aptitude to serve the grounds for transition to the *formation of the strategic partnership* of the parties thereof under conditions of substantial transformation of geopolitical and international legal structure of the world.

Due to the above, it becomes necessary to reveal the core features and the concept itself of the phenomenon "principles" of international law, since any type of international interaction is inevitably based upon the relevant principles. Besides, it no less matters to assess the achievements as well as challenges for the BRICS countries' development and how effectively the municipal laws are influenced by a variety of principles of international law in the course of mutual interaction of the parties. Unlike the scholars' writings that focus on general problems and trends of interplay between the international and domestic law envisaged not comprehensively but by way of perusing particular blocks (such as territory, armed conflicts, space or maritime law, international economic law, human rights violations along with the human rights international control, etc.), this paper is supposed to respond to the demands

[5] Cf., Emelyanov, A.I. *Peculiarities of BRICS Development in the Beginning of the XXI century,* BIG EURASIA: DEVELOPMENT, SECURITY, COOPERATION. Yearbook, Issue 1. Part 2. / RAS. INION Dep. of Scien. Cooperation; Gerasimov, V.I. (ed.). – M., 2018, at 256 (in Russian).

of the present moment for a special study of the issue of the influence exerted by the basic principles of international law on both the sectoral (branch) principles of international law and those that are properly inherent to cooperation between the BRICS countries in economics, science, technology, and innovation.

3 BRICS Group in the Current Geopolitical Landscape

The development of mutual relationships of Brazil, Russia, India, China, and South Africa as for legal foundation, guidelines, or forms of cooperation between states differs to some extent from those ones generally practiced, which are normally used to embrace both institutional and contractual grounds, meanwhile the BRICS countries predominantly make options in favor of flexible, not rigid (noninstitutional) basis for their interaction. The substantial feature thereof is multilateralism: the parties prefer bilateral and multilateral agreements in contrast to the institutionalization (which presumes coordinating the participants' ties through the established international institution). Moreover, the result of the above preference made by the grouping is in fact to be deemed as an "*atypical*" form for the contemporary international law and international relations, defined and classified as a "para-organization."

Nevertheless, the present period in the course of mutual cooperation is characterized by a qualitative leap forward—its previous framework is expanding after the alliance summit held in Beijing in June 2022, when Iran and Argentina applied to join cooperation programs with the "five." What are the chances of expanding the partnership in this regard, what will the group gain from the accession of two more states, and will it get the ability to become a new center of power are topical issues for the forthcoming period in the course of joint work of the BRICS members.[6] In addition to the extensive development of the grouping in the geographical sense, new spheres of public relations are being added to the diversity of activities within BRICS interaction that require common care (currently these are mainly sectors of economy with creation and application of high technologies, innovative achievements and "breakthrough" indicators of scientific and progress: aeronautics, high-speed

[6]According to mass media, referring in the publications to sources in the official circles of the respective states, Tehran is hopeful for Iran's partnership in the BRICS grouping would bring "additional advantages" to both sides. Thus, the country's foreign ministry noted that the share of the BRICS countries in the Iranian GDP was about 30%, and the total population of the states encompassed by the group accounted for nearly 42% of the world's population. In addition, Iranian President Ebrahim Raisi assured that "Iran's geopolitical and geo-economic position can make it a stable and reliable BRICS partner." The Iranian leader noted that Tehran was ready to provide the countries of the grouping with its opportunities to access new markets and meet energy needs. A similar statement was made by the President of Argentina, Alberto Fernandez: "We strive to become full members of this group of countries. We are a safe and responsible food supplier and a recognized player in the field of biotechnology and applied logistics." Available at https://iz.ru/1356676/kseniia-loginova/po-kirpichu-iran-i-argentina-podalngi-zaiavki-na-vstuplenie-v-briks (Nov. 19, 2022).

vehicles, microelectronics and information technologies, nanotechnology, food security and sustainable agriculture, biotechnology and veterinary medicine, basic research, mineral prospecting and exploration, remote sensing of the Earth from outer space, climate change, water resources and water purification technologies, etc.).

In connection with the above, regarding the progressive advancement of the grouping upholding the atypical form of organization in its cooperation processes, it will not be vain to highlight two circumstances. With regard to the first of them, no one could ignore the original "foundation" that was formed by the objectively merged long-term mutual attraction to each other between Russia, India, and China (RIC, once upon a time called the "Primakov trinity") and, as a result, bilateral ties that have been strengthened in every possible way in respective sectors and segments of their politics and economics. Thus, at present, the same did not disappear but received additional impact grace to the goals, guidelines, and programs of the BRICS in whole as a group. In this sense, the tasks as set forth today, for example, for Russian-Indian cooperation in public policy, trade, investments, science and technologies, and other fields, have distinctive peculiarities, including those determining the prospects for development of military-technical cooperation, viz., joint production of modern weapons, which in general invoked the actual qualification of their relationship as a "particularly privileged strategic partnership."

As far as the second point is concerned, it is helpful to remind that from the very beginning of the BRICS cooperation, the goals of creating a "classic" international organization have not been formulated, and the terminology of the documents related to the functioning of BRICS reflects the same as an objective trend of the world development toward formation of a polycentric system of international interaction along with the course toward strengthening the economic interdependence of states. In such system the noninstitutional structures of global governance and network diplomacy are increasingly being used.[7]

Nevertheless, in the sectors requiring more intensified joint activities, the elements of institutionalization are needed to be introduced without delay. As an example of actually operating pattern having some elements of institutionalization within BRICS is PartNIR. The cooperation within PartNIR is effected following up the vectors conditioned by the development of high technologies. At present the most advanced directions in science, technology, and innovations (STI) relate to arranging the zones of development of high technologies, digitalization of the economics, and development of artificial intelligence.[8] The system of components comprises structural and functional organs, bodies, and programs. The central positions are occupied by the BRICS STI Steering Committee, BRICS PartNIR Innovation Centre (BPIC); BRICS Centre for Industrial Opportunities for Development; and BRICS

[7] Cf.: The Concept of the participation of the Russian Federation in the BRICS grouping, approved by the President of the Russian Federation, para. 4 (2013).

[8] Cf.: Babayev K.V. The potential of BRICS+ in the field of BRICS technological partnership, Materials of the International scientific and practical conference, Issue 1 / RAN. INION. Scientific department. cooperation; Gerasimov, V.I. (ed). – M., 2023, at 24.

Young Polycentric Technology Transfer Center Network, iBRICS Network. There is a number of working groups: Digital Economy Working Group and the Working Group on ICT, Working Group on Digitalization issues (e.g. Cooperation on Digitalization of Manufacturing the PartNIR projects designed to out training programs to address challenges of NIR for inclusive collaboration with other relevant BRICS mechanisms), and the BRICS Institute of Future Networks.

Since the emergence and further advancement of BRICS following the path of expanding cooperation, in so far as time witnessed, considerably changed the outlines of contemporary world structure (comprising international legal order), having created better prospects and opportunities for participants (not only in "traditional" sectors—trade in goods, services, natural resources, industrial production tangible and intangible things, wealth, investments, etc.—but also in joint innovative activities in the course of cooperation in science and technology, intellectual property rights, etc., typical for "breakthrough" industries), it is the case to show the results of joint actions obtained up to date looking at from the legal point of view. For this purpose, the information disclosing the types, contents, dates, and quantum of international instruments (treaties, summits declarations, public acts of other organs of the group), made by the parties prior nowadays, is in a position to communicate a lot about the BRICS functioning.

In practice, the interaction of the regional blocks of the BRICS countries is already taking place. For example, agreements on cooperation between the EAEU and Vietnam, Iran, China, and other countries were signed; a joint statement on cooperation on the integration of the construction of the EAEU and the SREB was signed (2015); a memorandum of cooperation on trade and economic issues between the EEC and MERCOSUR (2018) and a memorandum of understanding between the EEC and the Commission African Union in the field of Economic Cooperation were made (2019); and contacts between the EU and ASEAN are developing, etc. In general, the interregional vector of cooperation is very promising for many of researchers, although it stands in the initial stage (however, it may be a serious mistake to artificially accelerate the process). What does really matter for the interregional cooperation development that is providing for certain organizational "collective measures" to raise a degree of institutionalization in order to accommodate both the integration and interregional cooperation of BRICS group to new geopolitical conditions and specifically those connected with the BRICS extending?

4 "BRICS+" and "BRICS-Outreach": Historical Antecedents and Major Features

According to Russian officials' evaluation, the BRICS+ and BRICS-outreach formats have a great potential for building sustainable ties with the interested multilateral associations and states with emerging markets and developing countries.[9] Chronologically, in 2013 South Africa became the first country under whose chairmanship the representatives of African regional organizations were invited to the BRICS summit, and by 2017 a tradition of developing partnerships in the regions of the alliance had been outlined and thereafter supported practically by all attendants of the forum. Then the officials of BRICS as a group initiated the discourse of the prospects of BRICS as *a platform for "integration of integrations*".[10] Notwithstanding this, the countdown for historical antecedents of the format BRICS-outreach may be conducted since 2011, when the idea of eventual attraction of new partners to the work of BRICS was expressed in the declaration (para 6) adopted at the BRICS summit in Sanya (Hainan Island, China, April 14, 2011).[11] "Before that, there were neither plans for global cooperation with third countries, nor even more, so with entire regions, in the rhetorics of the BRICS."[12]

There is a very important component in general assessment of actual position of the BRICS grouping in the world. It consists in the fact that "BRICS+" and "BRICS-outreach" embody simultaneously two diverse trends: aspirations for both globalism and regionalism. Previously, they have been traditionally viewed as opposite to each other outside the BRICS regions, and now the interdependence thereof is becoming clear. With due account to these circumstances, in science and practice concerning BRICS, a new round of exchange of views has unfolded, regarding the political, legal, organizational, and other qualifications of BRICS alliance as well as the current configuration of international relationship between the grouping referred to and outside nations. Thus, as per the Indian expert Sh. Naik's words, BRICS can be considered as *interregional interaction* [italics added, L.A.] of five countries that have united in an ascertained joint format of cooperation in order to solve common problems and achieve common goals in the international system, despite the lack of geographical proximity of the BRICS member countries, existing differences in culture, languages and identity". The author defines BRICS as an example of a "hybrid form of interregional interaction that exceeds the regions borders, but at the same time forms links between the countries, based on common goals and objectives for

---

[9] See Ryabkov S., *Priorities of the Russian Presidency in BRICS*, 2020, in: INTERNATIONAL AFFAIRS. 2020. BRICS/Russia. Special Issue. 2020 at 6. (In Russ.).

[10] Op.cit. *Ibidem*.

[11] *Declaration adopted by BRICS summit,* President of Russia, *available at:* http://www.kremlin.ru/supplement/907 (Jul. 20, 2023).

[12] See Lagutina M.L., *The regional dimension of cooperation between the BRCIS countries,* 13 JOURNAL OF INTERNATIONAL ANALYTICS 1, 67 (2022) (IN RUSS), available at: https://www.interanalytics.org/jour/article/view/414?locale=en_US (Jun. 28, 2023).

the al formation of a new world order and a system of global governance."[13] Regretful, but the conclusion leaves a lot to be desired in whatsoever concerns the elucidation of existing ambiguity related to the issue of "hybridness," namely, what makes the subject to be "hybrid" (how far does its heterogeneity go). Theoretical substantiation of regionalism related to BRICS as research subject-matter, obtained in Russian and foreign legal literature supplementary impulse in the course of last decades. A lot of proposals have appeared, both on the merits of various theories and on terminology intended specifically to denote the phenomenon itself concerning BRICS. Within the framework of new theories of regionalism, it has become possible to consider BRICS as a regional project of a new type, which different researchers define differently in their works: "alternative regionalism" (E.B. Mikhailenko), "hybrid form of interregional interaction" (Sh. Naik), "semi-globalism" (Y.D. Lisovolik), "global region" or "trans-regional forum" (M.L. Lagutina), etc.

The original approach to the interpretation of the concept of regionalism in connection with BRICS is demonstrated by the author from India, K. Meena, who suggested moving away from the geographical understanding of the category "region" and defined the latter as a "social construct" or "geopolitical fiction" ("geopolitical imagination"). On this basis, the BRICS countries identify themselves as a whole within the global world, despite the lack of territorial neighborhood. The major qualifying criterion, according to the author's opinion, is that there should be the availability of common features (homogeneity) of the participants. As a result, the strategic regionalization of BRICS in relation to the West is ensured (the West vs. The Rest), since the decisive factor of BRICS cooperation—a kind of global governance of the developing world—was adjacent to emerge.[14] Within the framework of "*new concepts of regionalism*," it has become popular to consider BRICS as a regional project of a new type, which various researchers in different ways defined in their works.[15]

The XIV BRICS summit stated that the world today is experiencing changes unprecedently accelerated in a century. As it was noticed by President Xi Jinping, the head of China which chaired the grouping at that time, "…over the past 16 years, the giant BRICS ship has been steadily moving forward,…has embarked on the right course of mutual support and mutually beneficial cooperation. Standing at the crossroads of history, it is necessary not only to look back at the path we have traveled and remember first of all why we created BRICS, but also to look forward to a common future as a more comprehensive, close, practical and inclusive high-quality partnership in order to jointly embark on a new stage of the path of cooperation".[16] In addi-

[13] Naik, Sh., *Rising BRICS: a path to Multipolar World Reality?*, COMPARATIVE POLITICS 9, No. 1, at 100–108 (2018).

[14] See Meena, Kishnendra, *Regions, Regionalization and BRICS,* REVOLUTIONS: GLOBAL TRENDS AND REGIONAL 3, No. 1, at 18–42 (2015).

[15] More details in this respect, see Lagutina M. L. Regional Dimension of BRICS cooperation, op.cit, 69–74.

[16] See XIV BRICS Summit materials, at http://brics2022.mfa.gov.cn/eng / (Nov. 11, 2022); also cf. Beijing Declaration of the XIV BRICS Summit of June 23, 2022; Joint Statement of the Ministers

tion, the term "expansion" has a second dimension, which gave rise to new forms of interconnections, viz., "BRICS+" and "BRICS outreach".[17] The latest summit showed that other like-minded states from Asia, Africa, Latin America, and the Middle East are ready to participate in the functioning of the group. In political comments in this respect, it is noticed that "more and more like-minded people will join the BRICS+ format."

The antecedents for emergence of a new scale in international cooperation and, accordingly, the onset of qualitative changes in the results thereof are, first of all, the complexity and diversity of spheres and multiplicity of ties within cooperation, taking into account external and internal needs, achieving fundamental strategic goals and task performance in ensuring national interests, and, finally, strengthening the overall economic and political weight of the country in the global scale. An even more important indicator of the process under consideration is its geopolitical dimension, namely, the redistribution of powers and "world control centers" and the formation of new groups of states and their allied ties, both inside existing political and economic entities and outside them, forming new alliances or between them, which objectively "undermines" the unipolar world order and works to create its polycentric alternative: multipolarity.

Over the years, the worth of relationship within the framework of the BRICS group for each of the participants, step by step, has been acquiring a special value as an asset (being in conformity with specific national goals, interests, and needs). As for the grouping taken at whole, it obtains a flexible mechanism of interstate interaction that meets the spirit of the times—"winds of change"—devoid of dictate and based on the principles of collegiality, equality, mutual respect of interests, and an *innovative tool of global governance.*[18] For the Russian Federation, which faces unprecedented increase of unjust and internationally completely wrongful acts, tending to turn into a permanent "squall" of so-called "sanctions" or all kinds of "restrictive measures and regimes" forwarded against the sovereign state by the "collective West," the relationships with the alliance countries acquire the necessary stability

---

for Foreign Affairs/International Relations of the BRICS countries "Strengthening solidarity and cooperation, responding to new opportunities and challenges in the international environment" dt. of May 19, 2021 BRICS countries, at https://www.mid.ru/ru/foreign_policy/briks/1814106 (accessed Nov. 21, 2022).

[17] Back at the Johannesburg Summit (July 2018), China proposed a new format for countries that suggest an ambition to cooperate with BRICS in a specific area. It is called PartNIR, which means "Partnership in the field of the New Industrial Revolution." The project, strictly saying, is a challenge to the international economic system, which relies on the availability of only one "decision-making center" in the contemporary world order: the United States. The afore-referred initiative of China was preceded by Russian domestic document dt. of 2013 and titled "The Concept of the participation of Russian Federation in the BRICS grouping," which provided in part of development of scientific, technical, and innovative cooperation the new wording related to the format counted not only for five BRICS member states but mentioned also "smaller multilateral groups, involving, in case of mutual interest, partners from among non-BRICS states" (para. 24).

[18] See Stepanov O., *BRICS Unification and Global Governance in a multipolar world,* International life (2020), BRICS. The Russian Presidency. Special issue, at 10 (2020).

and, moreover, ensure formation of a strategic partnership, which implementation is provided by the official documents thereof. The said characteristics become more and more justified as paramount, especially at present, under modern conditions qualified to be the crisis from many points of view. It is worth emphasizing in this regard that strategic interests are inherent to all participants of BRICS as an alliance of the reformers of the world economy and adepts of the new world order. Such statement without any exaggeration represents a key feature for the grouping in question.

While defining the phenomenon of "BRICS-outreach" purported to disclose its subject matter, the researchers from Ghent Institute for International Studies (GIIS) [Ghent University, Belgium] channeled their analysis to the comparative approach. They wrote: "We focus on two research puzzles: a) the motivations and b) the form and degree of the institutionalization of BRICS outreach. We define outreach as collaborative interaction among BRICS and other actors within and outside the BRICS area and focus on outreach to governments of non-BRICS countries and national top officials representing regional organizations. First, we offer a theoretical framework based on the experiences of the Group of 7/8 (G7/8) and the Group of 20 (G20), considering both commonalities and differences with BRICS. Second, we provide a detailed empirical analysis of BRICS outreach over time. Third, we explain BRICS in light of the theoretical framework and enrich it based on our findings. Methodologically, we draw empirical information from official documents, news media and academic literature. We argue that the outreach activity of a major power grouping is reflective of its internal cohesion, as well as of how it defines its own position in the world and how it is perceived by others."[19] These positions, deserving the serious attention to be paid to, coincide in much with the ideas expressed earlier in this paper. The authors afore-referred confirmed the allegations exposed herein in so far as the nonrigid (flexible) legal basis of the BRICS cooperation is concerned. However, there is no possibility to admit the mere positivists' agreeing with the presupposed so-called overall institutionalization of BRICS.[20]

There is another reason to disagree with the mentioned experts—it is the theoretical justification of the BRICS-outreach format. Referring to the theory of "group hegemony" expressed by the Canadian scholar Ellison Beilin, they proceed from the identity of BRICS and G7, by saying: "This group (c.q. the G7) has taken over the role of a declining great power (c.q. the US), and is characterized by a concentration of economic power, group identity and fidelity to economic liberalism."[21]

It should not be correct, if to ignore admitted distortion, i.e., almost nonavailability of similarity between the BRICS alliance and the G7, except, indeed, that both are noninstitutionalized forums of states, which exhausts the common elements, and the rest of the characteristics drastically differ. Hence, the main result of such a comparison is the assessment of the "orientation of hegemony": in G7 (as well as in G8 or

---

[19] Zhao H., Lesage D., *Explaining BRICS Outreach: Motivations and Institutionalization,* 15 International Organisations Research Journal 2, 68–91 (2020) (in English).

[20] Op. cit. at 68.

[21] *Ibid.* at 69.

G20) it bears an external character, which provides the meaning "hegemony in relation to the rest of the world." On the contrary, the involvement by BRICS into cooperation of the outside nations (originally nonparticipants) is based on a completely differing policy and ideology, i.e., ensuring the consolidation of their own positions in order to find out opportunities for an adequate response to the challenges of the new geopolitical landscape. As it appears, in this case it is unreasonable to treat it as strictly saying "hegemony." Consequently, as a result, the nature of "BRICS+" or "BRICS-outreach" has a peculiarity, though it may change in the future. At the same time, there is no doubt about the interstate nature of interaction in both the first and the second formats, and therefore they are fully subject to the principles and norms of international law.

Regarding the definition itself of the format "BRICS-outreach" according the scholars' approach, it may be defined as "collaborative interaction among the actors (governments and institutions) and other actors within and outside the BRICS area, such as other governments, multilateral institutions, business and civil society".[22] The focus preferred by the authors in their consideration of the "outreach" practices was set on the governments of non-BRICS countries and regional organizations represented by the competent organs.

5 "Principles," Basic Principles, and Jus Cogens in General International Law

Principles and Basic Principles of International Law

Despite the increasing denial both of international law as such and inclusively its principles, not only in the West but rarely also in Russia, and the widespread approach of domestic legal science concerning the legal principles of mutual cooperation of the BRICS countries, it is necessary to place them within the framework of the principles of international law. At the same time, a substantive analysis is required, in the course of which it is important to segregate the political and legal significance, role, and place of the BRICS' cooperation principles in the system of international law and their correlation with the basic principles of international law, i.e., those set forth by the UN Charter.

The problems related to the discourse indicated above determine the mainstream in further development of the fundamental part of the theory of international law, because it is directly connected with many vital aspects prevailing nowadays in the international relationships. The vital role of principles of law is vividly illustrated by two fragmented quotations that belonged to a very prominent lawyer and recently deceased the judge of the International Court of Justice Antônio Augusto Cançado Trindade: "One cannot study international law making abstraction of its foundations...Nor can one study the foundations of international law making abstraction of

[22] Zhao H., Lesage D., *Explaining BRICS Outreach: Motivations and Institutionalization*. P. 68–69.

its basic principles." And for supplement: " ….the truth is that, without those principles, there is no legal system at all, be it national or international. They give expression to the idea of an *objective justice*, paving the way to the application of the *universal* international law."[23]

The interaction of various states in the field of science, technology, and innovation constitutes a significant portion of international economic cooperation in the contemporary reality, laying down in some cases the foundations for further development of promising areas of strategic partnership and even integration ties. It is an axiom that in the development of this kind and in general, in order to create certain prerequisites for scientific and technical cooperation (STC), the principles of legal regulation as special instrument that provides the necessary impact on relevant public relations play a pivotal role.

Noting changes in such kind of statements for the case of BRICS grouping. There is also the task of doctrinal elaboration of the issue of the system of international legal principles, structural elements, their features, etc. Prima facie, the issue of substance comes to the forefront of international legal theory: what is the principle? In addition, the problem of differentiation of principles in the system of international law is acute. Finally, the special role of the dominating category of principles—the *basic* principles (alternatively sometimes called otherwise, as "generally recognized principles and norms international law"[24])—both for the functioning of the system of positive international law itself and international legal theory, requires clarification of understanding.

Of course, in one publication it is not possible even briefly to embrace the spectrum of all listed areas in total, though the placement of reference points in the analysis to be effected appears as the only appropriate way. In particular, the central discourse should be the formulation of a number of provisions with regard to substantiating the availability of normativity in the principles of international law as their inherent property, functional purpose of the principles within the system of international law, their place, differentiation, etc.

Primarily, we are talking about the guiding norms that have an unreservedly binding character, which in Soviet and Russian doctrine are traditionally referred to as "basic principles."[25] In this regard, there is a need to compare this concept with the peremptory norms of international law, which in Western teachings are mainly

---

[23] Trindade A. A. Cançado., *Prologue: An overview of the contribution of international tribunals to the rule of law* (accessed from the electronic resource, downloaded from Elgar Online at Oct. 4, 2022).

[24] More details on the issue of differentiation of the terms and concepts afore-referred, cf.: Anufrieva L.P., *Enigma of the Constitution of the Russian Federation 1993*: "Generally Recognized Principles and Norms of International Law" – in: *Pravo. Zhurnal Vysshey shkoly ekonomiki.* No 3, at 4–25. (2019) (in Russ.).

[25] Cf.: Pushmin E. A. *O ponyatii osnovnykh printsipov sovremennogo obshchego mezhdunarodnogo prava. – Sovetskiy ezhegodnik mezhdunarodnogo prava.* Moscow, 1980, pp. 72–85 (in Russ.). From the latest works published in Russia on the raised problem, see Anufrieva L.P., Principles in Modern International Law (certain issues of concept, nature, genesis, substance, and scope). Moscow Journal of International Law, 2021. No 1. P. (in Russ.), 6–27; Anufrieva L.P. Following

defined by means of the term "jus cogens." At the same time, this does not mean that the latter is absolutely alien to Russian science, and expatriate doctrine does not operate with the notion "basic principles." It is important to make an explanation here: the term "basic principles" "comes into the picture" only once in the Resolution of the UN General Assembly (hereinafter, UN GA) dated October 24, 1970, containing the "Declaration on Principles of International Law concerning Friendly Relations and Cooperation between States in Accordance with the Charter of the United Nations." It indicates that the seven principles interpreted by are "basic" ones, although neither in the UN Charter nor in the "Declaration of Principles by which States – Participants would be guided in their Mutual Relations" (contained in the Helsinki Final Act of the CSCE, 1975) such a phrase itself or its definition is used. In the light of the above, there is an ambiguity: are the analyzed concepts—"basic principles" and jus cogens—identical and synonymous, and therefore, so is the same with the terms as well as (and this is the most important thing!)? What is more inherent to the essence of international law? Do the UN Charter and the Declaration 1970 contend the exhaustive list of basic principles for international law, etc.? There is a lot of queries. Among the relevant examples of using the term there is the work of the most prominent Uruguayan international lawyer Eduardo Jiménez de Aréchaga "Sovremennoye mezdunarodnoye pravo," in which the author refers to the "general principles of international law governing the conduct of States," interpreting them as prescriptions included in the category of fundamental norms. Prominent Italian international lawyer Antonio Cassese also uses terminology similar to the Russian one and refers to the principles in question as "basic" (but literally calling them "fundamental," L.A.), "regulating international relations."[26] By the way, the positions expressed by A. Cassese clarify the queries outlined hereinabove. Against this background, it is needed also to recognize that the concepts "basic principles," "expressing the essence of legal provisions on international relations," as well as "general principles of international law" are not alien to German science.[27]

Jus Cogens in International Law The ideas that there are specific imperative norms[28] in the international community, rules of a binding order, have been expressed since the end of the nineteenth century. This phenomenon became known in positive international law and legal literature as jus cogens. J.C. Bluntschli, P. Fauchille,

---

up the discussion on the stricto sensu "principles" in modern international law, and beyond the same .... – MOSCOW JOURNAL OF INTERNATIONAL LAW, 2021. No 2, at 6–34 (in Russ.).

[26] Cf.: Aréchaga de, Eduardo J. *Sovremennoye mezhdunarodnoye pravo.* /transl. from Span. Moscow: Progress Publishing House, 1983 (in Russ.) [Aréchaga de, Eduardo J. *Modern International Law]*; Cassese, Antonio. *International Law.* 2nd ed. Oxford: Oxford University Press, 2005, at 46–48.

[27] Cf.: *Völkerrecht =International law* / V. G. Vittstum, M. Bote, R. Dol'tser et als. Moscow: *Infotropik Media*, 2015, book 2, -1072 p. (in Russ.).

[28] The term "peremptory" (*imperious*) is deemed as "imperative, final; binding; decisive, absolute, positive; not allowing for a question, revision or any alternative; self-evident, not requiring support by any evidence"; for semantic approach cf.: *Black's Law Dictionary* (6th ed. 1990), at 1136.

A. Verdrosss, and many others wrote on this subject.[29] Both the scope and in fact the very existence of this concept have been debated by the international legal community for many years.[30] Detailed review of historical evolution of jus cogens was included into the first report of the Special Rapporteur of the UN International Law Commission[31] to which the proliferation of the concept as such within contemporary international law was due.

It will not be superfluous to mention again in this respect: the concept of "basic principles of the international law" seems more appropriate for Russian and former Soviet doctrines, whereas the term "jus cogens" ("mandatory law," "binding law," "peremptory norms," "binding norms") prevails in Western literature, materials of the UN International Law Commission (hereinafter ILC), and law enforcement practice.[32]

However, the theses exposed hereinbefore may be to some extent refuted by cases of a diverse approach. For example, in the article of Rafael Nieto-Navia, the idea of equalizing "the fundamental principles of international law and jus cogens" slips through. He wrote as follows: "The concept of jus cogens in international law encompasses the concept of peremptory norms in international law. In this regard, the opinion was formed (I. Brownlie, *added L.A.*) that there are some fundamental principles of international law that form 'a body of jus cogens.' These principles are those from which it is accepted that no State may derogate by way of treaty." It is appropriate to add hereto the opinion of Sir Hersch Lauterpacht. In the commentary to draft Article 15 on the law of treaties, he regarded norms of *jus cogens* "as

[29] Namely, it was found that there existed a binding law, and violation of which rendered illegal the object of certain treaties: "The notion of *jus cogens* in international law encompasses the notion of peremptory norms in international law" (see Bluntschli J.C. *Le Droit International Codifié*. (1874), 238–240). A view has been expressed that certain overriding principles of international law exist which form "a body of *jus cogens*" (Aréchaga de, Eduardo J. Op.cit.; Cassese, Antonio. *International Law.* 2nd ed. Oxford: Oxford University Press, 2005, at 48.

Cf.: Fauchille P. *Traité de Droit International Public*. Vol. I, 1ère partie. 1922. p. 22). And, besides, "these principles are those from which it is accepted that no State may derogate by way of treaty. As a result they are generally interpreted as restricting the freedom of States to contract while 'voiding' treaties whose object conflicts with norms which have been identified as peremptory" (cf.: Verdross A. *Forbidden Treaties in International Law*//American Journal of International Law (далее: hereinafter—AJIL). 1937, Vol.31, 571 ff.).

[30] See Meron T., *On a Hierarchy of International Human Rights,* 80 American Journal of International Law (AJIL) 1, January 1986, at 1–23.

[31] See General Assembly, ILC, 68 Sess, Geneva, May 2–June 10 and July 4–August 12, 2016. First report on *jus cogens* by Dire Tladi, Special Rapporteur. Doc. A/CN.4/693. Chap. (IV), at 9–27 (2016).

[32] Cf.: First report on *jus cogens* by Dire Tladi, Special Rapporteur. Doc. A/CN.4/693; UN General Assembly. International Law Commission. Sixty-ninth session. Geneva, May1–June 2 and July3–August 4, 2017. Second report on *jus cogens* by Dire Tladi, Special Rapporteur. Doc.A/CN.4/706. https://undocs.org/pdf?symbol=en/A/CN.4/706 (accessed Oct. 01, 2021); UN General Assembly, International Law Commission. Seventieth session. Geneva, April 30–June 1 and July2–August 10, 2018. Third report on peremptory norms of general international law (*jus cogens*) by Dire Tladi, Special Rapporteur. Doc. A/CN.4/714.

constituting principles of international public policy."[33] The provisions exposed in I. Brownlie's well-known *Principles of Public International Law* discover the author's support of the view "that certain overriding principles of international law exist, forming body of jus cogens,"[34] which means nothing else but presumption of equivalence alleged by the author between the concepts "*principles*" of international law and its norms *jus cogens*. Finally, the most remarkable notes in the context of the debated discourse are contained in the Trinidad and Tobago statement intimated at the 56th meeting of the *Committee of the Whole* in the framework of the United Nations Conference on the Law of Treaties, where it was declared: "General multilateral treaties such as the United Nations Charter could also be a source of norms having the character *jus cogens*."[35] "At the same time, it is essential to draw attention to one major point: although the wording implicitly contained at least a hint of availability of jus cogens norms in the principles of the UN Charter, however, the fact that no explicit indication was made regarding the basic principles which prima facie should be treated as jus cogens, cannot be accepted."

Better understanding of both concepts "principle" and "jus cogens" in their comparison may be reached in the course of diligent perusal of the of the UN IL Commission reports related to the topic under its program "jus cogens." The First Report prepared by the Special Rapporteur D. Tladi is devoted to the historical evolution of the concept, methodological approach, theoretical basis for the peremptory character of jus cogens, the core elements of jus cogens, and conclusions (Chapters III, IV, V, and VII), creating the necessary general impression of the subject. Chapter III of the Second Report of the Special Rapporteur exposed the criteria of jus cogens and read as follows: (1) "Rules of international law may be modified, derogated from or abrogated by agreement of States to which the rule is applicable unless such modification, derogation or abrogation is prohibited by the rule in question (*jus dispositivum*). The modification, derogation and abrogation can take place through treaty, customary international law or other agreement." (2) "An exception to the rule set forth in paragraph 1 is peremptory norms of general international law, which may only be modified, derogated from or abrogated by rules having the same character." Draft conclusions (3, 7) as proposed by the Special Rapporteur[36] provided the following theses: (3) "Peremptory norms of international law (*jus cogens*) are those norms of general international accepted and recognized by the international community of States as a whole as those from which no modification, derogation or abrogation is permitted." (4) "Norms of *jus cogens* protect the fundamental values of

[33] See *The Commentary to the Draft Articles on the Law of Treaties,* Yearbook of the International Law Commission (1966) vol I (United Nations publication, Sales No. 67. para. 4 of the Commentary to draft Article 15.

[34] Brownlie I., *Principles of Public International Law, (*Sixth ed) Oxford, Oxford University Press, 488 (2003).

[35] See the Official Records of the United Nations Conference on the Law of Treaties, First Session, Vienna, March 26–May 24, 1968: Summary Records of the Plenary Meetings and of the Meetings of the Committee of the Whole (United Nations publication, Sales No. E.68.V.7), para. 63.

[36] See A/CN.4/693, para. 74.

the international community; are hierarchically superior to other norms of international law and are universally applicable."[37] The testimonies to the above allegations may be supported by the relevant judicial practice both international and domestic ones. In the case *Prosecutor v. Furundžija*, the International Criminal Tribunal for the Former Yugoslavia (ICTY)[38] described *jus cogens* norms as those that "enjoy a higher rank in the hierarchy of international law than treaty law or even 'ordinary' customary rules."

Thus, the major criterion for identification of peremptory norms, namely, of those jus cogens, is that they are norms of *general international law*, which are explicitly spelled out as yet as in 1969 in Article 53 of the Vienna Convention on the Law of Treaties. Besides, one of the substantial details flowing from the conclusions formulated by the doctrine and actual practice of modern international law in connection with the juxtaposition of jus cogens and basic principles of the international law contains in unreservedly stating that neither of them is contradictory to, firstly, the conciliatory (compromise/consensus) nature of international law, or, secondly, hierarchically positioning thereof at the superior level, or, thirdly, generally accomplished fact of its acceptance and recognition by the international community, etc. The same is totally applicable to the basic principles of international law residing in the UN Charter [Art. 2]. Would it be admissible to deny rigid force thereof for the regulatory purposes in case, when required, applicable to the relationship within any of BRICS' formats or between members of the group? The question, being rhetorical, does not need an answer. Naturally, the cooperation between the BRICS countries, or between the latter and the non-BRICS nations as well as relationships between any other parties should be based upon the principles of general international law and/or jus cogens.

Nevertheless, generalization of conclusions should be a great mistake, since there is no unanimity among states and scholars in supporting the theory of jus cogens. The relevant examples are represented by France which back in the 1960s intimated its disagreeing with the concept and subject matter in connection with jus cogens. Such a position sustained little changes till now. In particular, as it was underlined in the course of debate at the VI Committee of the UN General Assembly, France was particularly critical toward the Special Rapporteur's approach, suggesting that it gave no due consideration to the practices and opinions of states and, instead, adopted "an overly theoretical or ideological approach" to *jus cogens.*[39] Still on the question

[37] Second report on *jus cogens* by Dire Tladi, Special Rapporteur. Doc. A/CN.4/706.

[38] For example, the Tribunal with reference made to the to the US national courts practice (Filartiga v. Pena-Irala, Youssef v. Secretary of State for Foreign and Commonwealth Affairs SC 27-Jan-2016 cases) expressly linked the status of the prohibition of torture as a *jus cogens* norm importance of the values it protects," noting that "[c]learly, the *jus cogens* nature of the prohibition against torture articulates the notion that the prohibition has now become one of the most fundamental standards of the international community" (cf.: Judgement, Case No. IT-95-17/1-T, T.Ch., 10 December 1998, paras. 153 and 154. The same with approval was quoted by the European Court of Human Rights in *Al-Adsani v. United Kingdom* (Application No. 35763/97), judgment of 21 November 2001, para. 30.).

[39] Doc. A/C.6/71/SR.20, para. 77.

of the practice and opinions of states, France contended in its statement that the Special Rapporteur, "despite [France's] well-known reservations ... concludes that France is not a persistent objector."[40]

In response, Dire Tladi emphasized as follows: "It is true, as France noted, that the practice of France was of particular interest to the Special Rapporteur. This was because France was known as having objected to the very idea of *jus cogens*. Yet actual practice, as seen from the statements of France itself, shows this to be inaccurate. The assessment was not concerned with whether France is or is not a persistent objector and nowhere does the first report draw any conclusions in this respect. All that the report states, with regard to France, is the well-documented fact that, at the adoption of the Vienna Convention, France did not object to the idea of *jus cogens*. Rather, France expressed concern about the lack of clarity concerning how it would be applied and the possibility for its abuse" (para 17).

As far as the criteria of the jus cogens norms, they have evoked divergences from the side of governments of states. In this respect, the most sophisticated points may be forwarded by opinions of states regarding the disclosure of the elements of the jus cogens aimed to ascertain the hierarchical superiority thereof during debates on the International Law Commission materials.[41] The criticism expressed against the wording of some elements related to the issue of hierarchical superiority drew serious attention. The United States feared that the debated elements, in particular, the notion that *jus cogens* norms are universally applicable and reflect the fundamental values of the international community, would open the door to attempts to derive *jus cogens* norms from vague and contestable natural law principles, without regard to their actual acceptance and recognition by states. The quoted details of the discussions taken place at the meetings of the UN ILC manifest considerable difficulties on the ways of elaborating consensus on the key issues of international law. Even at present, after many years of the ILC working on the topic "jus cogens," the doctrine and official practice of nations do not stop to intimate objections in connection with different sides of the envisaged subject. Not less disputable are expected the matters arising from the draft conclusions concerned the way in which jus cogens rules are

[40] See written statement of France (on file with the Special Rapporteur): "In his report, Mr. Tladi is particularly interested in the French position. Despite my country's well-known reservations with regard to the concept of *jus cogens*, he concludes that France is not a persistent objector ... and that France has accepted it in principle. He does not, however, take into account the reservations expressed about this concept by the French delegations, *especially in recent years*." (emphasis added), Second report on *jus cogens* by Dire Tladi, Special Rapporteur. Doc. A/CN.4/706. Paras 16–17 *[Footnote 16. p.5/47-6/47]*.

[41] As an example: for China the problem with the elements was that they were "obviously at variance with the basic elements of *jus cogens* set out in article 53 of the Vienna Convention." The elements *of one of the draft conclusions* were seen as adding new core elements or requirements. With respect to hierarchical superiority, China questioned whether this "new" element would imply that *jus cogens* should prevail over the Charter of the United Nations, given that Article 103 of the Charter provides that obligations under the Charter prevail over other obligations" (see Second report on *jus cogens* by Dire Tladi, Special Rapporteur, at 14. Doc. A/CN.4/706).

to be identified and the legal consequences flowing from them, which have the universal importance.

In this connection, in continuation of devolving the topic, it might be referred to the essay of one of the most ardent objectors of the concept "jus cogens" from the United States, A. d'Amato.[42] Another representative of the academic science, being to some extent in opposition to the corpus of protagonists of jus cogens concept, an analyst who has never hidden his skepticism about this subject, at least judging by the titles of his works, is a Swedish scholar Ulf Linderfalk.[43] However, nowadays trying to assess the problem objectively, he had to state: "...whilst the concept of jus cogens was steadily growing last years in the direction of getting more and more the importance in science of public international law, lawyers remain hugely divided both over what precisely confers a jus cogens status on a norm, and what this conferral implies in term of legal consequences."[44] In his new ground-breaking book, U. Linderfalk definitely lays down the way for future, succinctly exploring the reasons for this divide in order to facilitate more rational and productive further discourse.

With due account to the above, it will be rather logical to wonder whether there is still a need in jus cogens research, especially in connection with the relationship of the BRICS countries. The answer should be quite lapidary: jus cogens expresses the idea of the existence of an international *lex superior.* The assumption is that jus cogens norms have an authority which exceeds that of ordinary international law. It lies in the very nature of a hierarchically superior law that it is applicable without any limits as to either subject or situation.[45] Resultant the disclosed legal hierarchy, it may have far-reaching consequences for construction of any international system of legal norms and accordingly regulation of the relevant relations. The same fully extends to cooperation between the BRICS countries and their ties with respective partners.

---

[42] Anthony D'Amato, *It's a Bird, it's a Plane, it's Jus Cogens!,* 6 Connecticut Journal of International Law 1-6 (Fall 1990), No1, electronic copy also available at: http://ssrn.com/abstract=1653507.

[43] Linderfalk U., *The Effect of Jus Cogens Norms: Whoever Opened Pandora's Box, Did You Ever Think About the Consequences?,* 18 The European Journal of International Law, 5, at 853–871 (2008).

[44] See Linderfalk U., *Understanding Jus Cogens in International Law and International Legal Discourse.* I. Introduction, Faculty of Law, Lund University, Elgar International Law series, Lund, 256, (2020).

[45] Ibidem.

6 The Principles of International Law Underlying the BRICS Cooperation

The theses outlined above in the present article have created a logical vector of further analysis of the subject. The prevailing task of current BRICS' regulation of its links consists in the formats of cooperation preferred to, viz., in selecting organizational facilities to achieve the economic goals set forth by the BRICS summits as the relevant major objectives and determining the adequate legal foundation required to be in conformity with the main stream of cooperation.

The BRICS group, as was reiterated, along with other alliances, groupings, and informal forums, does not constitute a legally formalized association—an international organization in the proper sense of the word. Nevertheless, the cooperation of the said countries within the framework of the BRICS cannot be deprived of any legal basis at all, which is composed of a package of principles agreed and formulated jointly by the parties.

The relevant aspect, covering the nature, classification, list and legal content of such principles, and their relationship with the principles of general international law, is a serious theoretical problem in modern jurisprudence, not only in terms of content but also in terms of volume. In particular, there is no doubt that, being realized as an integral part of global interstate economic cooperation, cooperation in the economic sphere of the BRICS countries is based on the principles of international economic law (IEL). Consequently, they as the branch (i.e., sectoral) principles, when coordinating the cooperation of the parties, extend their efficiency to mutual relationship of the BRICS countries both to the grouping (between themselves) and to their relations with the third parties in the field of economics. In this regard it is worth underlining that the principles of the IEL within the economic sphere have universal effect. In comparison with them, the principles of cooperation accepted, recognized, or developed by the BRICS countries properly for their relationship between themselves cannot be characterized by such an effect as universal, unless there is no assumption of the partners' address to basic or called "generally recognized" principles of international law as universal peremptory norms. Hereinafter, we will focus on the provisions concerning precisely such specific principles inherent to BRICS cooperation, which constitute at the present stage a distinguished legal basis for the relationship of the grouping under consideration.

Economic interaction, embracing a wide variety of areas, steadily extends the limits of cooperation, which sometimes aimed at ambitious targets. According to the presentations of some foreign experts, one common to all the BRICS countries' target is reviewing the global economic system, the basic component whereof is modernization of financial institutions by way of reforms within the Bretton-Woods system.[46] Apart of that, there is another subject of common interest, as joint activity

[46] Seyad, S., *A Critical Overview of the Objectives and Future Direction of the BRICS and its New Development Bank*, 31 JOURNAL OF INTERNATIONAL BANKING LAW & REGULATION, 9, at 495–506 (2016).

in "innovative" areas, such as the creation of new technologies and development of basic scientific research. There is no doubt that the principles of international cooperation should be construed as an integral part of the entire system of legal regulation of BRICS interaction, in whatsoever form it would be performed.

The models of progressive development of BRICS mutual relationships incorporate both traditional legal mechanisms and instruments and principles and forms of cooperation or requiring to rely on the innovative ones adapted to modern conditions, changing targets, needs, and demands of the parties involved therein. It means that all heads of principles available in the international law—basic principles and norms of IL, its branch (sectoral), and special principles—are, therefore, applicable without exemptions.

"The "triple problem" of principles in international law resultant from its relevant differentiation (availability, firstly, of basic principles, as well as of those related to regulation of specific fields of international relations – sectoral and special principles – secondly, and peremptory fundamental norms, including, in particular, both general ones and norms jus cogens, - thirdly), could partially be deemed as a gap in international law theory, requiring prompt and targeted scientific research". The fact is, that along with the basic (generally recognized) principles of international law which penetrate into and go through the entirety and integrity of the normative system, there are ~~(action and)~~ special principles of international law sector, branch, or fields of law, i.e., branch (sectoral) principles. There is no need to point out that the legal foundation for operation of each and every international organization or an integration community is constituted by their charters, statutes, or other acts which determine the limits of an institution's capacity. Due to this, the BRICS grouping, along with of the other nonformal entities (e.g., G7, G8, "G20", etc.[47]), in turn is subject to operate following their own principles formulated by the relevant official documents (summit declarations), if once they committed to would have shared the partnership therein. The list, contents, and scope of the aforementioned guiding rules acting as "principles" may vary and be differentiated depending on their species, legal nature, value, and effect. However, substantively the main relevant condition for validity of the said shall be deemed fundamental principles of international law underlying the whole system thereof.

In Russian domestic theory, in terms of scientific research of the principles as a category of international law and, prima facie, the principles enshrined in the UN Charter, the relevant approach thereto is consistently used as to the main guiding norms applicable to the entire system of international law, which, along with the above, possess normativity, general acceptance/recognition, imperativeness, attribution to general international law, property to protect universal values, and the impossibility of being changed due to simple agreement of the parties and other special qualities (primarily consistency with the basic principles of international law).

---

[47] The views which treat BRICS and other similar grouping having no elements of institutionalization and therefore, denying its capacity, not rarely are expressed in legal literature. It seems to be justified (in connection with this, cf.: Shinkaretskaya G. G., *On the legal status of BRICS*, 10 Modern law, at 140–145 (2015).

The list and content of the above categories of guiding norms as principles may vary and differentiate depending on their species, which determines the legal significance and hierarchical force; however, satisfaction of the requirement of compliance with the basic (systemic) principles of international law is an indispensable condition of legal validity for them. Thus, the principles of trade and economic, scientific and technical, industrial and technological, and innovative cooperation within the framework of the BRICS textually differ from the formulas of the principles of the UN Charter, referred to in the literature on international law as the "basic principles." Nevertheless, this does not mean that the principles of BRICS cooperation retreat or, moreover, contradict the essence of the principles of the UN Charter.

The contemporary international reality objectively creates conditions for supporting the course of strengthening the "basic pillars" in the international system and international law in the form of a sovereign state, principles of respect for sovereignty, sovereign equality, and equality. It is also important to emphasize that the course of this stage in the development of BRICS somehow determines the question of the need to accelerate the development of a fundamental framework for cooperation between the participating states. Based on the political results of the recent summit meetings of the leaders of the BRICS countries, formally enshrined in the summit documents, it is necessary to identify the prerequisites for identifying some of the leading principles of economic cooperation of the BRICS countries, put forward by the practice of mutual relations. Thus, the statement of the task regarding the implementation of "purposeful and concerted efforts to increase the dynamics of comprehensive and multilevel cooperation" has created a need for the principle of development and multilateralism. The goal of establishing a more just, equitable, honest, democratic, and representative international political and economic order, set at previous summits and stages of cooperation, led to an unambiguous formulation of the principles of honesty and justice in order to ensure peace and stability at the international and regional levels, mutual respect and mutual understanding, equality, solidarity, openness, inclusiveness and mutually beneficial cooperation, consideration of interests, and respect for the right of each state to choose ways of development.

The allegations afore-referred indicate that the principles fixed in the documents are not yet legally complete formulas that can be used as the basis for determining the legality or illegality of the behavior of the BRICS states as subjects of international law and in cases where international liability procedures are activated. These are more likely to be "declarations" (declarative ambitions) and "program guidelines," rather than legal rules. It seems that while they occupy an intermediate position between the so-called soft law and hard law (i.e., law stricto sensu), simultaneously, it is counterproductive to deny possibility for such provisions to acquire in future the quality of the principles of international cooperation of an informal grouping overcoming continuously the following stages: firstly, identifying the need; secondly, realizing the need for legal objectification of the corresponding goal and task; and, finally, outlining the scope of legal norm (norms) and formulating its (their) content.

Similarly, the above does not mean denying the existence of legally binding norms of international law in the current framework of cooperation between the

BRICS countries. The matter consists in the differences immune to the mechanisms for obtaining legal binding character by the rules of conduct. The latter ones related to the grounds of BRICS cooperation, could get their binding character not due to incorporation into the summit declarations or other commonly agreed by the nations inter-state documents, which, in their turn, are of recommendatory, not binding nature, but resultant from the fact that consequently they were enshrined in the acts of international law that have such properties as universality, general acceptance and recognition by the international community as a whole, and therefore, normativity in legal terms

In particular, the principles of equality, mutual benefit, reciprocity, independence in determining the forms of participation in cooperation with other states, as well as coordination, integration, and partnership represent a refraction in the sectoral principles of international economic law of basic principles of BRICS cooperation. At the same time, both the former and the latter satisfy the main criterion of validity of the legal framework of interaction, which was mentioned earlier—compliance with "hard law"—mediated by the basic principles of modern international law, which are fixed in the UN Charter, the Final Act of the CSCE, etc., or peremptory norms of general international law (jus cogens). This is directly applicable to Xiamen, Johannesburg, Beijing, etc., declarations that provide for "a just and equitable international order with the central role of the United Nations on the basis of the purposes and principles enshrined in the Charter of the United Nations and compliance with international law, commitment to the principles of democracy and the rule of law in international relations." On the other hand, nowadays the international law does not yet have the "principle of inclusiveness," which is often mentioned in BRICS documents. Therefore, at this stage, such provisions cannot be considered as normative. Along with this, the appearance on a broad international scale of an appropriate act or a number of acts containing binding regulations on inclusivity, in case of compliance with the requirements, might change the existing situation.

The states declare respect for the development paths chosen by the BRICS countries, understanding and supporting each other's interests, and advocating for equality and solidarity (paragraph 3 of the Xiamen Declaration of September 4, 2017). The principles of mutual respect, sovereign equality, democracy, inclusiveness, and strengthening cooperation are used by the BRICS countries in the name of ensuring peace, a more just international order, sustainable development and inclusive growth, stability, maintaining the central role of the United Nations, implementing the goals and principles E enshrined in the UN Charter, observing international law, and promoting democracy and the rule of law rights (paragraphs 5–6 of the Johannesburg Declaration of July 26, 2018). As it is seen, the cited provisions of the documents are aligned with the principles of the UN Charter, incorporating its norms with the same content, gradually forming the legal foundation of cooperation, and reinforcing the theses formulated above about the existence of systemic links between the principles of BRICS cooperation with the basic (generally recognized) principles of international law.

Chapter 3
Eurasian Countries and Human Rights Protection: Perspectives and a Possible Mechanism for Cooperation

S. Marochkin, Yu. Bezborodov, R. Khalafyan, and M. Likhachev

Abstract The growing interconnectedness of the world presents challenges for states, including environmental threats, armed conflicts, and human rights protection. In response, regional cooperation and the establishment of institutions have become important trends in the interstate system. The Eurasian region, with its geopolitical significance and vast potential for interstate cooperation, has witnessed essential integration in the twenty-first century. However, while the Eurasian countries share common interests in various fields, cooperation in human rights protection remains underdeveloped but promising. This paper explores the perspective of human rights protection in Eurasia. It discusses the necessity of developing this issue, examines universal and Eurasian concepts of human rights, and assesses the potential of existing Eurasian institutions to establish a specialized mechanism for human rights protection. The paper also addresses the institutional structure of this mechanism, considering whether it should be a separate body or integrated within existing organizations. The proposed mechanism could be implemented incrementally, progressing from advisory to judicial bodies. The research methodology involves critical theoretical analysis, genealogy of knowledge, deconstruction, prognosis and modeling, and comparative legal analysis using appropriate national and international legal materials. The findings contribute to the exploration of Eurasian cooperation and human rights protection.

The research was supported by Russian Science Foundation (Project № 25-28-00797), URL: https://rscf.ru/project/25-28-00797/.
This article was previously published in Law Science—Selected Papers Volume 3, Issue 2 (2024).

S. Marochkin (✉)
University of Tyumen, Tyumen, Russian Federation
e-mail: s.y.marochkin@utmn.ru

Y. Bezborodov · R. Khalafyan · M. Likhachev
Ural State Law University named after V. F. Yakovlev, Yekaterinburg, Russian Federation

T. Du, X. Fei (eds.), *The BRICS Legal Cooperation and Perspectives*,
https://doi.org/10.1007/978-981-95-4356-4_3

Keywords Eurasian integration · Universal and Eurasian concepts of human rights · Mechanism for human rights protection · SCO

1 Issue of the Eurasian Human Rights Protection

Challenges of international concern, such as environmental crises, armed conflicts, and human rights protection, require joint efforts of states at the universal, regional, and subregional levels. The opposing forces of universalism and regionalism have become emblematic for the first decades of the twenty-first century. Cooperation in addressing the universal issues has sharply slowed down, if not stagnated. The confrontation between states, especially the superpowers, has increased and reached an extreme point. The current state of the world leads to an even more radical assessment: "[…] it seemed that the humanity, having learned from history, was stepping into a period of the 'end of history.'"[1] The states have failed to address and tackle the common global problems properly due to a high degree of mistrust, opposition, and ambitious aspirations. The world is going through times of turbulence and uncertainty.

The trends in interstate system are the strengthening of regional cooperation and creation and development of regional and interregional institutions. International relations tend to move from universal to group (regional) cooperation and the creation and development of regional and interregional structures and organizations. Contemporary international relations are predominantly formed by bilateral and group interactions, rather than global ones. A significant increase in the number of regional interstate associations is evident, and now almost every country is involved in at least one regional association.

The first quarter of the twenty-first century has witnessed the growth of the Eurasian integration. The Eurasian region is playing an increasingly important role in the global political process. The region holds significant geopolitical importance due to its large states, vast territory, diverse culture, and historical experience, as well as its potential for economic growth. It is characterized by political and ideological heterogeneity and instability. Eurasian countries share common interests in the economic, political, military, cultural, and humanitarian fields. This has led to the widening of the "Asian world" influence in the international arena during the second half of the twentieth century and the first decades of the twenty-first century.

The region has great potential for interstate cooperation, and the beginning of the twenty-first century is marked by the growth of collaboration at the macro-, micro-, and interregional levels in various formats and directions including Commonwealth

---

[1] Rein Mullerson, *On Some Geopolitical and Societal Tendencies Threatening Peace and Stability*, 22(3) Chinese JIL 375 (2023).

of Independent States (CIS), Eurasian Economic Community (formerly), Eurasian Economic Union (EAEU), Collective Security Treaty Organization, Eurasian Customs Union (formely), and Shanghai Cooperation Organization (SCO).[2]

However, cooperation on human rights remains underdeveloped despite being a crucial issue on the global agenda and an essential element of states' international reputation. Therefore, the Eurasian states need a mechanism for human rights protection. This mechanism could enhance humanitarian cooperation in the region and promote regional human rights standards in line with international standards. At the SCO summit in New Delhi (India) on 4 July 2023, the UN Secretary General stressed the need for common efforts to address global issues, such as security, human rights, and sustainable development.[3]

The member states of the SCO maintain the importance of the human rights issues. In particular, under the Dushanbe Declaration on the 20th anniversary of the SCO in 2021,[4] the states expressed their intention to expand information exchange and take coordinated steps in the forensic field, including joint activities (paragraph 3.7). Additionally, the Declaration reaffirmed the universality, indivisibility, interdependence, and interconnectedness of human rights, the obligation to respect them, and to oppose "double standards" (paragraph 5.9). The agenda to celebrate the anniversary of the Organization did not emerge overnight. It had been discussed and developed over the years. In the same vein, the Bishkek Declaration of the SCO Council of Heads of State of 2019[5] supported the goal to develop practical cooperation in compliance monitoring of legislation, law, and justice and to strengthen the independence of domestic courts and forensic activities.

These declarations aim to promote the internal approaches of Eurasian states to international human rights issues. All states pay a particular attention to human rights in special chapters of their national constitutions, and some even allow individuals to appeal before international bodies to protect their rights violated domestically (Kyrgyzstan, Uzbekistan, and Russia).

Regarding Russia (RF), the right of citizens to appeal to interstate bodies to protect their rights and freedoms, after all available domestic remedies have been exhausted (as stated in Article 46(3) of the Constitution), remains unsecured following its withdrawal from the European human rights protection mechanism (European Convention on Human Rights and European Court of Human Rights (ECtHR)). This constitutional article specifies and promotes one of the foundations of the constitutional order of the country—the individual, his/her rights, and freedoms shall

[2] *See, e.g.*, SERGEY MAROCHKIN & YURI BEZBORODOV (EDS.), THE SHANGHAI COOPERATION ORGANIZATION: EXPLORING NEW HORIZONS, at 1–2 (London & New York, Routledge, 2022).

[3] https://news.un.org/ru/story/2023/07/1442572?utm_source=UN+News+-+Russian&utm_campaign=760d207df0-EMAIL_CAMPAIGN_2023_07_05_12_04&utm_medium=email&utm_term=0_6a23d2f3b7-760d207df0-%5BLIST_EMAIL_ID%5D (last visited on December 10, 2023).

[4] http://www.kremlin.ru/supplement/5699 (last visited on December 10, 2023).

[5] http://www.kremlin.ru/supplement/5421 (last visited on December 10, 2023).

be the supreme value. The recognition, observance, and protection of human and civil rights and freedoms shall be an obligation of the state (Article 2 of the RF Constitution). The Federation Council (the upper chamber of the Russian parliament), the Association of Lawyers of Russia, and some other official national institutions related to the protection of human rights have proposed the creation of a Eurasian Court for the Protection of Human Rights, which would serve as an analogue to the ECtHR.[6]

It is unlikely that cooperation in the field of human rights protection in the Eurasian region can move on quickly and expansively, through the establishment of a special court or the expansion of the functions of an existing one (the EAEU Court). The region includes the countries with a common authoritarian legacy but with different histories, civilizations, cultures, political systems, levels of economic development, and influence in the world. Many of them lack experience in participating regional mechanisms for the protection of human rights, all of them have peculiarities in their understanding the essence and relationship of an individual with the state. Additionally, some of them have a controversial human rights record.

A critical approach to the nature of Eurasian regional organizations may reveal them as mere authoritarian imitations of Western organizations. This "mimicry" may be of some benefit for authoritarian survival. This borrowing and retooling can help facilitate "adaptive authoritarianism."[7] "Instead of deep, sovereignty-eroding regional integration, with extensive delegation to international organizations, we see thinner models of cooperation that demand little of members and can be discarded once their political purpose has been served... Instead of third-party dispute resolution, we are observing a softer 'dialogue and mutual respect' framework that is less rule-bound and more focused around negotiated solutions to international problems… Accompanying weaker dispute resolution is an emphasis on softer commitments and dialogue. Iterated negotiation allows power to be exercised behind the veneer of win-win rhetoric. And instead of a logic of commitment and hands-tying, international law plays a thinner, coordinating role."[8]

Nonetheless, it is important to consider future possibilities. In this regard, the potential and opportunities for expanding the Eurasian organizations' areas of cooperation are largely unrealized but still relevant: economic cooperation, migration,

---

[6] (Russian) Kommersant, April 18, 2022, June 2, 2022; KOSACHEV NAZVAL EDINSTVENNUYU UTRATU ROSSII OT VIKHODA IZ SOVETA EVROPI at https://ria.ru/20220411/evropa-1782842167.html; YURISTI PREDLAGAYUT SOZDAT'NA EVRAZIISKOM PROSTRANSTVE ANALOG ESPCH at https://rg.ru/2022/03/16/iuristy-predlagaiut-sozdat-na-evrazijskom-prostranstve-analog-espch.html (last visited on December 10, 2023).

[7] Tom Ginsburg, *Authoritarian International Law?*, 114(2) American Journal of International Law 241 (2020). See also on the issue—Heike Krieger, *Populist Governments and International Law*, 30(3) European Journal of International Law 971–996 (2019); TOM GINSBURG, DEMOCRACIES AND INTERNATIONAL LAW (2021).

[8] Tom Ginsburg, *Authoritarian International Law?, supra* note 7, 257.

labor market development, energy partnership, and humanitarian efforts, including human rights, scientific, and cultural interaction.[9]

We believe that the regional human rights cooperation is crucial for Eurasian states to gain global recognition. The willingness of states to undertake commitments on human rights is the starting point. Rather than simply following others, it is important for states to clearly demonstrate their approach to human rights issues.

2 Understanding Human Rights: Origin and Perspectives

2.1 European Roots of the International Human Rights Idea

Whether universal or parochial, human rights are generally essential. The globalized world has no choice but to establish common human rights standards and to implement them in a consistent and at the same time compromised (taking into account regional and national specificities) manner.

The modern international legal concept of human rights originated from the liberal humanist ideas of the Enlightenment, although the prerequisites of the modernist human rights doctrine were laid down by thinkers of the European Renaissance.[10] The gradual disintegration of feudalism, the emergence of the modern European state, and the invention of the human rights (originally rights of a man) are interconnected tectonic processes.[11] From that time on the human being is considered as "the point of reference of any legal action" (an action taken against human being).[12] Whether within the disputes as to the *ius naturale* and *ius positivum* division or the

---

[9] *See* SERGEY MAROCHKIN & YURI BEZBORODOV (EDS.), *supra* note 2.

[10] MICHAEL HAAS, INTERNATIONAL HUMAN RIGHTS LAW. A COMREHENSIVE INTRODUCTION, at 26–30 (London, NewYork, Routledge, 2014); Martti Koskenniemi, *Rights, History, Critique* in ADAM ETINSON (ED.), HUMAN RIGHTS: MORAL OR POLITICAL? at 41–42 (Oxford, Oxford University Press, 2018); Dinah Shelton, *Introduction* in DINAH SHELTON, THE OXFORD HANDBOOK OF INTERNATIONAL HUMAN RIGHTS LAW, at 2 (Oxford, Oxford University Press, 2013). For rights of a man and human rights dissection *see* LYNN HUNT, INVENTING HUMAN RIGHTS: A HISTORY, at 15–35 (W. W. Norton & Company, 2008); for distinguishing individual rights and human rights *see* ANNE PETERS, BEYOUND HUMAN RIGHTS: THE LEGAL STATUS OF THE INDIVIDUAL IN INTERNATIONAL LAW, at 456–457, 467–469 (Cambridge, Cambridge University Press, 2016).

[11] WILGELM G. GREWE, THE EPOCHS OF INTERNATIONAL LAW, at 167 (Berlin, New York, 2000); FREDERECK H. RUSSEL, THE JUST WAR IN THE MIDDLE AGES, at 44–45 (Cambridge: Cambridge University Press, 1975); *see also* LARRY SIEDENTOP, INVENTING THE INDIVIDUAL. THE ORIGINS OF WESTERN LIBERALISM (Cambridge, Massachusetts: The Belknap Press of Harvard University Press, 2014).

[12] WILGELM G. GREWE, *supra* note 11, 168. *See also* ROSI BRAIDOTTI, THE POSTHUMAN, at 13–14 (Cambridge, Polity Press, 2013).

critique of the monopoly of state in the legal realm (statism), the individual and his/her rights were and are inescapably at the center of the discussion.[13]

It is true that the origin of the doctrine of human rights is Eurocentric. And today it remains so in its foundations and basic provisions. Historically, not only European thought but also political history of the European countries served as a driver for the development of this doctrine. The same is true for international law as a whole. And this is a historical fact, although the injustices of the past, especially in its colonialist and racist dimensions, are obvious.[14] However, the ideological distortions and abuses of the past do not deprive by default the doctrine of human rights of its claim to universality. It is precisely these "European" human rights that have received universal legal recognition during the twentieth century. The current system of international law with sovereign equality of states contains tools (including tools of regional integration) to promote diverse human rights ideas.

2.2 *From the Idea to Practice: the Crystallization of Human Rights in the International Legal Order*

A milestone in the human rights doctrine was the tragedy of the World War II and the creation of a truly global institution: the United Nations. The fears and doubts of the so-called idealists and revisionists of the Interbellum were realized: the state could be and had been used against its creator and ultimate unit—the human being.[15]

The UN system was one of the first and most significant efforts to make this right and "to save succeeding generations from the scourge of war, which twice in our lifetime has brought untold sorrow to mankind" (the Preamble of the UN Charter). Although human rights are mentioned seven times in the UN Charter,[16] there is no list of human rights in the document, and the basic obligation is formulated not in terms of protection or fulfilment but in terms of "international cooperation…in

[13] Steven Hall, *The Persistent Spectre: Natural Law, International Order and the Limits of Legal Positivism*, 12 (2) European Journal of International Law, 269, 269–307 (2001); for the critique of the international legal positivism *see* ROLAND PORTMANN, LEGAL PERSONALITY IN INTERNATIONAL LAW, at 59–60, 128–131 (Cambridge: Cambridge University Press, 2010).

[14] Rossana Deplano, *Is international legal research international?* in ROSSANA DEPLANO ET AL. (EDS.), RESEARCH METHODS IN INTERNATIONAL LAW, at 78–95 (Cheltenham, UK, Northampton, MA, USA: Edward Elgar Publishing, 2021).

[15] For the review of the idealists and revisionists of the Interbellum—J. Brierly, N. Politis, J. Spiropoulos, A. Alvarez, H. Krabbe, G. Scelle, H. Kelsen *see* JANNE E. NIJMAN, THE CONCEPT OF INTERNATIONAL LEGAL PERSONALITY: AN INMQUIRY INTO THE HISTORY AND THEORY OF INTERNATIONAL LAW, at 122–130 (the Hague, 2004). *See also* JAMES L. BRIERLY, THE SHORTCOMINGS OF INTERNATIONAL LAW. THE BASIS OF OBLIGATION IN INTERNATIONAL LAW AND OTHER PAPERS, at 68 (Oxford, Clarendon Press, 1958); HANS KELSEN, GENERAL THEORY OF LAW AND STATE, at 93, 108 (Cambridge, Harvard University Press, 1945).

[16] Preamble, Articles 1, 8, 13, 55, 62 and 88, 77 of the UN Charter.

promoting and encouraging respect for human rights and for fundamental freedoms" (Article 1.3 of the UN Charter).

The International Bill of Human Rights was the product of the joint work of representatives of different states and cultures.[17] In 1946, the Human Rights Commission was established to draft the text of the Universal Declaration and included representatives not only of the Western European liberal tradition but also of the USSR, Chile, China, Egypt, India, Iran, Lebanon, Panama, the Philippines, Uruguay, and Venezuela. Among the authors of the final text there were the widow of the American leader E. Roosevelt, the Indian human rights activist H.J. Mehta, Lebanese Ch. Malik, Chilean H. Santa Cruz, Chinese P.C. Chang, French lawyer R. Cassin, and Canadian J. Humphrey.[18] We may argue about the depth of influence of each of them, but the fact is obvious—the provisions of the Declaration were the product of the followers of different legal traditions.

Under the pressure from the socialist camp, Articles 22–27 of the Declaration guaranteed social, economic, and cultural rights.[19] The claim to universality of human rights standards is expressed in Article 28: "Everyone is entitled to a social and international order in which the rights and freedoms set forth in this Declaration can be fully realized." The Global South and China had insisted on the stipulation of a personal duty of an individual before the community, "in which alone the free and full development of his personality is possible" (Article 29).[20] The voting results in the UN General Assembly of the Universal Declaration of Human Rights were promising: none of the 58 members of the Organization dared to vote against; 48 states supported the resolutions with 8 abstentions and 2 absences (Honduras, Yemen).[21]

Among the abstaining countries were the socialist countries which did not object to the enumerated rights per se, at least not openly, but focused mainly on the absence of the people's right to self-determination and the mechanisms for the minorities' protection.[22] Anyway, the Universal Declaration's claim to universality is confirmed by the fact that four fundamental human rights documents adopted at

---

[17] JAMES V. SPICKARD, THE ORIGINS OF THE UNIVERSAL DECLARATION OF HUMAN RIGHTS, at 15 (University of Redlands, 1999).

[18] Universal Declaration of Human Rights. Selected Papers. (1948), at https://legal.un.org/avl/ha/udhr/udhr.html (last visited on December 10, 2023); Manfred Nowak, *Universal Declaration of Human Rights* in CHRISTINA BINDER ET AL. (EDS.), *ELGAR ENCYCPLOPEDIA OF HUMAN RIGHTS*, at: https://www.elgaronline.com/display/book/9781789903621/9781789903621.xml (last visited on December 10, 2023).

[19] See JOHN P. HUMPHREY, HUMAN RIGHTS AND THE UNITED NATIONS: A GREAT ADVENTURE Dobbs Ferry, at 72–73 (New York, Transnational Publishers, 1984); Karin Mickelson, How Universal Is the Universal Declaration?, 47 University of New Brunswick Law Journal, 19, 20 (1998).

[20] *Ibid.*

[21] *Ibid.*

[22] Chandler Green, *70 Years of Impact: Insights on the Universal Declaration of Human Rights*, at: https://unfoundation.org/blog/post/70-years-of-impact-insights-on-the-universal-declaration-of-human-rights/ (last visited on December 10, 2023).

the regional level recognize the commitment to the ideas of the Declaration (European Convention on Human Rights of 1950, American Convention on Human Rights of 1969, African Charter on Human and Peoples' Rights of 1981, and Arab Charter on Human Rights of 2004).

In any case, it is too simplistic to regard the Universal Declaration as a purely European document reflecting Western values. Even among so-called Western countries, the Declaration was not overwhelmingly acclaimed.[23] Anyway, the relevance of human rights issues extends beyond the disputed universalism and effectiveness of the Universal Declaration and even the corpus of human rights law generally. Human rights are embedded in the international legal order as a whole and guide its operation and implementation.

Under the concept of human rights, international law itself has undergone radical metamorphoses. The contraction of the domaine réservé,[24] the internationalization of crimes against humanity,[25] and the emergence of issues of international concern,[26] *jus cogens*, and *erga omnes*[27] are based on the recognition of universal values and universal morality. The international legal emancipation of the human and the individualization of international law are undisputable trends.[28]

In the second half of the twentieth century, human rights went beyond the realm of interstate cooperation and have become a fundamental aspect of the international legal discourse. Today, human rights are an essential element of the global security agenda, a factor in addressing environmental crises (through environmental human

---

[23] Mark Goodale, *The Myth of Universality: The UNESCO "Philosophers' Committee" and the Making of Human Rights*, 43 (3) Law & Social Inquiry, 596, 609 (2018); Åshild Samnøy, *Human Rights as International Consensus. The Making of the Universal Declaration of Human Rights 1945–1948* in REPORT CHR, MICHELSEN INSTITUTE, at 95 (Bergen: Chr. Michelsen Institute, 1993); *see also* Tai-Heng Cheng, *The Universal Declaration of Human Rights at Sixty: Is It Still Right for the United States?,* 41 (2) Cornell International Law Journal, 251, 289 (2008); HERSH LAUTERPACHT, INTERNATIONAL LAW AND HUMAN RIGHTS, at 25 (New York, Fredrick A. Praeger, 1950); Karin Mickelson, *supra* note 19, 19–48.

[24] Katja S. Ziegler, *Domaine Réservé* in ANNE PETERS (ED.), MAX PLANK ENCYCLOPEDIA OF PUBLIC INTERNATIONAL LAW, at https://opil.ouplaw.com/home/MPIL (last visited on December 10, 2023).

[25] *See* the Charter and Judgement of the Nurnberg Tribunal—History and Analysis: Memorandum Submitted by the Secretary General in International Law Commission. A/CN.4/5, at 71 (1949); Crimes against Humanity. International Law Commission First Report. A/CN.4/680, at para. 27 (2015); "Crimes against Humanity," Article 7 of the Rome Statute of the International Criminal Court (1998).

[26] Articles 12, 13 of the Statute of the League of Nations 1919; the preamble to the Rome Statute of the International Criminal Court (1998).

[27] See International Law Commission. First Report on Jus Cogens. A/CN.4/693, at paras. 71–72 (2016).

[28] Gerhard Hafner, *The Emancipation of the Individual from the State under International Law* in RECUEIL DES COURS DE L'ACADÉMIE DE DROIT INTERNATIONAL (volume 358) (2011); ANNE PETERS, *supra* note 10, 1–10.

rights), a dimension of regional integration, an instrument of international criminal justice, and a crucial point of interstate political dialogue.[29]

2.3 *Relativism v. Universalism*

Some scholars and activists "provincialize" the idea of human rights and deny their universality due to the complexity and diversity of the sociocultural and political-legal landscape of each society.[30] Is legal relativism a significant obstacle to the universalization of human rights because cultural differences make these rights highly dependent on the background and conditions of a particular society? Probably not.

Firstly, the history of different countries provides examples of controversial but partly efficient human rights transformations: Afghanistan in the 1960s, Iran in the 1960–1970s, Gorbachev's reforms in the Soviet Union in the 1985–1991, and Yeltsin's transformations in Russia in the 1990s. Anyway, these processes were about democratization (as declared), human rights, and freedoms with meaningful if not overwhelming public support. The same is true of the current human rights policies.

Secondly, human rights rhetoric is present, at least verbally, in most regional organizations—Southeast Asia, Arab, and Islamic cooperation.[31] The states of "non-Western world" aspire to membership in the UN Human Rights Council and are

[29] Responsibility to Protect. UN General-Secretary. Annual Report. September 20, 1999. SG/SM/7136. GA/9596; UN Security Council practice to include gross human rights violations in the notion of the breach of peace and here at to peace under Chapter VII of the UN Charter: *see* Alain Pellet, Alina Miron A. *Sanctions* in ANNE PETERS (ED.), MAX PLANCK ENCYCLOPEDIA OF PUBLIC INTERNATIONAL LAW, at https://opil.ouplaw.com/home/MPIL (last visited on December 10, 2023)); for humanitarian intervention as casus belli *see* Syria Action. United Kingdom Government Legal Position. April 14, 2018, at: https://www.gov.uk/government/publications/syria-action-uk-government-legal-position/syria-action-uk-government-legal-position) (last visited on December 10, 2023).

[30] For legal relativism and its critique *see* JOANNE R. BAUER, DANIEL A. BELL, THE EAST ASIAN CHALLENGE FOR HUMAN RIGHTS (Cambridge, Cambridge University Press, 1999); Jack Donnelly, *The Relative Universality of Human Rights*, 29 Human Rights Quarterly, 281 (2007); Miranda Fricker, *Styles of Moral Relativism—a Critical Family Tree* in *Oxford Handbook of the History of Ethics* (Oxford, Oxford University Press, 2013); Anthony J. Langlois, *Human Rights Universalism* in *The Ashgate Research Companion to Ethics and International Relations* (Routledge, 2009); Joseph Raz, *Human Rights without Foundations* in *The Philosophy of International Law* (Oxford, Oxford University Press, 2010); Amartya Sen, *Human Rights and Asian Values*, 217 (2/3) The New Republic, 33 (1997).

[31] ASEAN Declaration on human rights (2012), at: URL: https://asean.org/our-communities/asean-political-security-community/rules-based-people-oriented-people-centred/human-rights/; Organization of Islamic Cooperation and Cairo Declaration on human rights in Islam (1990), at: URL: https://oic-iphrc.org/home/*; League of Arab States and Arab Charter on human rights 2004 (last visited on December 10, 2023).

sensitive to its criticism; they are willing to use universal human rights mechanisms to advance their agenda.[32]

Thirdly, the very essence of the concept of human rights protection is inherently close to most societies.[33] Proponents of the universality of human rights challenge cultural relativism, referring to several empirical factors: (1) "unsolvable" differences in human rights are in reality often focused on derivative issues (such external discrepancies can be neutralized by shifting the focus from one aspect of a right to another while preserving its essence), and (2) rejection of human rights often relates to sociopolitical or economic problems rather than to denial of liberal values; in such a case the root of the problem lies in the inappropriate context rather than in ideology and public opinion.[34]

Fourthly, the human rights issue is a means of political rhetoric. Such an immanent politicization of human rights ensures both their high flexibility and their dependence on space and time where and when they are implemented. Human rights standards focus on a normative minimum that allows for specification with regard to regional particularities. The instruments of such specification are a balance between private and public interests, margin of appreciation doctrine, regional consensus, evolutive interpretation, proportionality requirement, etc.[35]

2.4 Alternative Concepts of Human Rights

However, the modern concept of human rights is not completely Eurocentric. It is not the content of the doctrine of human rights, but rather its normative and institutional instruments, the skillful and delicate national policies on the issue that make the universal human rights possible, allow the promotion of a regional and even local humanitarian and axiological agenda through the regional mechanisms.

The modern concept of human rights emphasizes human dignity but not personal freedom as an end in itself.[36] Human dignity and more broadly the dignity of life itself are the foundation of human rights in the twenty-first century. Freedom is only

[32] Philip Leach, *The Continuing Utility of International Human Rights Mechanisms?*, in EJIL: TALK!, at: https://www.ejiltalk.org/the-continuing-utility-of-international-human-rights-mechanisms/; for interactive dialogue on problematic countries *see* Human Rights Council. Official page, at https://www.ohchr.org/en/press-releases/2022/03/human-rights-council-holds-interactive-dialogue-iran-and-starts-interactive (last visited on December 10, 2023).

[33] MICHAEL HAAS, *supra* note 10, 15.

[34] Lars G. Binderup, *Universalism and (Cultural) Relativism* in CHRISTINA BINDER ET AL. (EDS.), *ELGAR ENCYCPLOPEDIA OF HUMAN RIGHTS* at: https://www.elgaronline.com/display/book/9781789903621/9781789903621.xml (last visited on December 10, 2023).

[35] YUVAL SHANY, THE UNIVERSALITY OF HUMAN RIGHTS: PRAGMATISM MEETS IDEALISM, at 14–19 (Jacob Blaustein Institute for the Advancement of Human Rights, 2018).

[36] CHARLES R. BEITZ, THE IDEA OF HUMAN RIGHTS, at 34–36, 82–84 (Oxford, Oxford University Press, 2009); Stephen Riley, *Human Dignity as a Sui Generis Principle*, 32 (4) Ratio Juris, 439 (2019).

a means, albeit an important and valuable one, for the protection of the dignity of life.

The universality of human rights is not an empirical fact but a long way normative claim that involves compromises and requires accuracy, moderation, and consistency. The means of such a path may be different (for different countries, cultures, regions), but the goal is undoubtedly the same—the human well-being and the dignity of life.

In the promotion of human rights, the focus is not on detailed positive regulation but rather on the deliberate evolution toward the goal. "Black or white" and "all or nothing" approaches do not work here: it is not a zero-sum game. Sensitive issues requiring preparation can be postponed to a more appropriate time. For example, the international standard itself does not require the abolition of the death penalty or the legalization of same-sex partnerships. These are only means that vary. Universality is about moderate uniformity and different paths to a common goal.

Understanding international human rights standards requires the demythologization of the human rights dogma. In formulating standards, it is important to avoid clichés and ideologies about "Western values," "Westernization," "individualism" (as opposed to collectivism), and "liberalism." Human rights are about a normal life for everyone. Even in the so-called Western world, there is no uniform in understanding of the values of the liberalism and individual freedom, and in Asia there is no uniform approach to the so-called Asian values.[37] Is the Philippines leader F. Marcos with his "Bread before Freedom" so far from the American President F. Roosevelt with his "Freedom from Want?"[38]

Even major efforts to promote Asian standards of human rights took the current international human rights doctrine as a point of reference.[39] Although criticized, the universal approach is taken as something relevant and authoritative.[40] The Asian

---

[37] Louis Kraar, *What Pacific Century?*, 140 (10) Fortune, 198 (1999).

[38] (Russian) Tigran Oganesian *Sistema zashchity prav cheloveka v ASEAN: perenos kontseptsii "aziatskikh tsennostey» na subregional'nuyu pochvu [ASEAN human rights protection system: transferring the concept of «Asian values" to sub-regional grounds]*, 9(1) Mezhdunarodnoye pravosudiye [International Justice], 81 (2019); FRANKLIN DELANO ROOSEVELT. THE FOUR FREEDOMS. 6 JANUARY 1941, at https://www.americanrhetoric.com/speeches/fdrthefourfreedoms.html (last visited on December 10, 2023).

[39] Bilahari Kausikan, *Asia's Different Standard,* 92 Foreign Policy, 24 (1993); Ann Kent, *China's Human Rights in the "Asian Century"* in *Human Rights in Asia,* at 188 (Cheltenham: Edward Elgar Publishing, 2011); Garry Rodan, *Political Accountability and Human Rights in Singapore* in THOMAS W.D. DAVIS & BRIAN GALLIGAN, HUMAN RIGHTS IN ASIA, at 81–85 (Edward Elgar Publishing, 2011). For the opposite view—on Asian states' skepticism as to development of universal international law generally—*see* Simon Chesterman, *Asia's Ambivalence About International Law & Institutions: Past, Present, and Futures*, 27 (4) European Journal of International Law, 945, 948, 971 (2017); Chu Li-lu, *Refute the Absurd Theory Concerning International Law*, People's Daily (1957, 18 September); *see* also Hungdah Chiu, *Communist China's Attitude toward International Law*, 60 (2) The American Journal of International Law. 245, 248 (1966).

[40] Michael D. Barr, *Lee Kuan Yew and the "Asian Values" Debate*, 3 Asian Studies Review, 309, 314 (2000).

states' focus on economic and social rights provides a good example of how the universal doctrine of human rights can be instrumental in the cross-cultural dialogue.[41] The Eastern scholars' and politicians' criticism of Eurocentric emphasis on "individual–society–state" conflict should be taken into account by shifting the focus to the public dimension of individuality and the collectivist connotations of the international human rights standards.[42] The Western protagonists of the universality should not ignore that issue sensitive for the European democracies may be less important for the global agenda and *vice versa.*[43]

This is the ideological basis of the concept of human rights to be implemented through the proposed human rights mechanism in the Eurasian space.

3 Are There Opportunities and Potential for the Eurasian Organizations to Help Protect Human Rights?

3.1 Human Rights Potential of the Eurasian Region

Russia's withdrawal from the Council of Europe in March 2022 was accompanied not only by critical attacks against the European Court of Human Rights (ECtHR) but also by statements on the creation of an alternative international mechanism at the regional level. In the Euro-Asian region, which includes the SCO member states, there is an obvious vacuum in the international human rights dimension; therefore, ideas about the creation of regional human rights mechanisms within the BRICS, the SCO, the EAEU, or the CIS began to emerge in the academic and political realm. All these associations could be significantly enhanced by the inclusion of a human rights institution in their structure; and they all have certain advantages and disadvantages in implementing this cooperation route. Eventually the proposal to revive a human rights body under the auspices of the CIS has prevailed, although it did not seem to have widespread support.[44] However, among the options being dis-

[41] John D. Ciorciari, *Institutionalizing Human Rights in Southeast Asia*, 34 (3) Human Rights Quarterly, 695, 699 (2012).

[42] Wai-Teng L. Leong, *From "Asian Values" to Singapore Exceptionalism* in *Human Rights in Asia: A Reassessment of the Asian Values Debate*, at 121– 140 (New York, Palgrave MacMillan, 2008); Fareed Zakaria, *Culture Is Destiny: A Conversation with Lee Kuan Yew*, 73 (2) Foreign Affairs, 109 (1994); Bilahari Kausikan, *Asia's Different Standard*, 92 Foreign Policy, 24 (1993).

[43] Yash Ghai, *Understanding Human Rights in Asia* in *International Protection of Human Rights: A Textbook,* at 547–574 (Turku, Åbo Akademi University, Institute for Human Rights, 2012); MAROCHKIN and BEZBORODOV (EDS.), THE SHANGHAU COOPERATION ORGANIZATION, *see supra* note 2.

[44] (Russian) VICTORIA IL'INA, KOSACHEV: INSTITUTY PO ZASHHITE PRAV CHELOVEKA MOGUT FORMIROVAT'SJA V SNG I EAJES [KOSACHEV: INSTITUTIONS FOR THE PROTECTION OF HUMAN RIGHTS CAN BE FORMED IN THE CIS AND THE EAEU], at https://rg.ru/2022/04/11/kosachev-instituty-po-zashchite-prav-cheloveka-mogut-formirovatsia-v-sng-i-eaes.html (last visited on December 10, 2023); (Russian) SERGEJ STEPASHIN

cussed, the most viable option so far remains the SCO. Its influence is growing both at the regional and global levels due to diplomatic achievements, economic progress, and the institutional streamlining of structures within the Organization.

The nature and objectives of the activities of other regional organizations with the participation of Russia meet the requirement for the creation of a human rights body to a lesser extent. The EAEU is aimed at the sustainable economic development of the member states, ensuring competitiveness of national economies, and creation of a common market for goods, services, capital, and labor (Article 4 of the Treaty on the Eurasian Economic Union). BRICS is an informal association of states, it is poorly institutionalized, and as a result it cannot serve as a basis for the creation of a human rights protection body. The CIS members states recognize the Commonwealth's purpose to ensure human rights and fundamental freedoms (Article 3 of the Charter of the Commonwealth of Independent States), but given the real weight and current state of the Organization, it is difficult to assume that an effective human rights mechanism can be formed on its basis.

Recently, the measures have been taken to enhance the human rights dimension of the CIS. On 14 October 2022 the CIS members states signed the Protocol on Amendments to the Convention on Human Rights and Fundamental Freedoms of 26 May 1995 and adopted the Rules of the Human Rights Commission.[45] The amendments were motivated by the desire to expand the composition of the Commission with representatives of the countries that are not parties thereto (Armenia, Kazakhstan, and Uzbekistan). However, the intention to include new partners failed: Armenia and Tajikistan put reservations to the Protocol and thereby did not recognize the competence of the Commission to review the appeals of the state parties and individual claimants. The Protocol has not yet entered into force. However, regarding the current situation in the Commonwealth, it is doubtful that the Commission would live up to the high expectations for the CIS as a whole.[46]

Some experts emphasize the need for a human rights protection mechanism in the EAEU, since some members of the Union prioritize the protection of the rights

---

PREDLOZHIL "RASSHIRIT' GEOGRAFIJU" ZASHHITY ROSSIEJ PRAV CHELOVEKA [SERGEY STEPASHIN PROPOSED TO "EXPAND THE GEOGRAPHY" OF RUSSIA'S PROTECTION OF HUMAN RIGHTS], at https://alrf.ru/news/sergey-stepashin-evraziyskiy-sud-mozhet-stat-effektivnym-instrumentom-zashchity-prav-cheloveka-/ (last visited on December 10, 2023); (Russian) MARINA CAREVA, SERGEJ STEPASHIN: "EVRAZIJSKIJ SUD MOZHET STAT' EFFEKTIVNYM INSTRUMENTOM ZASHHITY PRAV CHELOVEKA" [SERGEY STEPASHIN: "THE EURASIAN COURT CAN BECOME AN EFFECTIVE TOOL FOR PROTECTING HUMAN RIGHTS"], at https://www.vedomosti.ru/society/articles/2022/06/02/924936-stepashin-zaschiti-rossiei-prav (last visited on December 10, 2023).

[45] "Protocol on Amendments to the Convention of the Commonwealth of Independent States on Human Rights and Fundamental Freedoms" (1995), at http://publication.pravo.gov.ru/Document/View/0001202211140001?ysclid=lq0q68pr9o863192481 (last visited on December 10, 2023); Decision of the Council of Heads of State of the CIS "On a new version of the Regulations on the Human Rights Commission of the Commonwealth of Independent States" (2022) https://cis.minsk.by/reestrv2/doc/6636#text (last visited on December 10, 2023).

[46] The Convention has been signed by seven States, of which four have ratified (Belarus, Kyrgyzstan, Russia and Tajikistan, except Armenia, Moldova and Georgia).

of governmental bodies rather than individuals. It is proposed to adopt the Charter of Economic and Social Rights, entrusting the Court of the EAEU a competence in human rights protection competence.[47] Although the EAEU Treaty mentions consumer rights (Article 60) and the rights of workers with the Union (Article 98), such protection would be too specific to attain the essential level of the general human rights protection.

As Tan Hsien-Li points out, "…ASEAN and the EAEU are demonstrably more developed in terms of ambition, outlook, and strategy … The member states of both organizations have consolidated their cooperation efforts and taken steps to formalize their status as organizations with legal personality… They have done so in order to secure the gains of deeper economic integration, the complex processes of which require *the stability and predictability that legalization and institutionalization* [emphasis added] can provide to an organizational system… [T]he SCO, SAARC, PIF, MSG, and APEC… are more fluid in their agenda and outlook and have remained as political and diplomatic entities… Political flexibility is more attractive to these five APROs [Asia-Pacific regional organizations] due to strategic factors such as the presence of competing powers within the organization or in the wider region… In certain cases, *the flexibility and informality pave the way to a wider ambit of potential cooperation*" [emphasis added].[48]

The presence of China among the SCO members as an external center of power and balance significantly distinguishes the Shanghai organization from the CIS and the EAEU. Nevertheless, cooperation and exchange of information among the countries advance growth of trust between China and states of Central Asia, strengthening ties with India, Iran, and Pakistan.

The long-lasting period since the formation of the CIS and the Russia's adhesion to the Convention on the Protection of Human Rights and Fundamental Freedoms of 4 November 1950 (ECHR) would surely impact the country's choice of the track of its further development and influence the approaches of other post-Soviet states to human rights. Meanwhile, the emerging debates on a new regional mechanism for the protection of individual rights raise the question of the design of a potential counterpart (at least a hypothetically effective if not equivalent) to other influential regional human rights bodies (ECtHR, Interamerican Court of Human Rights, African Court of Human and People's Rights). In our opinion, it is the SCO that is the most appropriate to confront this challenge taking into account the Organization's current development and prospects as well as the nature and interests of the third countries in the region.

---

[47] (Russian) Tatiana N. Neshataeva, *Evrazijskij jekonomicheskij sojuz: organy, praktika, pravo [The Eurasian Economic Union: bodies, practice, law]*, 27(5) Zhurnal rossijskogo prava [Journal of Russian Law] 187–201 (2003).

[48] Tan Hsien-Li, *Regional Organizations* in SIMON CHESTERMAN, HISASHI OWADA & BEN SAUL (eds.), THE OXFORD HANDBOOK OF INTERNATIONAL LAW IN ASIA AND THE PACIFIC, at 56 (Oxford, Oxford University Press, 2019).

The establishment of a special SCO human rights mechanism conforms to the "soul" of the Organization and its institutional framework. There are some factors to be kept in mind.

First of all, the essence of the "Shanghai spirit" of the SCO is the cooperation of member states based on mutual respect, diversity of cultures and civilizations of Christian, Buddhist, and Muslim religions, as well as the desire for joint development based on nonconfrontation, mutual consultations, equal relations, development, decision-making, and international treaties through consensus and transparency. These are unique features of the SCO partnership.

Secondly, by its very nature, the SCO is neither a military block (like NATO) nor an international security body (like OSCE, ASEAN Regional Security Forum). According to the SCO Charter, its purpose and objectives are to strengthen mutual trust among the member states, consolidate multidisciplinary cooperation, facilitate comprehensive and balanced economic growth and social and cultural development, and promote human rights and fundamental freedoms (Article 1). In other words, from the point of view of the purpose and essence of the SCO, there are no obstacles to the further evolution of the Organization in the human rights dimension. The SCO Charter establishes the prerequisites for the development of countries in various directions, including in the humanitarian sphere. Therefore, there is no need to expand the competence of the SCO to cover human rights issues (which would be necessary if supranational body for the protection of human rights in the Eurasian Economic Union was created).[49]

The Organization's internal acts set out guidelines for the development of the states in various spheres, including the humanitarian one. For example, the Development Strategy of the SCO until 2025[50] declares that the member states will pay special attention to enhancement of the SCO as a multi-format regional organization conceived not as a military and political block nor economic integration association with supranational governance bodies.

However, respect for human rights and freedoms is not among the SCO principles. It would be appropriate to include this principle into the text of the Charter as a new means for the interaction of member states. Especially since the goals and objectives of the SCO (Article 1 of the Charter) include "the promotion of human rights and fundamental freedoms in accordance with the international obligations of the Member States and their national legislation."

Thirdly, although the efforts of the SCO states were initially aimed at regional security,[51] it cannot be denied that the mechanism of human rights protection would be an integral part of the activities in the sphere of enforcement of international

---

[49] Mark Entin, Dmitry Galushko, *International Human Rights Protection and Regional Integration: European and Eurasian Integration Processes Compared,* 7 (1) Journal for the International and European Law, Economics and Market Integrations. 38 (2020).

[50] "THE DEVELOPMENT STRATEGY OF THE SCO UNTIL 2025", at https://rus.sectsco.org/20150710/11817.html (last visited on December 10, 2023).

[51] (Russian) Vladimir I. Vasilenko, Vladimir V. Vasilenko & Aleksey G. Poteenko, *Shanhajskaja organizacija sotrudnichestva v regional'noj sisteme bezopasnosti (politiko-pravovoj aspekt)*

peace and security. For this reason, it is hardly acceptable to question the legal significance of the interests of the individual and her/his protection. The growing importance of international human rights law, as noted in the Report of the International Law Association on United Nations Reform, required a new reading of the collective security provision enshrined in Article 1 of the UN Charter in the light of the concept of personal safety.[52]

A threat to inextricable link between enforcement of security and human right protection activities is envisaged by the SCO treaties. According to them, now international "evils" include new, vague crimes of separatism and extremism, and the treaties expand the set of actors whose "political" behavior would nevertheless render them available for extradition under bilateral treaties.[53] In other words, in case of unfairness, states can abuse of their competence when taking appropriate measures. The specified feature of compulsory military and other nonviolent measures implemented on a collective basis should be taken into account by the SCO. The establishment of a human rights protection body will represent an important guarantee of the interests of individuals.

The representatives of the Organization illustratively drew attention to this problem. According to the SCO Secretary General, "[while s]olving security-relating challenges the SCO attaches increasing importance to issues of joint development in its activities… At the same time, the social component is increasingly coming to the fore, and the main task of the SCO is to ensure the well-being of people and the growth of their well-being."[54] There are enough grounds to install new measures for human rights protection in a more effective and decisive way, through a special human rights body.

Fourthly, the fact that the founders did not envisage a separate human rights body should not reduce its potential significance for the future development of the Organization. There are a lot of examples when the control bodies were established after the creation of an international organization (e.g., the ECtHR at the Council of Europe). Sometimes states declared in the constituent act the formation of such a body in the future (Article 14 of the Statute of the League of Nations on the PCIJ, Article 14 of the ASEAN Charter on the ASEAN Human Rights Body). By virtue of para 3 of Article 4 of the SCO Charter, the Council of Heads of State may decide to establish other bodies of the Organization.

In the history of the SCO, we see the gradual expansion of the areas of cooperation of the member states, and the third countries show their interests in the activities of the Organization. This is not the case with the CIS, which faced the withdrawal

---

[Shanghai Cooperation Organization in the Regional Security System (political and legal aspect)] (Moscow, Prospect, 2014).

52 Vera Gowlland-Debbas, *Accountability of the Security Council*, in RALPH WILDE (ed.), Report of the International Law Association Study Group on United Nations Reform, at 39 (2011).

53 Tom Ginsburg, *Authoritarian International Law?*, *supra* note 7, 253.

54 (Russian) RASHID ALIMOV, *Shanhajskaja organizacija sotrudnichestva: stanovlenie, razvitie, perspektivy [Shanghai Cooperation Organization: formation, development, prospects]*, at 23 (Moscow, The Whole World, 2017).

of countries therefrom despite its deliberate subject matter competence. The CIS Convention on Human Rights and Fundamental Freedoms of 26 May 1995 was signed by a small number of states (Russia, Tajikistan, Belarus, and Kyrgyzstan) that were not interested in it. The membership in the EAEU is motivated by economic considerations; therefore, the changes in the system of its bodies may be met with skepticism by some countries (e.g., by Kazakhstan which cannot but put emphasis on economic cooperation).

Fifthly, the current international legal regulation is marked by closer attention to the interests of the individual; the humanization of international law is a *Zeitgeist*. The SCO does not pass events and decisions by that affect individuals. Quite specific statements have already been made. Measures against the COVID threat, development of science and technology, and business initiatives are discussed within the SCO.[55] Under Article 11 of the Agreement on Long-term Good-Neighborliness, Friendship and Cooperation of the SCO Member States of 16 August 2007, the contracting parties intend to develop cooperation in promoting human rights and fundamental freedoms in accordance with their international obligations and national legislation. The creation of a human rights body in the SCO will be a logical step in the promotion of these purposes.

H. Hanqin notes the expansion of cooperation on the subject matter level of the SCO. She believes that "[i]n addressing regional and global threats, such as the global financial crisis, energy and food security, and climate change, the SCO has come up with common positions of its member States and proposed common views for future international actions, thus broadening the scope of their co-operation."[56] Given the nature and character of the SCO's activities, there are no obstacles to its institutional evolution.

Sixthly, it does not duplicate similar international structures where member states of the SCO participate. Attempts by states to establish a properly functioning international body for the human rights protection have not yet been successful: the commissions on human rights provided for in Article 33 of the CIS Charter of 22 January 1993 and in Article 16 of the Treaty on the Establishment of the Union State of Russia and Belarus of 8 December 1999 are not functioning. Compared to the

[55] "STATEMENT OF THE SCO COUNCIL OF THE HEADS OF THE MEMBER-STATES ON THE COMMON RESISTANCE AGAINST THE NEW CORONAVIRUS INFECTION (COVID-19)" (2020), at https://eng.sectsco.org/20201110/690356.html (last visited on December 10, 2023); "STATEMENT OF THE COUNCIL OF HEADS OF STATE OF THE SHANGHAI COOPERATION ORGANISATION ON STRENGTHENING COOPERATION IN SCIENCE, TECHNOLOGY AND INNOVATION" (2021), at https://eng.sectsco.org/20210917/782613.html (last visited on December 10, 2023); "JOINT COMMUNIQUÉ FOLLOWING THE 21ST MEETING OF THE SCO HEADS OF GOVERNMENT (PRIME MINISTERS) COUNCIL" (2022), at https://eng.sectsco.org/20221102/Joint-communiqu-following-the-21st-meeting-of-the-SCO-Heads-of-Government-Prime-Ministers-Council-922225.html (last visited on December 10, 2023).

[56] XUE HANQIN, CHINESE CONTEMPORARY PERSPECTIVES ON INTERNATIONAL LAW: HISTORY, CULTURE AND INTERNATIONAL LAW, at 217 (Leiden & Boston, Martinus Nijhoff Publishers, 2012).

EAEU as an international economic integration organization, the SCO in terms of the provisions of the constituent act and practice reflects the broad cooperation of the states, including the humanitarian field. Therefore, the possibility of including the human rights function in the SCO seems more realistic.

Seventhly, the SCO practice proves the readiness of the member states for fruitful cooperation in improving joint activities in the field of protection of human rights and freedoms. This was highlighted in the Samarkand Declaration of the Heads of State Council of the SCO of 16 September 2022 and the Dushanbe Declaration on the 20th Anniversary of the SCO of 17 September 2021.[57] This practice would certainly be enhanced by the creation of an international body for the protection of individual rights in the SCO.

The SCO bodies are mainly composed of heads of state and specific departments. However, meetings of the heads of parliaments and courts are also envisaged. On 10–12 March 2023 the XVIII Meeting of the Chairmen of the Supreme Courts of the SCO member states was held in New Delhi, India, where informatization, access to justice, and law enforcement were discussed.[58]

International organizations in the post-Soviet space provoke some debates. Against this background, the SCO's position is assessed less critically. For example, having criticized the Eurasian regional organizations because of their authoritarianism, A.V. Obydenkova and A. Libman noted that "Eurasian organizations either explicitly refuse to use any value basis (EAEU, which presents itself as a purely economic organization), or use the rhetoric of democracy while filling their vocabulary with a different content (CIS), or concentrate on security and sovereignty as the main values (SCO). Eurasia does differ from other NDROs [non-democratic regional organizations] as it represents a series of cases where a leading State is powerful enough to create concerns about manipulation, but not strong enough to coerce other countries into membership. In case of the EAEU and the CIS, this issue is particularly pronounced…."[59]

Eighthly, the common past of some SCO countries and their traditions in state building and management could facilitate technically the creation of a body on human rights. It can influence the interpretation and application of human rights law. In this regard, it is possible to implement the declared idea of the Eurasian concept of human rights, which recognizes Asian values along with universal legal

---

[57] "Samarkand Declaration of the Heads of State Council of the SCO" (2022), at https://eng.sectsco.org/20220920/Documents-signed-during-the-meeting-of-the-Council-of-Heads-of-SCO-Member-States-that-you-can-find-922248.html (last visited on December 10, 2023); "Dushanbe Declaration on the 20th Anniversary of the SCO" (2021), at https://eng.sectsco.org/20210917/782639.html (last visited on December 10, 2023).

[58] "The XVIII Meeting of the Chairmen of the Supreme Courts of the SCO member states," at http://rus.sectsco.org/political/20230313/933456/XVIII-Soveschanie-predsedateley-Verkhovnykh-sudov-gosudarstv-chlenov-ShOS-.html (last visited on December 10, 2023).

[59] ANASTASSIA V. OBYDENKOVA & ALEXANDER LIBMAN, AUTHORITARIAN REGIONALISM IN THE WORLD OF INTERNATIONAL ORGANIZATIONS: GLOBAL PERSPECTIVES AND THE EURASIAN ENIGMA, at 266 (Oxford, Oxford University Press, 2019).

values, including priority of the community and state over the individual, the prevalence of public order over personal rights and freedoms, the common well-being, special attention to morals and religion, and admiration for strong political leaders.[60]

These views are apparently in line with the Chinese perception of statehood and individual rights. In this case, the countries of Central Asia and China could form a perfect entente, promoting the declared values through the activity of the SCO international human rights body. T. Oganesyan put attention on the current contradictions in views and noted that today a new stage had begun in the debate on "Asian values," adhered to by most of the Asian states. These values had developed as a separate phenomenon and are presented in various forms (literature, media, official documents). At the same time, opponents of "Asian values" believe that this concept is used to justify government attack on freedom of speech and media.[61]

The establishment of an institutional framework for the protection of rights within the SCO would be an acid test for the human rights record in these countries, including Russia, and present a real opportunity to strut their stuff as to the declared view of human rights. Anyway, "universality does not equal uniformity, and most human rights norms are defined in a way that necessarily entails a degree of flexibility in their interpretation and implementation."[62]

3.2 *Benefits for the SCO and for the Member States*

The proposed modification in the SCO system would positively affect the activities of the Organization in general and correspond to the interests of states. A special mechanism for the protection of human rights would contribute to the deepening and expanding of cooperation among them. The SCO countries have repeatedly declared their commitment to the protection of human rights at the global level and the support of the UN. For example, under paragraph 5 of the joint statement of the foreign ministers of the Russian Federation and the People's Republic of China of 11 September 2020, "[t]he sides will continue developing cooperation on promoting and protecting human rights and advancing the equal treatment of all categories of human rights in the UN human rights agencies."[63]

---

[60] *See* Oleg Vinnichenko, Elena Gladun & Zhumabek Busurmanov, *Convergence of Western and Asian legal values in the SCO perspective,* in SERGEY MAROCHKIN & YURI BEZBORODOV (EDS.), *supra* note 2, 77–79.

[61] Tigran Oganesian, *supra* note 38, 87.

[62] Hurst Hannum, *Human Rights* in SIMON CHESTERMAN, HISASHI OWADA & BEN SAUL (eds.), *supra* note 48, 140–141.

[63] "JOINT STATEMENT BY THE FOREIGN MINISTERS OF THE RUSSIAN FEDERATION AND THE PEOPLE'S REPUBLIC OF CHINA" (2020), at https://www.mid.ru/ru/foreign_policy/un/1441881/ (last visited on December 26, 2023). See also: "THE MOSCOW DECLARATION OF THE COUNCIL OF HEADS OF STATE OF THE SHANGHAI COOPERATION ORGANISATION" (2020), at https://eng.sectsco.org/20201110/690356.html (last visited on December 26, 2023); "THE QINGDAO DECLARATION OF THE SCO COUNCIL OF THE

The effective role of the Organization in ensuring peace and sustainable development, promoting regional cooperation, and strengthening good-neighborly relations was noted by the UN General Assembly.[64] The SCO's efforts to create its own human rights structure could be extremely useful for strengthening its influence in regional and subregional relations and its reputation.

Establishing a human rights protection body can be a response to criticisms of the SCO members and their policies. It would also make the human rights situation in the national legal systems more transparent to the international community, allow moving from declarative, mainly political, documents to international treaties imposing clear, specific obligations, and diversify the subject matter of the SCO agreements, dedicated to the measures against drug trafficking and terrorism. Whatever efforts are made by the participants in terms of the humanitarian agenda, they should be supported by specific actions demonstrating the seriousness of the intentions expressed at regular multilateral meetings.

From S. Yee's point of view, the modern stage of the development of international relations (the post-Cold War era) is characterized by such a concept of international law as co-progressiveness. It replaced the idea of coexistence at the height of the Cold War, cooperation during the period of détente. The conception is based on the gradual moral and ethical progress of humanity, leading to universal prosperity. Under this conception, the state plays an enormous role in human rights protection. The author explains: "[b]y human flourishing is meant the situation where an individual lives his or her life driven by a worthy project, goal or value… I proposed that we consider the role of 'induced liberty,' in the sense that efforts to seek meaning do not result from any innate quality of the atomic individual, but are induced, though not to be coerced, by the community, its culture and history, and its web of relationships. Thus, without the State the individual would not have thought about many choices. Sovereignty thus informs and influences the perception of personhood. From this perspective, strong States are essential to human flourishing."[65]

Such a perception of a person's position may raise debates. However, the approach does not solve the question of how to defend human rights at the international level and how to restrict the state. Nonparticipation in such mechanisms and their low efficiency prove the contrary. The creation of a new human rights body in the SCO may be a worthy response to current criticism.

HEADS OF MEMBER STATES" (2018), at https://rus.sectsco.org/files/442935/442935?ysclid=lqm6tn5ygk988994319 (last visited on December 10, 2023).

[64] "Cooperation between the United Nations and the Shanghai Cooperation Organization". UN General Assembly Resolution. 17 March 2021. A/RES/73/334.

[65] Sienho Yee, *The International Law of Co-progressiveness: The Descriptive Observation, the Normative Position and Some Core Principles,* 13(3) The Chinese Journal of International Law 488 (2014). The review of the book made by: Sergey Yu. Marochkin, Sergey A. Stepanov, *SIENHO YEE, TOWARDS AN INTERNATIONAL LAW OF CO-PROGRESSIVENESS, PART II MEMBERSHIP, LEADERSHIP AND RESPONSIBILITY. BRILL & NIJHOFF, 2014*, 16(1) The Chinese Journal of International Law 125–129 (2017).

Moreover, the statements made by its main participants, Russia and China, are somewhat contradictory to the claims of growing humanitarian cooperation in the SCO. In the Declaration of two governments on the Promotion of International Law of 25 June 2016, the parties formulated their vision of a just and equitable international order. In the carefully compiled list of basic ideas, such as sovereign equality and refraining from the threat of force, condemnation of military intervention and unilateral sanctions, and inviolability of the immunities of states and officials, there is no mention of respect for the rights and interests of the individual, implementation of human rights obligations, and susceptibility to gross and systematic violations of human life and dignity.[66] The creation of a new human rights body in the SCO could make clear the real situation.

Now human rights obligations are implemented through individual efforts of countries. It is clear that this is not enough for the SCO: the establishment of a special body for the protection of human rights is valuable not only in itself but also radically changes the architecture of the Organization, which should not be fixated on combating terror and suppressing drug trafficking. It is impossible to develop full-fledged multilateral cooperation ignoring human rights issues since "[a]bsolutely every integrative association faces the need for real protection of human rights at different periods of its development."[67] International regional organizations in Europe, Africa, and America, which do not define themselves as military blocs and bodies, provide for similar judicial and nonjudicial institutions. The situation with a human rights mechanism in Asia is quite difficult, but some results have been already archived.

Perhaps the proposed human rights mechanism should focus primarily not on the protection but promotion of human rights ideals and values within the SCO agenda. At the same time, it is obvious that a human rights body should be not a fiction but a bearer of political and legal values.

The creation of a human rights mechanism in the SCO should not require its members to accept all obligations at once. It is possible to recognize the competence of the body only partially by accepting its separate competences. The members of the Organization are states that, despite the similarities, have differences in the development of legislation, influence of religion, and cultural life. The creation of a special human rights body does not contradict the specific approaches of countries to human rights.

It is clear the comprehensive development of the cooperation in the SCO meets the interests of Russia and China. According to the Concept of the Foreign Policy of

---

[66] "THE DECLARATION OF THE RUSSIAN FEDERATION AND THE PEOPLE'S REPUBLIC OF CHINA ON THE PROMOTION OF INTERNATIONAL LAW" (2016), AT https://www.mid.ru/ru/foreign_policy/position_word_order/1530748/?lang=ru (LAST VISITED ON DECEMBER 10, 2023).

[67] (Russian) Anatoliy Kovler, Yana Lebedeva, *Zashchita prav cheloveka stricto sensu sudami integracionnyh ob"edinenij: opyt sravnitel'nogo analiza [The protection of human rights stricto sensu by the courts of integrational organizations: experience of comparative analysis]*, 12(4) Mezhdunarodnoye pravosudiye [International Justice], 36–50 (2022).

the Russian Federation, a comprehensive deepening of ties and strengthening of coordination with friendly sovereign global centers of power and development, which are located on the Eurasian continent, are particularly important for achieving strategic goals and major objectives of the foreign policy of the state (para 51).[68] According to the Joint Statement of the Russian Federation and the People's Republic of China on the Twentieth Anniversary of the Treaty of Good Neighborliness and Friendly Cooperation between the Russian Federation and the People's Republic of China of 28 June 2021,[69] the parties intend to continue their joint efforts to promote the use by the UN human rights mechanisms of an even-handed approach to systemic advancement of human rights and counter politicization of the international human rights agenda, the policy of double standards, and the use of the human rights issues as a tool for interfering in the internal affairs of sovereign states. Russia and China will be great pacemakers in the far-reaching reform of the Organization in this regard.

International practice provides examples of different human rights protection mechanisms within interstate organizations. Overall, the specific approaches of countries to human rights values and the possible difference in their perception should not undermine the idea of international protection of the individual as such.[70]

As mentioned above (see Section I), some SCO member states have enshrined in their legislation the constitutional right to appeal to interstate bodies for the protection of human rights (Article 41 of the Constitution of Kyrgyzstan 2010, Article 46 of the Constitution of Russia 1993, Article 55 of the Constitution of Uzbekistan 2023). A limited number of SCO members with such norms in the national legislation hardly meet approval. However, such a gap can be partially filled by accepting of the right of individuals to submit communications on violations of human rights to the bodies that monitor each treaty compliance. The right of individual petition with respect to the International Covenant on Civil and Political Rights has been accepted by Kazakhstan, Kyrgyzstan, Tajikistan, and Uzbekistan. In addition to the universal system of protection of human rights, the possibility of exercising the right to appeal to intergovernmental bodies can be guaranteed at the regional level, particularly in the SCO.

---

[68] "THE CONCEPT OF THE FOREIGN POLICY OF THE RUSSIAN FEDERATION APPROVED BY THE DECREE OF THE PRESIDENT OF THE RUSSIAN FEDERATION" (2023), at https://www.mid.ru/ru/detail-material-page/1860586/?lang=en (last visited on December 10, 2023).

[69] "JOINT STATEMENT OF THE RUSSIAN FEDERATION AND THE PEOPLE'S REPUBLIC OF CHINA ON THE TWENTIETH ANNIVERSARY OF THE TREATY OF GOOD NEIGHBORLINESS AND FRIENDLY COOPERATION BETWEEN THE RUSSIAN FEDERATION AND THE PEOPLE'S REPUBLIC OF CHINA" (2021), at http://static.kremlin.ru/media/events/files/en/Bo3RF3JzGDvMAPjHBQAuSemVPWTEvb3c.pdf (last visited on December 10, 2023).

[70] (Russian) Anatoly Kovler, Evgeniy Fokin & Veronika Cherenkova, *Organy mezhdunarodnogo pravosudiya v integratsionnykh sistemakh sovremennogo mira [Bodies of international justice in the integration systems of the modern world]*, 9(2) Mezhdunarodnoe pravosudie. [International Justice], 44–61 (2019).

A special body for the protection of human rights in the SCO, on the one hand, would strengthen the legal status of citizens of the member states, their security. On the other hand, it would ensure the implementation of the obligations assumed by the states.

The exchange of experience is possible among SCO countries that are involved in other international human rights bodies (e.g., in the Independent Permanent Human Rights Commission of the Organization of Islamic Cooperation). It was heralded in the New Delhi Declaration of Council of Heads of States of the SCO of 4 July 2023[71] that Central Asia as *the core of SCO* [emphasis added] supports the efforts of the regional countries to ensure prosperity and peace, sustainable development, and the formation of a space of good neighborliness, trust, and friendship.

Yang Cheng says that "the Shanghai spirit should be regarded in the light of its development. The essence of the Shanghai spirit is not static… new practices have widened the extent of the Shanghai spirit and have also provided rich philosophical and intellectual resources for international relation theories."[72] At the same time, he admits that "SCO members lack the necessary elements for regional identity such as common or similar historical memories, cultural traditions, and religions… This is closely connected with the institutional designs and operations of the SCO. For the public, the SCO is a lofty geopolitical and economic design, scarcely related to their daily life… Although members all agree with the Shanghai spirit, and they hope to promote cooperation in all fields within the SCO framework in order to push forward their own development, still it is difficult for them to make choices between relative and absolute gains or between economic interests and strategic calculations, or issues concerning choosing China or Russia or the United States as a priority partner, since a 'sense of belonging' identity does not yet exist."[73]

The EAEU Court considers constitutional traditions of the member states relevant. According to E. B. Dyachenko and K. V. Entin, including human rights as a general principle of the Union law enables the EAEU Court to verify the decisions of the Eurasian Economic Commission for compliance with fundamental human rights. Such control will be carried out by the courts of the member states, the need for a mechanism for dialogue between national courts and the EAEU Court. A similar approach can be adopted in the SCO to ensure a high standard of protection.[74]

---

[71] "THE NEW DELHI DECLARATION OF COUNCIL OF HEADS OF STATES OF THE SCO" (2023), at file:///C:/Users/Legion/Downloads/NEW%20DELHI%20DECLARATION%20%20OF%20THE%20COUNCIL%20OF%20SCO%20HEADS%20OF%20STATE%204%20JULY%202023%20.pdf (last visited on December 10, 2023).

[72] Yang Cheng, *The Shanghai Spirit and SCO Mechanisms: Beyond Geopolitics*, in MICHAEL FREDHOLM (ed.), THE SHANGHAI COOPERATION ORGANIZATION AND EURASIAN GEOPOLITICS: NEW DIRECTIONS, PERSPECTIVES, AND CHALLENGES, at 206–207 (Copenhagen, NIAS Press, 2013).

[73] Yang Cheng, *supra* note 72, 215–216.

[74] (Russian) Ekaterina B. Dyachenko, Kirill V. Entin, *Tolkovanie s oporoj na konstitucionnye tradicii gosudarstv-chlenov i zashchita prav cheloveka Sudom Evropejskogo Soyuza i Sudom Evrazijskogo ekonomicheskogo soyuza [The interpretation through constitutional traditions of the member States and the protection of human rights by the European Union Court of Justice and*

3.3 Obstacles to Human Rights Integration

At the same time, it is important to take into account factors complicating the development of human rights protection in the SCO.

Some SCO countries share common features due to their previous USSR experience, such as geographical proximity, the interaction within a former state, the common language (Russian) and educational space, and close ties in the field of education and culture. The limiting factor is, as Marc Lanteigne puts it, "[w]ithin the SCO, there remain fundamental differences regarding both the ideal security identity of the organization and the degree to which non-security issues such as economic cooperation should be incorporated within its framework."[75]

Along with that, all countries have Westernized features of modern global civilization. Undoubtedly, this diversity and cultural richness is one of the powerful resources of the SCO's external "soft power." Multilateral human rights obligations can also serve as a unifying factor. As Duan Jielong believes, China aims to build a "harmonious world" that respects the UN Charter and the basic human rights and freedom provided for in human rights conventions.[76]

However, the lack of common values and language complicates cooperation within the SCO and impedes the creation and functioning of the humanitarian cooperation. Note that the official languages of the SCO are Russian and Chinese. If the Russian language is actively used in the post-Soviet space of the SCO, the Chinese language cannot serve unifying for the rest of the Organization—Russia, Central Asia, India, and Pakistan.

Humanitarian cooperation within the SCO is hindered by economic competition between China and Russia, as well as with Central Asian countries. The Central Asian governments are striving to maintain a balance between different centers of power. The complicated relations between Uzbekistan and Kyrgyzstan should not be ignored. The same is true for partnership between India, Pakistan, and China. It is still relevant that "the need to eliminate the significant gap between the political and economic tracks of the Organization's activities remains an urgent task."[77]

Court of the Eurasian Economic Union], 25(4) Zhurnal rossijskogo prava [Journal of Russian Law], 185 (2021).

[75] Marc Lanteigne, *Russia, China and the Shanghai Cooperation Organization: Diverging Security Interests and the 'Crimea Effect'*, in HELGE BLAKKISRUD & ELANA WILSON ROWE (eds.), RUSSIA'S TURN TO THE EAST DOMESTIC POLICYMAKING AND REGIONAL COOPERATION, at 132 (Cham, Springer, 2018).

[76] Duan Jielong, *The Concept of the 'Harmonious World': An Important Contribution to International Relations*, in SIENHO YEE & JACQUES-YVAN MORIN (eds.), MULTICULTURALISM AND INTERNATIONAL LAW: ESSAYS IN HONOUR OF EDWARD MCWHINNEY, at 62 (Leiden & Boston, Martinus Nijhoff Publishers, 2009).

[77] (Russian) Konarovsky M. *Rossija – ShOS: nekotorye jelementy strategii [Russia and the Shanghai Cooperation Organization: Some Elements of Strategy.]*, 11(4) International Organisations Research Journal 154 (2016).

Thus, due to the complexity of the region, there are several obstacles to the creation of human rights mechanism within the SCO. One of them is the civilizational heterogeneity of the SCO countries: the multinational culture of Russia, the unique millennia-old Chinese civilization, and patriarchal religious culture in the countries of Central Asia.[78]

The SCO unites states with different levels of democratic institutions, which strongly affects the Organization's policy. The focus is on the declaration and demonstration of high intentions regarding human rights, but there is lack of real actions. Low activity in the law-making sphere and high activity in the geopolitical sphere are relevant for the SCO.

The research allows for some hypothetic conclusions. There are grounds for the creation of the SCO human rights body, which would serve as a guarantee for the protection of individual rights and align with the interests of the member states. However, a number of unresolved issues are a serious obstacle to institutional change. Therefore, the SCO's human rights activities can be performed if there is a political will of the states, especially Russia and China.

4 The SCO Human Rights Protection Mechanism: Possible Perspectives

There is a great experience of different human rights protection mechanisms worldwide at regional and global levels. And it should be taken into account. The SCO may and ought to be open to achievements, to correct mistakes, and to introduce own schemes.

In international law, the main but not the only function of all human rights mechanisms is monitoring the fulfillment by states of their international treaty obligations.[79] It can be carried out in different forms: (1) reports of states on the implementation of their human rights obligations; (2) claims of member states on violations of such obligations by other member states; (3) complaints of individuals, groups of individuals, and nongovernmental organizations on violations of their rights by the state; (4) facts finding related to alleged or established violations of human rights through special bodies; and (5) individual complaints within the framework of a special international judicial procedure. It is obvious that the last *modus* seems to be the most effective at the regional level as compared to the universal one.

The SCO member states declare their commitment to the generally recognized principles of international law and supplement them with the principles of

[78] SERGEY MAROCHKIN & YURI BEZBORODOV (eds.), *supra* note 2, 88.

[79] Simma Bruno, *Human Rights Before the International Court of Justice: Community Interest Coming to Life?*, in CHRISTIAN J. TAMS & JAMES SLOAN (EDS.), THE DEVELOPMENT OF INTERNATIONAL LAW BY THE INTERNATIONAL COURT OF JUSTICE, at 301–326 (Oxford, Oxford University Press, 2013; online edn, Oxford Academic, 2014).

military cooperation in border areas, compromise based on mutual understanding and respect for the interests of each member state with the SCO's nondirectedness against other states and international organizations, prevention of any illegal actions against the interests of the SCO, and conscientious fulfillment of obligations under the Charter and other documents of the Organization. At the same time, as mentioned above, the SCO principles do not include respect for human rights and freedoms. In this regard, it would be appropriate to include this principle in the text of the Charter to ensure the interaction between member states. Moreover, among the goals and objectives of the SCO (Article 1 of the Charter) is "promotion of ensuring human rights and fundamental freedoms in accordance with the international obligations of the member states and their national legislation."[80] Thus, theoretically, the goals outlined in the SCO's founding documents may include human rights issues in the most general form. From the point of view of legal technique within the SCO, it is quite possible to create a niche for a special institution aimed at protection of human rights and freedoms.

The SCO countries are not members of any other regional mechanisms for the protection of human rights. The different approaches to human rights in Asian countries and the controversial human rights situation indicate the necessity of such a mechanism. However, the readiness of member states to assume new commitments in the field of human rights should be assessed realistically. Due to that a flexible mechanism from both a normative (standards stipulated) and a functional point of view (the human rights body's composition, competence, decisions, and their implementation) is needed. Therefore, the gradual and consistent implementation of the propounded mechanism is highly important: with the advisory and recommendatory competence at the first steps and with the incrementally enhancement competence at subsequent stages.

Thus, the main issues to be solved as to the design of the SCO human rights mechanism are:

- Whether it should be an expert body (a kind of UN committees) or a judicial one (a kind of European, Inter-American courts) or a structure of representatives of states (a kind of European Commission on Human Rights until 1998).
- Whether there should be a combination of structures: a single judicial body or a court supplemented by an expert body or a body of representatives of states. At the initial stage it seems proper to establish a two-tier structure: when a commission composed of experts (not representatives of states) transfers the most serious cases to the judicial authority; other cases are to be considered by a commission (a kind of the Council of Europe system before 1998). A promising scenario is the subsequent replacement of such a system by a permanent court of human rights.
- The legal force of the body decisions should be considered. The binding nature of the decisions of the human rights protection mechanism seems preferable.

[80] https://treaties.un.org/Pages/showDetails.aspx?objid=08000002803594e2 (last visited on December 10, 2023).

This would ensure higher compliance and uniformity of national practice. But at the initial stage the nonbinding decision scheme would be more realistic.
- The domestic implementation of the decisions of the protection mechanism. Following common practice, this issue should be left to the discretion of the member states. As an option, the former Russian practice on the execution of judgments of the ECtHR is relevant, when such international rulings were mandatory for the review of national judicial decisions by local courts.
- Support of the expert community and civil society structures. It is extremely important to support the work of the human rights mechanism by an independent expert body consisting of representatives of academia and civil society. Such a body may have an advisory status and consist of persons with high competence and experience in the field of human rights protection and international law. Such a structure would allow (a) to ensure the high academic quality of the decisions of the human rights mechanism; (b) to ensure the credibility of the mechanism before public; (c) to assist the mechanism in determining the key areas of its activities; and (d) to protect the mechanism from politicization of its work and decisions. The tools of the activity of such a structure are *amicus curia* conclusions at the request of the mechanism and *proprio motu*; participation in the election/appointment of members of the mechanism; participation in the preparation of regular reports on its activities; and preparation of reviews of the mechanism practice.

The coordination function within the entire human rights protection mechanism can be assumed by the SCO Commissioner for Human Rights (by analogy with the Council of Europe), acting in parallel with the judicial/nonjudicial human rights body. The Commissioner may focus on coordinating the mechanism, connecting its elements, communicating experience (through regular reports), and informing and advising support to the SCO member states and bodies.

It should be recognized that the SCO mainly unites states with undeveloped democratic institutions, and this cannot but affect the predominantly declarative and decorative nature of the Organization. Passivity in the law-making sphere and activity in the geopolitical sphere are the main international legal characteristics of the Organization.

Currently there is no indication that the SCO member states will willingly and eagerly participate in the human rights activities. Only if the initial interstate steps to overcome the reluctance succeed then other more decisive moves might be made with the creation of a special commission (committee) of experts holding recommendations. If the campaign is successful, then the Organization may proceed with the creation of a body with broader powers similar to UN committees. And only with positive experience therein, nothing prevents it from the creation of a special court in the future, which echoes the goals and principles of the SCO, on the one hand, and contributes to the social development of the entire Eurasian region, on the other hand.

Anyway, the sphere of ensuring human rights and fundamental freedoms in the SCO is a necessary and sought-after areas for the further development of the Organization.

5 Concluding Remarks

The human rights protection is a key issue in the global agenda and an indispensable element of the states' reputation. In the modern globalized universe, the influence of the "Asian world" has expanded in the international arena. The Eurasian region plays an increasing role in the global political process. But the Eurasian states' cooperation in the human rights is still undeveloped. The region needs to initiate a separate mechanism for human rights protection as most other large regions of the world have done (Europe, Northern and Southern Americas, Africa).

Among the existing institutions in the Eurasia (CIS, EAEU, SCO), the Shanghai Cooperation Organization has the most potential and the pertinent basis for a human rights mechanism. It faces conceptual issues of further development, and new global conditions necessitate the update of its policy. Ensuring human rights in accordance with international obligations and national legislation is a necessary and inevitable direction for the Organization's evolution.

Collective efforts to protect human rights are directly enshrined in Article 1 of the SCO Charter as one of the main goals and objectives of the Organization. Article 4 allows for the expansion of areas of cooperation, which could include the establishment of a special mechanism for the protection of human rights and freedoms.

The implementation of these intentions is more productive through the gradual insertion of a Eurasian human rights mechanism which could start with an advisory panel, progress to an international committee of experts, and eventually lead to an integral court with the SCO member states' participation.

We should be ready to wait as the process may not be timely and may not produce immediate results. However, it is important to anticipate potential future needs. When the regional states recognize this necessity and come to understanding it, some doctrinal suggestions and developments can be considered.

International legal affairs are largely dependent on the will of states. If the Eurasian countries are interested in building democratic institutions, promoting civil society, and strengthening justice, they can create a specialized body to consider claims of alleged violations and monitor the observance of human rights and freedoms. The acceptance of this necessity by governments is already a success that would pave the way to human rights.

Chapter 4
Central Asia and International Law

Vladislav Tolstykh

Abstract In recent years, the international relations of Central Asian states have been developing dynamically: along with positive trends (Eurasian integration, growth in mutual trade, cross-border cooperation), there have been negative processes (deterioration of the security situation, conflicts over water resources, etc.). Russia plays a large and often leading role in international legal policy in the region; however, recently, there has been a qualitative strengthening of the positions of China, Turkey, Iran, and Western countries. The article discusses the main features of the international legal policy of the Central Asian states, factors influencing it (economic specialization of the region, activities of external actors, intensity of ethnogenesis, influence of Islam, Soviet heritage), as well as particular legal problems. The latter include (Sect. 4) problems of distribution of water and energy resources, (Sect. 5) environmental problems related to the disappearance of the Aral Sea, (Sect. 6) uncertainty in the Caspian Sea regime, (Sect. 7) the problem of enclaves, (Sect. 8) the problem of minorities, and (Sect. 9) the absence of an integration project. The instruments of general international law are in most cases insufficient to address these problems: they are either imprecise or do not bind particular states. Regional instruments, in turn, are very often absent or characterized by a low level of legal technique. The existing legal vacuum contributes to the freezing of conflicts and contradictions and, in some cases, to their aggravation or exacerbation. The development of regional law in this regard seems to be a necessity: its conditions are the search for original ideas, cooperation of elites, and—as the most general solution—a separate integration project.

This article was previously published in Law Science—Selected Papers Volume 2, Issue 4 (2023).

V. Tolstykh (✉)
Institute of Oriental Studies, Russian Academy of Sciences, Moscow, Russian Federation

Shenzhen MSU-BIT University, Shenzhen, China

T. Du, X. Fei (eds.), *The BRICS Legal Cooperation and Perspectives*,
https://doi.org/10.1007/978-981-95-4356-4_4

Keywords International legal policy · Central Asian integration · Transboundary watercourses · Enclaves · Minority status · Right to self-determination

1 Introduction

International legal politics in Central Asia is understudied. There are a number of articles on specific problems of international relations in the region written by post-Soviet authors. While summarizing the contradictions on particular issues, these articles rarely address the legal dimension of these contradictions (applicable legal instruments, options for their interpretation, de lege ferenda proposals, etc.). The reason for this state of affairs is very simple: the instruments of general international law are too abstract; most of them are not adapted to the specific context of the region and cannot be used to resolve the conflicts in question. As for the regional treaties concluded in the post-Soviet period, they are few in number and characterized by an extremely low level of legal technique. To this should be added the traditional distrust of the Central Asian states in international courts and international law. The latter, of course, is used in political rhetoric but very rarely serves as a real regulator of interstate relations.

The main objective of this article, in this regard, is to identify the main contradictions in the region, establish their legal components, propose their preliminary legal qualifications, and develop de lege ferenda proposals. The actualization of the international legal discourse in the region is caused by a number of circumstances: first, the key external actors—Russia, China, and Turkey—are unable to guarantee the economic and political stability of the states in the region, which, therefore, have to organize the regional order on their own; second, some of these states (e.g., Kazakhstan and Uzbekistan) have ambitions that extend beyond the region and require legal substantiation; third, the constitution-building processes in Central Asian countries have largely been completed, and political elites can now focus on new tasks; fourth, some of the existing conflicts (e.g., the conflict between Kyrgyzstan and Tajikistan over the Vorukh enclave) are in a stage of aggravation.

The second section provides a general overview of the region (geography, economy, etc.), which demonstrates the specificity of the region. A characteristic feature of the region is the differentiation of its constituent countries, which makes it difficult for them to cooperate, including on legal issues. The third section examines the main factors influencing the international legal tradition in the region. These factors (individually and in combination) prevented the formation of Western-style political and legal institutions but guaranteed the region's viability for most of its history. The sharp turn in this history, which is taking place today, calls for a restructuring of the existing model.

The most important problems and approaches to their legal solutions are discussed next: the allocation of water and energy resources (fourth section), the problem of the Aral Sea (fifth section), the uncertainty of the legal status of the Caspian Sea (sixth section), the issue of enclaves (seventh section), and the problem of minorities (eighth section). The ninth section is devoted to the issue of regional integration, which could be a solution par excellence to all the abovementioned problems and which itself is a source of political contradictions (as different political elites are oriented toward different integration projects). The conclusion lists the difficulties hindering the resolution of these problems and expresses the hope that these difficulties can be overcome by a new generation of managers.

2 General Profile of the Region

Central Asia stretches from the Caspian Sea in the west to the Chinese (Pamir) border in the east. It borders Russia to the north and Iran, Afghanistan, and China to the south. The region includes five post-Soviet republics: Kazakhstan, Kyrgyzstan, Tajikistan, Turkmenistan, and Uzbekistan. Soviet scholars used the term "Middle Asia and Kazakhstan"; recently, the elites of the region have abandoned it in favor of the term "Central Asia," previously used only in Western scholarship. This substitution reflects a shift in political priorities: "Middle" implies being "between" recognized centers (Russia and China), while "Central" implies the self-sufficiency of the region and, at the same time, the rejection of the Soviet legacy.[1]

The regional landscape consists of steppes (Kazakhstan), deserts (the Karakum in Turkmenistan and the Kyzylkum in Uzbekistan and Kazakhstan), mountain ranges, and valleys (Kyrgyzstan, Tajikistan). The climate of the region is dry and sharply continental. The main population is Turkic, who adhere to Sunni Islam; the exception is the Iranian-speaking Tajiks. The Turkic ethnicity was the result of a mixture of Caucasoid (Iranian speaking) and Mongoloid elements and is heterogeneous: Caucasoid features are more distinct in Turkmens, while Mongoloid ones are more prominent in Kyrgyz.

The main branch of the economy is agriculture. The traditional activity of Kazakhs is nomadic cattle breeding; that of Tajiks and Uzbeks is irrigated farming; hence the differences in culture and lifestyle. Uzbekistan has a developed cotton industry (ranking sixth in the world); Kazakhstan is the largest producer of wheat. Kazakhstan, Turkmenistan, and Uzbekistan have large reserves of hydrocarbons; Kazakhstan has iron and nonferrous metals, including 30% of the world's reserves of chromium, 25% of manganese, and 14% of uranium; Uzbekistan has uranium and gold. Kyrgyzstan and Tajikistan have significant capacity for the production of hydro resources (dams, reservoirs, and power grids). The main indices of the Central Asian states and Russia (2021) are presented in Table 4.1.

[1] *See* Alexey Buraev, *K voprosu o primenenii termina "Central'naja Azija" v istoricheskih issledovanijah* [To the question of the use of the term "Central Asia" in historical research], 8 Vestnik Burjatskogo gosuniversiteta 142 (2011).

Table 4.1 Main indexes

Index	Kazakhstan	Kyrgyzstan	Tajikistan	Turkmenistan	Uzbekistan	Russia
Territory (km^2)	2,724,902	199,951	141,400	488,100	448,924	17,125,191
Population (million)/ density (people/km^2) [a]	19/6.93	6.6/32.6	9.66/64.5	6/12.8	34.4/76	146.15/8.54
GDP: total ($ billion)/person) (thousands of dollars) (IMF)	194/10.14	8.15/1.225	8.1/0.84	53/8.84	65.5/1.9	1647.6/11.27
Public debt (% of GDP) (IMF) [b]	26.3	68	51.3	32.2	36.4	18
Doing Business ranking: position [c]	25	80	106	No information	69	28
Human Development Index (UNDP) [d]	0.811	0.692	0.685	0.745	0.727	0.822
Democracy Index: overall score/position (EIU) [e]	3.14/128	4.21/107	1.94/159	1.72/162	2.12/155	3.31/124
Perceptions of corruption: position (Transparency Int) [f]	94	124	149	165	146	129
Homicide rate per 100,000 people (UNODC) [g]	3.2	1.75	0.9	1.1	1.4	6.8

Source

[a] https://www.imf.org/external/datamapper/profile/WEOWORLD

[b] https://www.imf.org/external/datamapper/GGXWDG_NGDP@WEO/OEMDC/ADVEC/WEOWORLD

[c] https://archive.doingbusiness.org/en/rankings

[d] https://hdr.undp.org/system/files/documents/global-report-document/hdr2021-22overviewrupdf.pdf

[e] https://www.eiu.com/n/campaigns/democracy-index-2021

[f] https://www.transparency.org/en/cpi/2021

[g] https://dataunodc.un.org/dp-intentional-homicide-victims

3 International Legal Tradition

The international legal tradition of Central Asia has been shaped by the following factors.

1. The region is crossed by the land route from China to the Middle East and Europe, which for centuries was the main direction of world trade (Silk Road). With the opening of sea routes around Africa in the fifteenth and seventeenth centuries and the launch of the Suez Canal (1869), the importance of this route faded; however, its sociopolitical inertia remains and manifests itself in the general underdevelopment of the state-legal tradition. Indeed, trade civilizations rarely form stable political formations: their elites are not interested in territorial control or the exploitation of large masses of the population and, as a consequence, in the development of a social contract that could stimulate the development of state institutions (including institutions of international law). Moreover, any stable entity located on a trade route inevitably becomes an obstacle to international commerce (e.g., the Ottoman Empire).[2] The fate of Central Asia in this sense is similar to the fate of Palestinian entities and Central American states.
2. The region is the center of a geopolitical figure whose corners are formed by the major regional powers: China, Russia, Turkey, and Iran, with the Western bloc acting as a global hegemon. As a result, politics in Central Asia are multi-vector, i.e., oriented toward several projects at once, and at the same time, it lacks its own project that could serve as an ideological basis for domestic and foreign politics.[3] Another consequence is the orientation toward Realpolitik rather than legal mechanisms: the formal force of laws and treaties does not determine policy but is rather its object, i.e., emerges and disappears depending on the dynamic political situation. Multi-vectorism implies the struggle of external actors for influence in the region (Big Game); the winner gets a chance to colonize the region (but never to absorb it). Colonization, in turn, presupposes their interaction with local elites who, therefore, may not seek support from their own population. The result, as in the previous case, is the absence of a social contract (a

---

[2] In 1453 A.D., the Ottoman Empire boycotted trade with China and closed Silk Road routes. Gabor and Masters state: "During the 15th and 16th centuries, when the Ottomans emerged as a great power, the primary goal of trade was the self-sufficiency of the empire. In keeping with this goal, the Ottoman Empire established three essential trade policies: ensure adequate supplies of primary goods within the empire; store primary goods in preparation for times of famine and scarcity; and, finally, avoid economic scarcity during wartime. As a natural result of these policies, Ottoman trade focused on imports, and most exports were prohibited." Ágoston Gábor & Bruce Masters, *Encyclopedia of the Ottoman Empire* 569 (2009).

[3] *See* Rachel Vanderhill, et al., *Between the bear and the dragon: multivectorism in Kazakhstan as a model strategy for secondary powers,* 96 (6) Int'l Aff. 975 (2020); Paradorn Rangsimaporn, *Central Asia and Southeast Asia: Exploring the Dynamics of Greater Engagement* 27–80 (2022); Emilbek Dzhuraev, *"Multi-Vectoral" Central Asia On the Other Side of Major Power Agendas,* in Monitoring Central Asia and the Caspian Area Development Policies, Regional Trends, and Italian Interests 15–33(Carlo Frappi & Fabio Indeo eds., 2019).

mechanism of regular communication between the elites and the rest of the population) and the lack of a legal order.

3. The region is predominantly Muslim. The religious perception is often superficial; norms of Sharia may conflict with local adats; elites are suspicious of religious radicalism. Traditions of Islam do, however, influence political life. These include the following: (1) dual legitimization of power, charismatic (appealing to the divine will) and rational (appealing to the opinion of the community); (2) the idea of the caliph—a religious leader distinct from secular leaders—emirs, khans, etc.; and (3) the idea of the ummah (the religious community) and its opposition to the rest of the world.[4]

   The influence of these ideas can be seen in the following: (1) rejection of the Western model based on the suppression of the religious element in politics, self-sufficiency of the sovereign, and equality of states;[5] (2) nonproliferation of ethnic separatism;[6] (3) perception of international relations as relations between the ummah and the outside world and relations within the ummah over leadership; (4) underdevelopment of formal institutions and predominance of direct diplomacy; and (5) a general lack of rationality.[7]

4. Since ancient history, ethnogenesis in the region has been extremely dynamic: peoples have been in constant flux, state formations have rarely lasted longer than two or three centuries, and large-scale invasions (Arabs, Turks, Mongols) completely changed the political map.[8] External challenges occasionally provided impetus for the synthesis of a unified nation; as they weakened, centrifugal

[4] Russian historian Bartold identifies three ideas that determine the political views of Muslims: (3) idea of a pious sovereign as a substitute (*caliph*) of God on earth, who owes his authority to God alone; (4) link between Mecca and Medina and the Muslim sovereign as the protector of these shrines; and (5) idea of a religious brotherhood, whose members are obliged to obey the leader (Vasilij Bartol'd, 6 *Sochinenija* [Works] 15–72, 303–319 (1966).

[5] This model is a direct result of the events of the sixteenth–seventeenth-century European history (Reformation, Thirty Years' War and English Revolution). The core of the Reformation (not experienced by Islam) was to close the social order from the manifestations of the divine will in order to make it self-organizing (self-contained).

[6] *See* Anatoly Novosel'cev, et al., *Puti razvitija feodalizma (Zakavkaz'e, Srednjaja Azija, Rus', Pribaltika)* [Ways of development of feudalism (Transcaucasia, Central Asia, Russia, Baltic)] 30 (1972).

[7] "The European conception of law is pluralist, and the recognition of the legitimacy of the existence of many states, side by side in a given region, is derived from it. This conception took shape within the unique circumstances of European history, and to a certain extent even contravened the monist ideal of a united Christian community. Islamic law is, conversely, monistic in essence, and only recognizes the legitimacy of a single all-embracing religion—Islam. The caliphate is ruled by a single sovereign—the caliph… International relations, according to this conception, are not relations of equality, but of subjugation between the caliphe and all other entities, to which a certain degree of autonomy is permitted, but not sovereignty." Elon Jarden, *The Israeli-Palestinian conflict in international law* in Israel and a Palestinian State; Zero Sum Game? 132 (Arieh Stav ed., 2001).

[8] "If we look at the history of Europe, the Middle Ages were marked by the consolidation of nationalities, which then developed into nations that have survived to the present day. It was around these or those nationalities that the known political communities were formed in Europe… The situation is quite different in West Asia, in particular in Transcaucasia and Central Asia. Here we constantly

tendencies resumed. Today, as it was a thousand years ago, the region is inhabited by two super-ethnoses—the Iranian one (Tajiks and Persians, in ancient times Khorezmians, Sogdians, Parthians, Saks, Massagetes) and the Turkic one (Uzbeks, Kyrgyz, Kazakhs, Turkmens). The history of the region is marked by the constant expansion of the Turks, accompanied by the active borrowing of elements from Persian culture.[9] Current political boundaries do not always align with the boundaries of these super-ethnoses—this situation is a source of constant tensions, whose destructive force, however, is mitigated by the influence of Islam, the weakness of state institutions, and general tolerance.

5. The political legacy of the USSR has both positive and negative aspects. The former includes the region's cohesion into a single economic complex, the creation and development of state institutions and political boundaries, friendly relations with Russia, joint integration projects, and a well-developed social sector. The latter include the ambiguous results of the national state delimitation of 1924, the destruction of traditional lifestyles and ties between peoples, negative environmental consequences of economic reforms (soil erosion, desertification, destruction of natural complexes, and the drainage of the Aral Sea), the vulnerable situation of displaced minorities, archaic political forms that imply extreme alienation of the population from politics, a lack of their own integration project, and economic dependence.

Combination of these factors forms a unique political landscape, whose features are (1) the coexistence and interpenetration of two types of institutions: autochthonous ones (clan system, adats, Islamic law) and borrowed ones (state and legal institutions in the proper sense of the word); (2) stability and latency of the former and instability and underdevelopment of the latter; (3) priority of the informal over the formal; and (4) lack of regular interaction between the elites and the populations. These features are manifested both at the domestic and regional levels. They also determine the international legal response (most often inconclusive) to the challenges faced by the states of the region. The most important challenges and responses to them are discussed below.

4 The Water-Energy Allocation: Too Many Cooks Spoil the Broth

The region's water needs are met by two rivers: the Syr Darya, which originates in the Tien Shan Mountains (Kyrgyzstan), and the Amu Darya, which originates in the Pamir Mountains (Tajikistan). Both rivers flow east-west through Uzbekistan,

---

observe the processes of either ethnos change or extreme narrowing of the territory and sphere of activity of the previously existing ethnic communities." Novosel'cev, et al., *supra* note 7, at 28.

[9] An example is the Turkic state of the Karakhanids (942–1212), which used Persian as language of interethnic communication and science.

Turkmenistan, and Kazakhstan, ultimately reaching the Aral Sea. The waters of the Syr Darya are collected in the Toktogul Reservoir, which is built on its tributary, the Naryn River (Kyrgyzstan). During the Soviet period, 75% of the runoff was produced during the growing season (April–September), while 25% occurred in winter (October–March). Of the total water resources, 46% were directed to Uzbekistan, 44% to Kazakhstan, 8% to Tajikistan, and 2% to Kyrgyzstan.[10] Additionally, "summer" electricity was supplied to Uzbekistan and Kazakhstan in exchange for fuel received by Kyrgyzstan from these countries.

In 1992, the Central Asian states signed the Agreement on the Joint Use of Water *Resources of the Central Asian States*, which preserved the Soviet-era regime. According to the Preamble, the parties "respect the established structure and principles of allocation and are guided by the current normative documents on water allocation." The determination of consumption limits was entrusted to the Coordination Water Commission. However, the Agreement did not address the issue of compensation. As a result, it proved to be ineffective. In 1993, when Uzbekistan stopped supplying gas to Kyrgyzstan due to outstanding debts, the latter increased its intake of "winter" water from the Toktogul reservoir to as much as 55%.

The 1998 Framework Agreement on the Use of Water and Energy Resources in the Syr Darya Basin addressed the issue of compensation. According to Art. 2, the parties should make annual decisions on water releases and compensation for energy losses. According to Art. 4, additional energy resulting from the water releases during the growing season should be transferred to Kazakhstan and Uzbekistan; compensation for it should be provided through the delivery of an equivalent volume of energy resources (coal, gas, fuel oil, electricity) to Kyrgyzstan or in a monetary equivalent upon agreement, in order to create the necessary annual and perennial water reserves in reservoirs.

Like the 1992 Agreement, the 1998 Agreement is not strictly binding. Its shortcomings include the reliance on bilateral agreements, which can be difficult to conclude; inflexibility (absence of mechanisms for flow adjustments in dry and high-water years);[11] failure to regulate the regime of infrastructure facilities and methods of compensation; and the confusing wording of Art. 4. According to Art. 7, "the operation, maintenance, and reconstruction of water and energy facilities

[10] *See* Scheme of complex use and protection of water resources in the Syrdarya basin and Resolution of the USSR State Planning Committee No. 11 (1982); *Protocol* No. 413 on the Syrdarya (USSR Ministry of Land Reclamation and Water Management, 1984); Protocol No. 566 on the Amudarya (1987).

[11] *See* Mar Campins Eritja, T*ransboundary Water Resourses Management in Central Asia and its Role in the Emergence of Conflicts Affecting Regional Stability*, 7 Paix et Sécurité Internationales 13, 34 (2019). In 2001, Kyrgyzstan transferred the agreed volumes of water to Uzbekistan and Kazakhstan, but their consumption was low, and they transferred less coal, gas, and fuel oil. As a result of this uncertainty, Tajikistan connected to the Iranian energy grid (2003) while northern Kazakhstan connected to Russia. *See* Ekaterina Borisova, *Istorija razvitija konfliktov po povodu vodnyh resursov v Central'noj Azii v postsovetskij period* [The history of the development of conflicts over water resources in Central Asia in the post-Soviet period], 9 *Rossija i musul'manskij mir* 122, 127, 129 (2014).

should be carried out in accordance with balanced ownership and legalized ownership." This provision is disadvantageous for Kyrgyzstan, which spends up to $100 million per year on the maintenance of the facilities.

Given the ineffectiveness of multilateral mechanisms, bilateral agreements have become the primary instrument for water-energy barter. Such agreements are concluded annually, not published, and sometimes not implemented; in such cases, flow regulation is carried out ad hoc (on request).[12] In the past few years, their conclusion seems to have become regular and orderly (this is probably credited to the new presidents who took office in Uzbekistan and Kyrgyzstan—in 2016 and 2017); they provide flexible and demand-oriented regulation (e.g., they take into account an expected low water). However, they are not based on a system of reciprocal obligations and involve regular coordination of interests, which requires considerable diplomatic efforts on the part of the downstream states.

In 2001, Kyrgyzstan adopted the Law "On Interstate Use of Water Bodies, Water Resources, and Water Management Facilities," which enshrined the following principles: recognition of the state's ownership of water resources; determination of water as a type of resource with economic value and as a commodity; payment for water use in interstate relations; interstate use of water resources based on agreements; pursuit of mutual benefit on an equitable and reasonable basis, etc. Kyrgyzstan expects to receive up to $350 million per year for water, arguing that the mere maintenance of hydropower plants (HPPs) and reservoirs costs it $120 million.[13] This approach provoked protests from Uzbekistan, which claimed losses of $770–800 million as a result of Kyrgyzstan's irrational water use, including flooding and pollution.[14]

The institutional hub for water distribution is the International Fund for Saving the Aral Sea (IFSA), established in 1993. Its headquarters are situated in Tashkent. Its structure comprises the Council of Heads of State, the Interstate Coordination Water Commission (ICWC), the Commission for Sustainable Development, and the Executive Committee. ICWC formulates water policies and approves consumption

[12] *See* Beate Jeshment, *Raspredelenie vodnyh resursov v Central'noj Azii: nerazreshimaja problema?* [Water distribution in Central Asia: an unsolvable problem] 9 (2011); Abdurasul Kajumov, *Deficit vodnyh resursov i dinamika mezhgosudarstvennogo sotrudnichestva v bassejne Naryna i Syrdar'I* [Deficit of water resources and dynamics of interstate cooperation in the Naryn and Syrdarya basin], 15 (4) *Central'naja Azija i Kavkaz* 92 (2012).

[13] *See* Sergey Zhil'cov, *Rol' vodnyh resursov transgranichnyh rek Central'noj Azii v razvitii regiona* [The role of water resources of transboundary rivers of Central Asia in the development of the region], 1 Ustojchivoe razvitie: obshhestvo, jekologija, jekonomika (Proceedings of the XV International Scientific Conference) 71, 82 (2019).

[14] According to Murphy and Mendikulova, Kyrgyzstan has no right to demand payment for water just because the Syr Darya originates on its territory; international law rejects the extreme position of exclusive sovereignty and the opposite position of territorial integrity; it enshrines the concept of limited sovereignty reflected in the concept of equitable and rational use. A riparian state, however, has the right to sell its share. The problem, however, is in determining that share. *See* Sharmila Murthy & Fatima Mendikulova, *Water, Conflict, and Cooperation in Central Asia: The Role of International Law and Diplomacy*, 18 Va. J. Int'l L 400, 440 (2017).

limits, reservoir operation schedules, and so forth. The executive bodies of ICWC include the Basin Water Management Organization "Amudarya" and the organization with the same name, "Syrdarya." In practice, these two entities lack real power and funds. In 2016, Kyrgyzstan suspended its participation in IFAS, citing that the organization does not consider its needs.

A general instrument is the 1997 Convention on the Law of the Non-navigational Uses of International Watercourses, which enshrines the principles of equitable and reasonable use, the prohibition of harm to other states, and the obligation of cooperation. Article 6 lists the factors for equitable and reasonable use: (a) ecological and other factors of a natural character; (b) social and economic needs; (c) the population dependent on the watercourse; (d) the effects of the use of the watercourses in one state on other states; (e) existing and potential uses; (f) the conservation, protection, development, and economy of the use of water resources; and (g) the availability of alternatives. All these factors should be considered together; in practice, however, states insist on prioritizing one factor over another.[15] As a result, the regulatory capacity of the Convention is low, and balancing the factors often requires recourse to a third party, such as international courts. Additionally, by binding the "upper" states, the Convention does not regulate the issue of compensation. Among the countries of Central Asia, only Uzbekistan has ratified it.

Thus, despite the abundance of instruments related to all three levels of legal regulation—general, regional, and bilateral—the problem of water allocation is far from being solved. This solution involves the implementation of common regulatory principles, transformation of the institutional structure, and the development of a new instrument.

The set of principles appears obvious: (1) multilateral (inclusive) settlement; (2) fair compensation for "upper" countries—in monetary form or in the form of fuel supplies; (3) taking into account environmental considerations; (4) integrity of the region's economic system; and (5) the need for a long-term solution. The relevant regime may include general obligations borrowed from the 1997 Convention and a number of additional obligations related to water-energy exchange, maintenance of infrastructure, and the procedure for annual withdrawals. The approach enshrined in the 1998 Convention seems optimal—annual limits; however, these limits should be determined by unilateral decisions of an international organization rather than by agreements of states.

The institutional mechanism established under the auspices of IFAS has several shortcomings: a very complex structure, weak interaction among departments, an emphasis on conciliation procedures, insufficient funding, an unclear regulatory

[15] According to Tarlock and Wouters, the concept of equitable and reasonable use assumes two interpretations: "classical allocation," under which each state receives its share of water and decides how to use it, and "shared benefits," under which states agree on the most rational use and share the profit. The second model was enshrined in the 1961 US-Canada Treaty: the parties agreed that Canada would regulate runoff, while the USA would generate electricity and pay compensation to Canada. *See* A. Dan Tarlock & Patricia Wounters, *Are Shared Benefits of International Waters an Equitable Apportionment?* 18 (5) Colo. J. Int'l Envtl. L. & Pol'y 523 (2007).

framework, and a lack of competencies for monitoring and dispute resolution.[16] Reform of this mechanism also appears to be necessary. The options include improving IFAS structures,[17] establishing a new organization with broader competencies, and creating a water-energy consortium that would integrate state entities, as well as agricultural and energy companies.[18]

To sum up, it is time to establish a new convention that would replace the 1992 and 1998 Agreements and would serve as a "water constitution" for Central Asia. Its strategic goal could be not only to ensure more effective interstate cooperation in the water and energy sector but also to improve the environmental situation in the region.

5 The Aral Sea: No Legal Shield Against the Damocles Sword of Environmental Disaster

The Aral Sea is a large saline lake fed by the Amu Darya and Syr Darya. At the beginning of the twentieth century, the state set a course for cotton cultivation. During the Soviet period, an extensive network of canals was built, significantly increasing water withdrawals from the Amu Darya and Syr Darya (from 60 to 120 km^3/year) and expanding the irrigated lands—from 4.5 million ha (1960) to 7 million ha (1990). As a result, river runoff sharply decreased—from 63 km^3/year (1960) to 3.2 km^3/year (2003): the surface of the Aral Sea has reduced from 69,000 km^2 (1950) to 7000 km^2; the volume has dropped from 1000 km^3 (1960) to 75 km^3 (2007); the salinity has increased from 10 to 100–200 g/L; the fishery has decreased from 60,000 t (1980) to 5000 t (1994); the coastline has receded by

[16] *See* Evgenij Vinokurov, et al., *Regulirovanie vodnojenergeticheskogo kompleksa Central'noj Azii* [Regulation of the water and energy sector in Central Asia] 79–81 (Reports 22/4, Evrazijskij bank razvitija, 2022).

[17] In 2010, the IFAS Executive Committee formulated the following proposals: clarifying the mandates of central and regional bodies, strengthening the role of central bodies, improving the distribution of seats of regional bodies among countries, international rotation of managers, internationalization of staff, streamlining coordination of national structures, improving communication with international organizations, improving transparency in allocation of international aid, etc. *See Sovershenstvovanie organizacionnoj struktury i dogovorno-pravovoj bazy MFSA: analiz i predlozhenija* [Improving the Organisational Structure and Contractual and Legal Framework of IFAS: Analysis and Proposals] 23 (Discussion Paper, 2010), https://unece.org/DAM/env/water/cadialogue/docs/rus/Draft_Paper_united_FINAL.pdf (last visited Aug. 15, 2023).

[18] The project of the Consortium was widely discussed in the late 90s. In 2005, the Water Coordination Commission published the draft of its Charter (*See* http://www.cawater-info.net/library/rus/carewib/02_iwec.pdf, last visited Aug. 15, 2023). In 2022, the Eurasian Development Bank returned to this idea and proposed to create a consortium, whose purpose would be the implementation of investment projects aimed at optimizing the use of water, as well as projects in the power sector aimed at creating a sustainable generating structure. *See* Evgenij Vinokurov, et al., *supra* note 17, at 88.

100 km; the adjacent lands have been subjected to desertification.[19] In 1989, the Aral Sea was divided into the Small (Northern) Aral and the Large (Southern) Aral. The Small Aral is located on the territory of Kazakhstan, and its condition is satisfactory (salinity is 9%, there is some fishing); the Large Aral is located on the territories of Kazakhstan and Uzbekistan.

The catastrophe was diagnosed in the Resolution of the Supreme Soviet of the USSR "On Urgent Measures for Ecological Rehabilitation of the Country" (27 Nov., 1989): "The situation in the Aral Sea region is practically beyond human control. The Priaralie has become a zone of ecological disaster." The Resolution called for the establishment of a governmental commission and the development of a concept for the restoration of the Aral Sea.

In 1993, the states of the region concluded the Agreement on Joint Actions to Solve the Aral Sea and Priaralie Problem, which defined common tasks (Art. 1) and established the International Fund for Saving the Aral Sea and the Interstate Council on the Aral Sea Basin Problems. The main forms of activity for these bodies were meetings and conferences.[20]

The states of the region also adopted a number of declarations—in Nukus (1995), Almaty (1997), Ashgabat (1999), Dushanbe (2002), and Almaty (2009). Along with general statements about their interest in solving the Aral Sea problem, the declarations defined the priorities of cooperation, including requests for assistance from the UN and other organizations and the development of a comprehensive program.

The 2006 Framework Convention on Environmental Protection for Sustainable Development in Central Asia enshrined principles of cooperation and some general obligations (equitable and reasonable use of resources, improving the environmental situation in the Aral Sea basin, etc.), obligating parties to provide to the Secretariat reports on implementation measures, and envisioned the working out of additional protocols. The Convention, focused on the individual responsibility of each state, looks like a step backward.

Under these conditions, Kazakhstan took unilateral measures to preserve the Small Aral and, in 2005, built the Kokaral Dam, which prevents water from the Small Aral from flowing into the Large Aral. The construction resulted in the deterioration of the Large Aral, which split into the eastern and western parts. Kazakhstan explained its actions by arguing that saving the Large Aral is impossible.

All five states participate in the 1994 UN Convention to Combat Desertification, 1992 Convention on Biological Diversity, 1992 Framework Convention on Climate

[19] According to other hypotheses, the Aral Sea catastrophe is related to the outflow of water from the Aral Sea basin to the Caspian basin, natural cycles of the Aral Sea, and global warming. *See* Alexey Kudinov, *Aral'skoe more: global'noe reshenie regional'noj problem* [The Aral Sea: a global solution to a regional problem], 2 *Jelektronnoe prilozhenie k 'Rossijskomu juridicheskomu zhurnalu'* (2023).

[20] Since 1995, IFAS has implemented four programs supported by the World Bank. Each program envisages a number of priorities: safe water supply, pollution control, improved management, drafting of legal instruments, etc. Their results are construction of local reservoirs, forest plantations, etc. The budgets of the programs are quite large; however, their effectiveness is difficult to assess.

Change, 1997 Kyoto Protocol, and 2015 Paris Agreement. However, none of these conventions can serve as an umbrella for coordination in saving the Aral Sea, simply because none of them obliges states to implement global projects to save natural sites. The efforts of international organizations are also insufficient; some experts even assess them as counterproductive.[21] For example, the Green Fund subsidies provided some time ago are clearly inadequate: they do not exceed a few million dollars and pursue localized goals.[22]

From a technical perspective, solving the Aral Sea problem is extremely challenging but possible. One idea is to divert the Siberian rivers southward; most scientists consider this idea dangerous, but there are supporters who point to the increased water availability of these rivers in recent years and the potential melting of Arctic ice. Another concept involves constructing infrastructure to transfer water from the Caspian Sea.[23] In any scenario, technical solutions must be coupled with changes in economic policy. Saving the Aral Sea relies on implementing radical reforms that transition to rational models of water use and alter the economic specialization of the region. Nonetheless, irrigated agriculture remains the primary occupation of the population[24] and a vital source of budget funding. All states in the region continue to promote it, despite public expressions of environmental concerns.

Thus, as in the previous case, the existence of a number of instruments adopted at the general and regional levels does not bring the problem closer to being solved. Moreover, unlike in the previous case, simply adopting a new convention or transforming the institutional mechanism cannot radically affect the situation. The solution to the problem thus remains outside the realm of international law: international legal solutions must be preceded by strategic political and economic decisions. At present, the states of Central Asia are not in a position to make such decisions.

---

[21] The most important programs are the EU Water Initiative: Water Policy Reforms in Eastern Europe, the Caucasus and Central Asia countries (2006), and German Water Initiative for Central Asia (Berlin Process, 2008). *See* Bakhodur Saidamirov & Andrey Toropygin, *Vodnye problemy Central'noj Azii: mehanizmy reshenija na raznyh urovnjah politicheskogo upravlenija* [Water problems of Central Asia: solution mechanisms at different levels of political management], 4 Evrazijskaja integracija: jekonomika, pravo, politika 34 (2018).

[22] The Fund has approved four projects for Uzbekistan. One of them is related to the Aral Sea and provides funding for crop diversification, water management, rehabilitation of degraded lands, etc.; the grant amount is relatively small ($ 68.8 million). Other projects have larger amounts of funding but less clear indicators; for example, the High Impact Programme for the Corporate Sector (1 billion for 7 countries) "seeks to forge a low-carbon pathway by promoting the uptake of high climate impact technologies and stimulating behavioural change at the corporate governance and management level." *See* https://www.greenclimate.fund/countries/uzbekistan (last visited Sept. 15, 2023).

[23] *See* Maksat Kalimoldaevet, et al., *Vodnye problemy central'noj Azii: analiz, metody poiska putej reshenija problem* [Water problems of Central Asia: analysis, methods of finding ways to solve problems] 6 Vestnik SamGU 239, 244 (2014).

[24] In Kazakhstan, the agricultural sector employs 15% of the population; in Kyrgyzstan—19, in Tajikistan 45, in Turkmenistan—21, in Uzbekistan—26 (2019). *See* https://data.worldbank.org/indicator/SL.AGR.EMPL.ZS (last visited Sept. 15, 2023).

6 The Caspian Sea: The Mountain Has Brought Forth a Mouse

The Caspian Sea is the largest saltwater lake on the planet; in a legal sense, this means that its regime is not regulated by the law of the sea, including the 1982 Convention on the Law of the Sea. Until recently, relations between the Caspian states were regulated, *first*, by the 1921 Russia–Persia Treaty and the 1940 USSR–Iran Treaty on Trade and Navigation, which established a 10-mile fishing zone and enshrined freedom of navigation;[25] *second*, by bilateral treaties on the delimitation of seabed and subsoil concluded in the 1990s and 2000s; and *third*, by the 2003 Tehran Framework Convention for the Protection of the Marine Environment of the Caspian Sea and the 2014 Agreement on the Conservation and Rational Use of Aquatic Biological Resources of the Caspian Sea. In 2018, Azerbaijan, Iran, Kazakhstan, Russia, and Turkmenistan signed *the Convention on the Legal Status of the Caspian Sea*, which enshrines a comprehensive *sui generis* regime. Its main elements are as follows.

1. The parties undertake to use the sea "for peaceful purposes" and adhere to the principles of "ensuring security and stability in the region"; "ensuring a stable balance of armaments among the Parties"; "non-presence of armed forces in the Caspian Sea that do not belong to the Parties"; "non-provision by a Party of its territory to other States to commit aggression and undertake other military actions against any Party" (Art. 3).
2. The water area is divided into internal waters, territorial sea, fishery zones, and common maritime space (Art. 5). The breadth of the territorial sea is 15 nautical miles, which is 3 miles more than in the general law. The breadth of the fishery zone is 10 miles from the outer boundary of the territorial sea; the fishery in it is regulated in much the same way as the fishery in the exclusive economic zone.
3. The Convention enshrines the principle of freedom of navigation beyond the territorial sea (provided for by general law), national treatment with regard to access to open ports (not provided for by general law), the right of free access to other seas, and transit through the territories of other parties. The procedure and conditions of the access are determined by bilateral agreements or by the law of transitory states.
4. The seabed and subsoil are delimited by agreements between adjacent states, with due regard to the generally recognized principles and norms of international law; a state has the exclusive right to construct and authorize the construction of

[25] The 1934 Order of the People's Commissariat for Internal Affairs of the USSR established the line "Astara - Hasan-Kuli" (423.2 km), which delimited the territorial waters and airspace between the USSR and Iran; in practice, fishing by Iranian vessels beyond this line was prohibited. *See* Larisa Ruban, *Problema razgranichenija Kaspijskogo morja: istoriko-pravovoj aspect* [The problem of delimitation of the Caspian Sea: historical and legal aspect], 5 Burenie i neft' 50 (2017).

artificial islands and installations within its sector (Art. 8). All existing agreements provide for delimitation along a modified median line (equidistance line).[26]

5. The Convention permits parties to lay pipelines on the seabed on the condition that their projects comply with environmental standards and requirements embodied in international agreements. Pipeline routes shall be determined by agreement with the party the seabed sector of which is to be crossed by the pipeline (Art. 14). A similar regulation is set out in Art. 79(4) of the 1982 Convention.[27]
6. The procedure of environmental impact assessment is enshrined in the 2018 Protocol to the 2003 Framework Convention: the state of origin must take into account the opinions of affected parties but can implement the project without their consent. The regulatory capacity of the Protocol, therefore, is questionable.
7. The monitoring functions are entrusted to "a mechanism of five-party regular high-level consultations under the auspices of their Ministries of Foreign Affairs to be held at least once a year" (Art. 19). Disputes are to be resolved through negotiation, and if unsuccessful, they may be submitted to settlement by other means; compulsory judicial jurisdiction is not provided for.[28]

The Convention was to enter into force after the submission of the fifth instrument of ratification (Art. 22); it has been ratified by all signatories except Iran. It seems that Iran's interest in the Convention was initially conditioned by the security guarantees, while Russia's interest was conditioned by the launch of Nord Stream 2. In return, both states made serious concessions in matters of delimitation and pipeline transit.[29]

In the last 3 years, the situation has changed dramatically. In 2020, Azerbaijan won the Second Karabakh War, and the Trans-Caspian pipeline project has become

[26] *See* 1998 Russia–Kazakhstan Agreement on the Delimitation of the Seabed of the Northern Part of the Caspian Sea; 2001 Kazakhstan–Azerbaijan Agreement on the Delimitation of the Seabed of the Caspian Sea; 2003 Russia–Kazakhstan–Azerbaijan Agreement on point of joint of the lines of demarcation of adjacent sites of bottom of the Caspian Sea; 2015 Kazakhstan–Turkmenistan Agreement on the delimitation of the Caspian Sea bed. The borders between Turkmenistan and Azerbaijan, as well as the borders between these two countries and Iran are unagreed.

[27] Previously, Russia insisted that pipeline construction required the consent of all littoral states because of environmental reasons. The most promising project is the construction of the Trans-Caspian Pipeline (Turkmenbashi–Baku), which would supply Turkmen and Kazakh gas to Turkey and the EU.

[28] *See* Vladislav Tolstykh, Pravovoj rezhim Kaspijskogo morja po Konvencii 2018 g. i interesy prikaspijskih gosudarstv [The legal regime of the Caspian Sea under the 2018 Convention and the interests of the Caspian states] 1 Rossijskij juridicheskij zhurnal 9 (2020).

[29] *See* Mohsen Hagbin & Alexandr Zhivotenkov, *Pozicija Irana po ratifikacii Konvencii o pravovom statuse Kaspijskogo morja v kontekste integracionnyh processov na Kaspii* [Iran"s Position on the Ratification of the Convention on the Legal Status of the Caspian Sea in the Context of Integration Processes in the Caspian], 12 (5) LOCUS: People, Sosiety, Culture, Meanings 122 (2021).

more realistic.[30] In February 2022, Russia recognized the Donetsk and Luhansk People's Republics. In response, Germany suspended the certification of Nord Stream 2, while the United States imposed sanctions against the company-operator. The hostilities in Karabakh have brought relations between Azerbaijan and Iran to the brink of war. Finally, the explosion of the Nord Stream pipeline in September 2022 has irreparably damaged Russia's gas transit to Europe, forcing it to focus on gas supplies to other regions (where its natural competitors are other Caspian countries).

Thus, at present, not only has Iran lost interest in the Convention, but also Russia, which had previously ratified it, is not interested in the Convention ever entering into force. As a result, many years of efforts to develop a legal regime have come to naught—the only consequence may be the principle of estoppel, which binds parties who have followed a certain line of behavior. However, the regulatory possibilities of this principle are extremely limited. The current situation is even worse than it was 30 or 20 years ago—tragic political events and an intensification of economic and transit competition have made the prospect of a common legal regime unrealistic, at least in the near future.

7 Enclaves: To Find a Black Cat in a Dark Room

The territory of Kyrgyzstan encloses several Tajik exclaves (Vorukh and Western Kalacha villages) and Uzbek exclaves (Sokh, Shakhimardan, Chon-Gara, Jangail); the territory of Uzbekistan encloses Kyrgyz (Barak) and Tajik (Sarvaksai) exclaves. The largest enclaves are Vorukh and Sokh, whose population is Tajik (40,000 and 80,000, respectively). The Kyrgyz village of Ak-Sai is located between Vorukh and the main territory of Tajikistan. Vorukh is the confluence point of two tributaries of the Isfara River.[31] A common issue for enclaves is conflicts over water and gravel usage, road and other construction, smuggling, and traffic control. Sometimes these conflicts escalate into armed confrontations (Vorukh, 2014, 2019, 2021, 2022; Sokh, 2013, 2020). These incidents remain localized and are quickly resolved by

[30] The construction project was also hampered by the conflict between Turkmenistan and Azerbaijan over three fields that are closer to the Turkmen coast but were developed by Baku oilmen during the Soviet period. Azerbaijan invokes the principle of *uti possidetis juris*. Turkmenistan proposed to submit the dispute to an international court. As a result, the parties have not managed to conclude a bilateral treaty on the delimitation. In 2021, however, they signed a Memorandum of Understanding for the joint development of the *Dostluk* ("Druzhba") field and are currently negotiating an agreement on this issue. This progress appears to be a direct result of Azerbaijan"'s victory in the second Karabakh war.

[31] The question of belonging is not clearly resolved: Kyrgyzstan refers to the 1955 protocols of the Parity Commission of the governments of the Kyrgyz SSR and the Uzbek SSR; Tajikistan insists on the use of the 1924–1939 maps. *See* Galina Ivanova, *Poterjali rubezhi* [Lost frontiers], lenta.ru (Feb. 22, 2022), https://lenta.ru/articles/2022/02/09/krg_tdj accessed (last visited Sept. 15, 2023).

central authorities. However, their regular occurrence demonstrates the absence of a legal framework within which the parties could operate.

Indeed, there is no systematic solution to the problem of enclaves at the level of general law: according to the few authors who have commented on this issue, the customary regime of enclaves includes only the right of transit, which is "a logical consequence of the recognition of the enclave by the surrounding State." This transit should be carried out by the shortest route and applied to civil servants and police officers.[32] Customs and currency control, use of transboundary watercourses, road construction, etc., are thus left to the discretion of the states concerned.

Perhaps the optimal bilateral solution is the Büsingen model, which implies a partial renunciation of sovereign rights by the mainland to the surrounding state.[33] In the case of the Vorukh enclave, it could involve the free movement of the border population, the inclusion of enclaves into the customs jurisdiction of Kyrgyzstan, and the use of the Kyrgyz currency (soms). The relevant zone could include the Batken district of Kyrgyzstan, parts of the Sughd district of Tajikistan, and possibly the Fergana district of Uzbekistan.

The Büsingen model, however, requires the development of a detailed and comprehensive legal framework and its consolidation through a bilateral treaty and domestic legislation. Currently, Kyrgyzstan and Tajikistan are not capable of establishing such a framework, both due to existing tensions in their relations and the absence of a well-established legal tradition and necessary legislative expertise. It should be noted that this issue is not unique to these two states alone but rather a widespread concern across the entire post-Soviet region.

An exchange of territories is also unlikely. Indeed, the "Ak-Sai, a portion of Tajik territory," deal is disadvantageous for Kyrgyzstan, which would lose control over a strategic road and access to Isfara and would also retain the disadvantageous ruggedness of the border area. The "Vorukh, a portion of Kyrgyz territory," deal, in turn, is disadvantageous for Tajikistan, since the plots that Kyrgyzstan can offer are either located in mountainous areas or lack water resources. In addition, the population of Vorukh is primarily composed of Tajiks.

As for the creation of transport corridors, it appears to be quite feasible but is unlikely to resolve all contradictions. Currently, Tajikistan accuses Kyrgyzstan of undermining the project to construct a new Vorukh–Khodjai A'alo road as an alternative to the Ak-Sai village route. They are also constructing the Ak-Sai–Tamdyk road, which hinders access to Vorukh and periodically blockades transit in the direction of Vorukh.[34]

---

[32] *See* Pierre Raton, *Les Enclaves*, Annuaire français de Droit International 186 (1958); Charles d'Olivier Farran, *International Enclaves and the Question of State Servitudes*, 4 Int'l & Comp. L.Q. 297 (1955).

[33] *See* Evgenij Vinokurov, *Teorija anklavov* [The theory of enclaves] 248–258 (2007).

[34] *See* Bahmanjor Nadirov, *Doroga v Voruh: doroga zhizni ili smerti* [Road to Vorukh: the road of life or death], ASIA-Plus (Aug. 3, 2021), www.asiaplustj.info/ru/news/tajikistan/security/20210803/doroga-v-voruh-doroga-zhizni-ili-smerti (last visited Sept. 15, 2023).

Attempts at bilateral settlements have been made, but each time they have failed. In 2001, Kyrgyzstan and Uzbekistan signed a memorandum on border delimitation that stressed the "expediency" of connecting Sokh with Uzbekistan. In exchange, Kyrgyzstan was offered an equal plot of land in Uzbekistan which, however, was a lifeless mountain range. As a result, the deal was rejected by Bishkek.[35] In 2014, the parties agreed on a Barak exchange, which, however, did not take place. In 2021, Kyrgyzstan offered Tajikistan the "Vorukh deal": an exchange of Vorukh for Kyrgyz territories in other districts of Batken oblast. This proposal was made by the head of the Kyrgyz State National Security Committee, Kamchibek Tashiev, and not by the President or the Kyrgyz Foreign Ministry, and was rejected by Tajikistan.

Judicial settlement of the problem of enclaves is unlikely: first, the parties would hardly agree to submit such an important issue to a mandatory decision of a third party; second, an international court is not competent to establish new obligations, for example, on the exchange of territories (such obligations can be formulated only by the parties themselves); third, decisions on territorial issues sometimes aggravate the conflict rather than resolve it (the 1899 Award on the dispute between Guyana and Venezuela is a good example).

Therefore, a mediation or conciliation mechanism may be more efficient. The problem, however, is that neither post-Soviet regional organizations (Commonwealth of Independent States (CIS) and The Eurasian Economic Union (EEU)) nor individual neighboring states (Russia or Kazakhstan) pay any attention to the issue of enclaves, even at the rhetorical level. The result is a significant gap in international legal regulation that appears unlikely to be filled in the near future. This, in turn, implies the likelihood of another escalation.[36]

8 Protection of Minorities: Stepchild of International Law

The main minorities in the region are Russians (4 million), Koreans (300,000 in Kazakhstan and Uzbekistan), Germans (200,000 in Kazakhstan), Ukrainians (260,000 in Kazakhstan), Uighurs (700,000), Dungans (120,000), Tatars (500,000), and Meskhetian Turks (140,000). Tajiks form a significant minority in Uzbekistan (1.5 million), Kazakhs in Uzbekistan (820,000), and Uzbeks in other republics (930,000 in Tajikistan and 640,000 in Kazakhstan). All minorities can be categorized into several groups: (1) representatives of titular nations (e.g., Uzbeks in

[35] *See* Alisher Babadzhanov & Stanislav Chernjavskij, *Problemy mezhgosudarstvennyh otnoshenij v Central'noj Azii (na primere tadzhiksko-uzbekskih i kirgizsko-uzbekskih otnoshenij)* [Problems of interstate relations in Central Asia (on the example of Tajik-Uzbek and Kyrgyz-Uzbek relations)]. 4 (13) *Vestnik MGIMO-Universiteta* 33, 34 (2010).

[36] On 13 March 2025, the presidents of Kyrgyzstan and Tajikistan signed a border treaty, which, according to media reports, settled all contentious issues. It was ratified by the Kyrgyz Parliament on 19 March. The text of the Treaty is not yet available to the public.

Kyrgyzstan), (2) Russians, (3) local communities (Uighurs, Dungans, etc.), and (4) deported peoples (Koreans, Germans, Poles).

Interethnic relations in the region are characterized by tolerance; however, this rule is not universal.[37] *First*, there are manifestations of systemic nationalism, i.e., nationalism that is conditioned by an a priori negative attitude toward another nationality. This includes discrimination in employment and condemnation of mixed marriages, among other things. *Second*, there are outbreaks of nonsystemic nationalism caused by everyday conflicts, and the background for this is the interethnic division of labor: guilt is imputed to the entire minority engaged in a particular trade.

The most serious incidents were (1) Fergana pogroms of 1989 (Uzbekistan), clashes between Uzbeks and Meskhetian Turks, which began due to an incident at a bazaar; (2) Osh events of 1990 (Kyrgyzstan), clashes between Kyrgyz and Uzbeks, where Kyrgyz claimed lands belonging to Uzbek farms, Uzbeks claimed autonomy, and the number of victims ranged from 1200 to 10,000; (3) Civil war in Tajikistan (1992–1997), which had not only a political but also a national dimension: thousands of Uzbeks and Russians fled the country; and (4) Clashes in Osh (Kyrgyzstan) between Kyrgyz and Uzbeks during the 2010 revolution, where the number of victims ranged from 1000 to 2000.

The constitutions of all five republics prohibit discrimination on the basis of nationality and focus on the notion of a civil nation (some constitutions do not even use the word "minority" and consider all ethnic groups living in the country as one nation).[38] The constitutions of Kazakhstan and Kyrgyzstan enshrine the official status of the Russian language.[39] Interethnic harmony is a priority of state politics,

[37] "The soviet internationalism turned out to be quite workable. Although minorities were under pressure, there was no perception that they were a dangerous element that needed to be rid of." Jendrju Vahtel', *Pochemu Central'naja Azija ne vstala na balkanskij put'?* [Why didn't Central Asia take the Balkan path?], *EUSP Online* (Jan. 15, 2014), https://eusp.org/news/razvitie-natsionalnykh-gosudarstv-v-tsentralnoj-azii (last visited Sept. 15, 2023).

[38] *See* Arts. 8 and 18 of the Constitution of Uzbekistan; Arts. 14 and 19 of the Constitution of Kazakhstan; Arts. 13, 24, and 32 of the Constitution of Kyrgyzstan; Arts. 6 and 17 of the Constitution of Tajikistan; Art. 28 of the Constitution of Turkmenistan.

[39] Art. 7 of the Constitution of Kazakhstan states: "1. The state language of the Republic of Kazakhstan shall be the Kazakh language. 2. Russian language shall be officially used on equal grounds along with the Kazakh language in state institutions and local self-administrative bodies" (also *see* Art. 10 of the Constitution of Kyrgyzstan).

especially in Kazakhstan (Art. 39 of the Constitution).[40] However, this priority and the established balance do not appear to be sustainable.[41]

First, the images of a great nation,[42] unfriendly neighbors, and a colonial past are convenient ways of addressing the legitimacy deficit, complex social situations, and injustices of post-Soviet borders.[43] *Second*, objective differences related to lifestyles, political sympathies, and ethnogenesis still exist and sometimes become incentives for conflicts. *Third*, minorities gravitating toward a neighboring country have a natural desire to live in it and reject attempts to assimilate them. *Fourth*, the Second Karabakh War (2020) and Russia's operation in Ukraine (2022) have intensified nationalist, pan-Turkist, and anti-Russian sentiments.

There are also some symptoms of a reorientation of official policy. The draft law "On the State Language," prepared by the National Commission on the State Language in Kyrgyzstan (2021), provides for the translation of outdoor advertising, consumer services, office documents, geographical names, education, and television broadcasting (at least 65%) into Kyrgyz. Russian retains the status of an official language but must be used in the manner stipulated by law and "if necessary."[44] On the one hand, the trend toward strengthening national identity is objective; on the other hand, it risks taking extreme forms, destroying civil peace, and, ultimately, provoking interstate conflicts.

General international law does not provide instruments and obligations to ensure interethnic consensus. It does not prohibit policies of national unification (assimilation), does not guarantee minorities the use of their language in the public domain,

---

[40] *See* Andzhej Vezhbicki, *Jetnichnost' i prava jetnicheskih men'shinstv v konstitucionalizme gosudarstv Central'noj Azii* [Ethnicity and Rights of Ethnic Minorities in the Constitutionalism of Central Asian States] 32 *Studia Politologiczne* 256 (2014). Gatliff notes the insufficiency of constitutional guarantees: none of the states have a specific antidiscrimination law; some retain the practice of indicating nationality when obtaining a passport or applying for a job. *See* Victoria Gatliff, *Discrimination on the Basis of Ethnicity and Language in Kazakhstan, Kyrgyzstan, Tadjikistan and Uzbekistan*, in Legacies of Division: Discrimination on the Basis of Religion and Ethnicity in Central Asia 68, 77–79 (Equal Rights Trust, 2017).

[41] *See* Serik Beisembaev, *Fenomen kazahskogo nacionalizma v kontekste segodnjashnej politiki: ot otricanija k ponimaniju* [The phenomenon of Kazakh nationalism in the context of today's politics: from denial to understanding], 10–11 (Soros Foundation-Kazakhstan, 2015).

[42] *See* Denis Maltsev, *Istoricheskie mify stran Srednej Azii* [Historical myths of the countries of Central Asia], 2 *Rossija i musul'manskij mir* 48 (2017).

[43] Megoran points out that the Kyrgyz nationalism is marked by a profound insecurity about the very survival of the country and the fear that Kyrgyzstan is primarily endangered by the weak state of the Kyrgyz language, internal disunity, and geopolitical threats. According to this vision, Uzbeks are seen to represent a fundamental existential threat to the state. The problem cannot be solved by persecuting criminals or attempting to reintegrate Uzbeks. The political and judicial system must be radically reformed and the economic situation improved. The Uzbeks will not be safe until the Kyrgyz feel that Kyrgyzstan is safe. The author makes some recommendations: to create inclusive forms of state building, to develop the Kyrgyz language, to negotiate with neighbors etc. *See* Nick Megoran, *Averting Violence in Kyrgyzstan: Understanding and Responding to Nationalism* (Russia and Eurasia Programme Paper, Chatham House, 2012).

[44] *See* http://koomtalkuu.gov.kg/ru/view-npa/1162 (last visited Sept. 15, 2023).

does not grant them the right to secession, and does not authorize the revision of unjustly established borders—a gap that stimulates civil conflicts. The minorities exposed to the risk of assimilation are thus faced with a difficult choice: to accept their fate and fade away slowly; to leave their homeland and emigrate to countries with a similar culture; or to take up arms and try to defend their right to live in their ancestral land. Each option carries risks not only for the minorities themselves but also for the states in which they live. The recent exodus of Armenians from Nagorno-Karabakh is an example of the tragedy of this choice.

In principle, the issue can become the subject of regional law. Elements of the relevant regime could include general documents (conventions and declarations) proclaiming the principles of nondiscrimination, periodic meetings of heads of state, an emergency response mechanism, consultations on the exchange of territory and population, a system of multilateral monitoring, and so on. However, there is no experience of working out such a regime in any region of the world.

9 Regional Integration: The Region "That Is Not"

A peculiarity of the region is the existence of parallel integration projects: along with its own project, terminated in 2005, there are common post-Soviet institutions dominated by Russia.

Commonwealth of Independent States (1991) By creating the CIS, the new states aimed to legitimize the dissolution of the USSR, prevent conflicts, and preserve economic and cultural ties. Initially, its members consisted of 12 former republics; many of them later withdrew. The CIS members have entered into numerous treaties on succession, pensions, and legal assistance. Currently, the potential of the CIS has been almost completely depleted.

Shanghai Cooperation Organization (SCO) (2001) The SCO was established through annual summits to combat extremism and to agree on a common position in relations with the West. The SCO members are four states of the region (except Turkmenistan), Russia, India, China, Pakistan, and Iran. Cooperation is limited to meetings, political statements, and treaties (2001 Convention on Combating Terrorism, Separatism, and Extremism).

The Eurasian Economic Union (EEU) Was Established in 2000 The EEU is composed of the Customs Union, which was formed in 2010, and the Common Economic Space, established in 2012. Its member countries include Russia, Belarus, Kazakhstan, Kyrgyzstan, and Armenia. The EEU Commission has the authority to make binding decisions but is accountable to two councils consisting of state representatives. The key accomplishments of the union include the adoption of the Customs Code, the implementation of a Common Tariff, and the elimination of customs controls at internal borders.

Collective Security Treaty Organization (CSTO) (1992) The members include Armenia, Belarus, Kazakhstan, Kyrgyzstan, Russia, and Tajikistan. Azerbaijan, Georgia, and Uzbekistan have left the organization. In 2010, the CSTO declined to provide assistance to Kyrgyzstan, which was troubled by internal unrest. However, in 2022, the CSTO provided assistance to Kazakhstan in a similar situation. The CSTO did not intervene in Karabakh in 2023, making further Armenian participation unlikely.[45]

The common features of all post-Soviet institutions are a fragmented legal framework and a loose organizational structure, a priority of intergovernmental dialogue over legal factors (to the detriment of legal ones), absence of elements of supranationalism, reliance on treaties as the primary form of cooperation, declarative nature, and low efficiency.

The Central Asian states also made several attempts to create their own structures. In 1992, Kazakhstan and Uzbekistan signed the Treaty of Friendship, Cooperation, and Mutual Assistance, which, along with phrases emphasizing respect for independence and strengthening friendship, aimed at forming the Asian economic space (Art. 7). In 1994, these states signed the Treaty on the Creation of the Common Economic Space, which was later joined by Kyrgyzstan. The Treaty included various general provisions such as "will ensure development" and "will promote," and it envisioned the free movement of goods, services, capital, labor force, and a common economic policy (Art. 1), albeit scheduled for the future under the Program for Deepening Integration. In 1998, Tajikistan joined the CES, leading to its renaming as the Central Asian Economic Cooperation. Key achievements of the CAEC included the 1999 Agreement on the Parallel Operation of Energy Systems and the 2000 Integration Strategy.

In 2002, the Central Asian states signed the Treaty on the Establishment of the Central Asian Cooperation Organization. Like previous texts, the Treaty contained many general declarations. The structure of the CACO mirrored that of the CIS and included several councils (composed of heads of state, prime ministers, and foreign ministers) who had to make decisions by consensus, along with the Committee of National Coordinators. In 2004, Russia joined the CACO. In 2005, the CACO summit decided to merge the organization with the EEU; Uzbekistan withdrew from the project.

The failure of these attempts has led many political scientists to conclude that Central Asia is "pathologically noncooperative"[46] and constitutes a region "that is

---

[45] "A serious obstacle to strengthening the Organization's position in the region is its normative principles of non-interference in the internal affairs of the member states, which is in serious contradiction with the needs of the CSTO's evolution… This is largely due to the fact that the CSTO member states fear an excessive reinforcement of Russia." Alexey Bezrukov, et al., *Integracionnye processy v Central'noj Azii: stolknovenie interesov vneshnih aktorov* [Integration processes in Central Asia: clash of interests of external actors], 11 (5) Gumanitarnye nauki. Vestnik Finansovogo universiteta 62, 66 (2021).

[46] *See* Martin Spechler, *Regional Non-Cooperation in Central Asia: A Pathology in Economic Developments and Reforms* in Cooperation Partner Countries: The Interrelationship Between Regional Economic Cooperation, Security and Stability 267 (NATO, 2001).

not."[47] The reasons for the failure are numerous and include an underdeveloped legal tradition, a lack of integration strategy, authoritarianism, and the desire of national elites to maintain control over the country's life, different economic and political systems, small mutual trade turnover, unresolved territorial, water, and interethnic conflicts, different vectors of foreign policy (ranging from openness and multi-vectorism in Kazakhstan to isolationism in Uzbekistan and Turkmenistan), competition between Kazakhstan (the "shield" of Central Asia) and Turkmenistan (the "soul" of Central Asia), the absenteeism of Turkmenistan due to its permanent neutral status, the influence and rivalry of external actors (the Second Great Game, this time involving Russia, China, and the USA), and the greater attractiveness of the EEU and CSTO.[48]

At present, the idea of Central Asian integration has become more relevant. Key external actors, primarily Russia, are unable to guarantee the economic stability of the region and are involved in major geopolitical conflicts. Constitution-building processes in Central Asian countries have largely come to an end, and political elites can now focus on addressing new challenges. Integration will provide solutions to the new challenges facing both the region as a whole and individual countries. After the change of the president in Uzbekistan in 2016, the country is attempting to revive the Central Asian project. The first summit of Central Asian heads of state after a long hiatus was held in 2018 in Astana. The focus has shifted to cooperation in specific areas, such as the modernization of communications and the removal of trade barriers.[49]

Indeed, the new integration structure could set several strategic goals:

---

[47] *See* Sebastian Krapohl & Alexandra Vasileva-Dienes, *The Region that Isn't: China, Russia and the Failure of Regional Integration in Central Asia*, 18 (5) Asia Europe Journal 347 (2019).

[48] *See* Gulbara Akunova, *Strany Central'noj Azii: trudnosti na puti sblizhenija* [Central Asian countries: difficulties on the way of rapprochement], 7 (5) Problemy postsovetskogo prostranstva 300 (2020); Dina Malysheva, *Problemy regionalizacii postsovetskoj Central'noj Azii* [Problems of regionalization of post-Soviet Central Asia], 13 *Kontury global'nyh transformacij: politika, jekonomika, pravo* 140, 144–145 (2020); *Filippo Costa Buranelly, Central Asian Regionalism or Central Asian Order? Some Reflections*, 8 Central Asian Affairs 1, 4–5 (2021); Jenis Kembayev, *Legal Aspects of the Regional Integration in Central Asia,* 66 Heidelberg Journal of International Law 967, 975–976 (2006). Tolipov criticizes approaches based on dualisms (upstream-downstream, Uzbekistan-Kazakhstan) and argues that the main reason for the failure was the predominance of the elitist component over the popular one; the leaderships of individual countries became isolated, presenting their states as a "bridge," "center," and "island"; Kazakhstan"s pseudo-leadership was distorted by its eclectic multi-vector policy while Uzbekistan"s pseudo-leadership—by its egoistic isolationism. The author identifies five problems: ontological one (denial of the existence of the region and possibility of integration), doctrinal one (lack of integration conceptions), conceptual one (the need to choose a model), institutional one (weakness of existing institutions), and political one (lack of political will) (Farhod Tolipov, *Central'naja Azija: teorija dezintegracii* [Central Asia: the theory of disintegration], in Central'naja Azija—25: mysli o proshlom, proekcija budushhego 24 (Marlène Laruelle & Aytolkyn Kurmanova eds., 2017).

[49] *See* Evgenija Makhmutova, *Central'naja Azija v poiskah sobstvennoj integracionnoj modeli* [Central Asia in search of its own integration model], 4 *Vestnik MGIMO-Universiteta* 78, 85 (2018).

- Creation of a common market
- Implementation of global infrastructure projects (such as construction of the Trans-Afghan Road and the Trans-Caspian pipeline)
- Coordination of water-energy exchange and development of water infrastructure
- Solving environmental problems (including the Aral Sea problem), mitigation and adaptation of the economy to climate change
- Development of a common foreign economic policy, resolution of economic disputes
- Unification of civil and commercial legislation, drawing up and concluding international treaties

More generally, the Central Asian integration project would contribute to the consolidation of Central Asia and its transformation into a major geopolitical player with a unified stance on the most critical issues of international cooperation.

The Central Asian integration project is often perceived as a utopia—indeed, many of the abovementioned obstacles seem insurmountable. A new generation of managers, aware of the inadequacy of the region's current political structure to meet the new challenges, however, can make this project a reality.

10 Conclusions

A purely legal solution to all these problems faces a number of difficulties.

The *first* issue is the lack of qualified historical, economic, and political science researchers who could serve as a foundation for international legal analysis. Most expert opinions are prepared with the assistance of international organizations and are often authored by foreign specialists. The objectivity of these opinions in this context may be questionable. Regarding surveys conducted by scholars from Russia and Central Asia, they still exhibit a relatively low level of analytical depth.

The *second* problem is the absence of open discussion, the general passivity of post-Soviet legal doctrine, which prefers to deal with scholastic issues rather than real problems, and a lack of demand for fundamental research on the part of states and international bodies. As a result, the discussion is relegated to the level of government agencies, whose position is often passive and unconstructive.

The *third* problem is that the post-Soviet international legal tradition is not adapted to practical tasks: the competent authorities and legal doctrine lack the necessary skills in lawmaking, interpretation, mediation, and judicial settlement. The decisions of the EAEU Court can be a good example: they are written in poor language, often lack information about the facts of the case, use vulnerable reasoning, and do not establish a *jurisprudence constante*.

The *fourth* problem is the shortage of actors who could elaborate and compromise on legal solutions. Russia's mediation (e.g., in the Karabakh conflict) is rarely accompanied by legal argumentation. Other states in the region refrain from intervening in conflicts that do not affect them. International organizations (such as the CIS and EEU) focus on economic issues, while their courts take a very cautious stance towards disputes between states.[50]

All these factors are interrelated and conditioned by more general causes: the inertia of the Soviet foreign policy tradition, oriented toward a diplomatic approach (rather than an international legal one), and the general disintegration trends taking place in the post-Soviet space. These factors, of course, can be overcome and sooner or later will be overcome. However, the development of the destructive effects of the contradictions considered above may outpace legal and political progress. The future of the region in this regard looks multifaceted.

---

[50] An example is the only decision of the EEU Court in an interstate dispute, rendered in a suit brought by Russia against Belarus, dated 21 February 2017, in which the Court found "the fact that the Republic of Belarus *has not fully implemented*" certain provisions of EAEU law.

Part II
The BRICS Scholars' Perspectives on Emerging Legal Issues

Chapter 5
Use of SEZs for Development: National Policies of China and India and the Potential Legal Implications

Rajan Sudesh Ratna and Jiangyuan Fu

Abstract Special Economic Zones (SEZs) have proliferated over the past decade and are leveraged as engines for development, especially in emerging countries, notably China and India. While much debate has focused on their evolution and economic performance, laws sustaining and contesting SEZs have received less attention in academic literature. There is no internationally accepted legal framework to regulate SEZs, and governments have formulated their own SEZ policies with their respective national developmental objectives. SEZ policies often involve shifts in regulatory powers in the legislature and significant room for executive discretion, thus raising questions about their legal regime at both the domestic policy level and international economic law. In Section 2, the article starts with the SEZ policy experiences in China and India and their economic performances. Section 3 compares the differences between SEZ policies in the two countries. In Section 4, the authors argue that despite the differences in design, institutional characteristics, and economic outcomes of SEZs in China and India, there are common concerns rooted in the legal regimes that underpin the potential conflicts with national policy and international obligations. In Section 5, it is concluded and recommended that policymakers should properly consider the legal regimes governing SEZs and recognize their potential conflicting regimes.

This article was previously published in Law Science—Selected Papers Volume 2, Issue 3 (2023). The authors shared equal contribution to this article, and the views and opinions expressed in this article are personal and do not reflect the views of organizations they represent. The authors are grateful for reviewers and editors for their valuable comments and the research assistance by Junyu Li and Siyi Wu is acknowledged. HUST Innovation Funds 2021WKFZZX030 is acknowledged.

R. S. Ratna
United Nations ESCAP South and South-West Asia Office, Delhi, India

J. Fu (✉)
Institute for Human Rights Law, School of Law, Huazhong University of Science and Technology, Wuhan, China

School of Law and Criminology, Maynooth University, Maynooth, Ireland
e-mail: Jiangyuan.fu@mu.ie

T. Du, X. Fei (eds.), *The BRICS Legal Cooperation and Perspectives*,
https://doi.org/10.1007/978-981-95-4356-4_5

Keywords SEZs · Subsidies · International trade and investment · Legal implications

1 Introduction

Special Economic Zones (SEZs) are geographically delimited areas within which governments facilitate industrial activity through fiscal and regulatory incentives, as well as infrastructure support.[1] The World Customs Organization's Revised Kyoto Convention defines these zones as "part of the territory of a Contracting Party where goods introduced are generally regarded, insofar as import duties and taxes are concerned, as being outside the customs territory."[2] Governments formulate their domestic policies for SEZs while keeping in mind the export potential of units that are set up in the zones. This is because they are also required to meet export obligations in order to avail tax benefits. SEZs have evolved in both breadth and depth since the establishment of the first modern SEZ in Shannon, Ireland. They can now be referred to by different names with various variations, such as free trade zones (FTZs), export processing zones (EPZs), industrial parks, and free ports, among others. Regardless of the name or type, SEZs have been intentionally designed as an important policy tool to promote economic development and growth. Therefore, the umbrella term "SEZ" is used in this article to denote a broad range of modern fiscal enclaves. Due to the rapid development of SEZs worldwide, they are no longer simply focused on incentive measures. Instead, they are now more about formulating special policies for carefully selected areas that can be transformed into international gateways. These policies differ from generic industrial promotion policies that are typically formulated.

There is no internationally accepted legal framework to regulate Special Economic Zones (SEZs). Therefore, each government formulates its own SEZ policy in alignment with its national developmental objectives. Through these policies, investments are solicited in demarcated areas by offering various incentives, which may include tax incentives, affordable land, land use preferences, duty-free imports of materials, as well as trade and investment facilitation. These incentives result in a reduction in the production cost of goods manufactured within these zones, making them more competitive than similar goods produced outside the zones within the same country. Some of these incentives may potentially violate certain multilateral obligations, such as being a trade-distorting subsidy of a country, which could lead to trade disputes in forum like the World Trade Organization (WTO).

Asia hosts three-quarters of the global SEZs, with China and India notably leading the way. India was the first country in Asia to recognize the effectiveness of

[1] UNCTAD, World Investment Report 2019: Special Economic Zones (2019), at https://www.un-ilibrary.org/content/books/9789210041584 (Last visited on August 9, 2022).

[2] Chapter 2 of Specific Annex D of Revised Kyoto Convention of World Customs Organization.

SEZs in promoting trade,[3] and both countries have a long history with SEZs. They have successfully utilized SEZ policies to achieve their developmental goals. This paper examines the evolution of SEZ policies in China and India, assesses their performance, and tracks how these policies have changed over time. Furthermore, the paper explores the similarities and differences between China and India's SEZ policies while considering their international obligations and trade disputes. Finally, the paper provides recommendations for the legal aspects that need to be taken into account when developing a successful SEZ policy.

2 SEZs in China and India

2.1 *Experience of China*

2.1.1 Evolving SEZ Policies in China

The development of SEZs in China started in the late 1970s as an integral part of its "reform and opening up" policy. Export processing zones (a subdivision and widely observed SEZ form) were already a common component of modernization programs in the majority of Asian countries.[4] Regional experiences undoubtedly helped shape China's decision to develop its own SEZs. The first batch of SEZs was established in Shenzhen, Zhuhai, Shantou, and Xiamen to leverage their geographical proximity to Hong Kong, Macao, and Taiwan. These SEZ pilots in remote southern cities were ideal for testing economic liberalization while minimizing potential political and economic risks spreading to other parts of the country.

The early success of SEZs encouraged further experimentation in 14 more cities along the east coast to attract foreign direct investment (FDI), promote export growth, and test new policies for the impending economic transition on a small scale of reform. The Yangtze River Delta and the Pearl River Delta were thus proven capable of substantial world manufacturing clusters and accompanied the further development of port terminal hubs. In 1988, SEZs expanded to the Hainan province, which is now being upgraded to become the largest free trade port in China.

In the 1980s, as the first decade of China's SEZ trial, local governments offered desirable incentives to investors. Preferential treatment granted to SEZs included tax incentives such as tax holidays, tax concessions, reduced red tape associated with market access, land use rights, and direct subsidies.[5] With these special

---

[3] As of 2019, China hosts more than 2500 SEZs, while India takes the third place next to the Philippines, hosting over 370 SEZs. See UNCTAD, supra note 1.

[4] Ann Fenwick, Evaluating China's Special Economic Zones, 2(2) Berkeley Journal of International Law 376, 376 (1984).

[5] These can be found in China's earlier SEZ regulations. See Regulations on Special Economic Zones in Guangdong Province (promulgated by Standing Committee of the Guangdong Provincial People's Congress, Sept. 16, 1980, effective Sept. 16, 1980); Regulations on Several Issues

arrangements, SEZs quickly became popular destinations for FDI. The SEZ pilot programs obviously provided a testing ground for rules and regulations related to foreign capital and trade liberalization.

In the 1990s, some of the original preferential policies were phased out. Starting from 1992, China established its commitment to building a socialist market economy and began to accelerate reforms and opening up. The SEZs model shifted to national-level new areas and proliferated across the country. SEZs became an important symbol of a new round of economic reforms. Many SEZs with various management models were created and diverged from each other according to dimensions and purposes but were subsequently diffused to the rest of China in the twenty-first century, including inland zones such as Yangtze River ports and border cities.

This is part of China's "Western Development" policy aimed at increasing incomes, alleviating social tensions, and fostering prosperity in the western regions of the country. It includes preferential treatment such as reduced or no customs duties, no import quotas,[6] looser foreign exchange controls,[7] unrestricted profit repatriation, tax incentives, duty-free allowances for production materials, land use, and the provision of better and more accessible infrastructure to attract investors.

The first decade of the twenty-first century witnessed the evolution of Special Economic Zone (SEZ) development in China. In 2001, as a result of China's accession to the World Trade Organization (WTO), the country was required to eliminate certain export subsidies and subsidies that promoted the use of domestic inputs instead of imported ones, including within SEZs. By 2021, the central government had abolished more than 2000 regulations and departmental rules, while local governments had repealed over 190,000 local policies and regulations.[8]

In the 2010s, SEZ development saw more breakthroughs and innovations. In May 2010, the establishment of the Horgos Special Economic Zone and the Kashgar

---

Concerning the Taxation Policy of Enterprises in the Shenzhen Special Economic Zone (promulgated by Shenzhen People's Government, Aug. 1, 1988, effective Sept. 1, 1988). Regulations of the Shenzhen Special Economic Zone on Land Management (promulgated by the People's Congress of Guangdong Province, Jan. 3, 1988, effective Jan. 3, 1988).

[6] Products are not subject to export quota and licensing control in special regions. *See* Article 11 of Customs Supervision Measures for Bonded Zones (promulgated by the General Administration of Customs, Aug. 1, 1997, effective Aug. 1, 1997); Article 21of Regulations of Zhuhai City on the Zhuhai Bonded Zone (promulgated by the Zhuhai People's Congress, May 21, 1998, effective July 1, 1998).

[7] Article 6 of Provisional Measures for Foreign Exchange Management in Bonded Zones (promulgated by the State Administration of Foreign Exchange, Jun. 29, 1991, effective Jun. 29, 1991, expired by Procedures on Foreign Exchange Control in Bonded Areas on Jan. 1, 1996); Article 2 of Notice of the State Administration of Foreign Exchange on Issues Related to Foreign Exchange Management in Bonded Zones (promulgated by the State Administration of Foreign Exchange, Sep. 1, 1998, effective Sep. 10, 1998, expired by Measures for Foreign Exchange Control in Bonded Areas in 2002).

[8] MINISTRY OF COMMERCE, GOVERNMENT OF CHINA, CHINA HAS FULLY FULFILLED ITS COMMITMENT TO THE WORLD TRADE ORGANIZATION (WTO) ACCESSION, at https://www.gov.cn/xinwen/2021-10/28/content_5647459.htm (Last visited on August 9, 2022).

Special Economic Zone in Xinjiang marked a significant milestone in the expansion of SEZs from coastal areas to inland regions.

In 2013, the Shanghai Free Trade Zone (FTZ) was launched, marking a new generation of wide-area SEZs with comprehensive reforms in trade and investment, as well as in their legal and regulatory frameworks. It is the first pilot FTZ in China, covering four special customs supervision areas in Shanghai and later expanding to include high-tech parks and finance and trade zones. The FTZ was designed with extensive reforms beyond traditional SEZs, with a focus on trade facilitation. It also introduced measures to enhance the investment management systems through a negative-list approach, financial innovation aimed at capital account convertibility, liberalization of financial services, and a more convenient and efficient legal environment.

More recently, the Communist Party of China Central Committee and the State Council released the Overall Plan for the Construction of the Hainan Free Trade Port. Subsequently, the Hainan Free Trade Port Law of the People's Republic of China took effect on June 10, 2021. Hainan is taking bold steps toward becoming the largest island-wide SEZ in China, with comprehensive reforms and the highest level of openness. In the same year, to further advance the reform of simplifying administrative procedures, decentralizing powers, optimizing the business environment, and accelerating the transformation of government functions, the Standing Committee of the National People's Congress introduced the Decision on Authorizing the State Council to Temporarily Adjust the Application of Relevant Legal Provisions in Pilot Free Trade Zones.[9]

The establishment of the Shanghai Free Trade Pilot Zone and the Hainan Free Trade Port in China serves as "experimental fields" for the implementation of higher-level openness policies across various domains, including economics, urban development, ecology, society, industry, taxation, and legal systems. These zones feature high-quality innovation-driven development systems and demonstrate China's strong determination and proficiency in SEZ innovation and opening up. They also represent concrete practices through which China promotes the construction of an open world economy, reinforcing the country's commitment to advancing high-level openness. China's high-quality openness model aligns with the global aspiration for collaborative and shared development vision.

Instead of having a unified national regulatory SEZ framework, China's approach to regulating SEZs has been more reactive and piecemeal in nature, with legislations specific to zones in the form of local regulations, such as the "Regulation on China (Shanghai) Pilot Free Trade Zone" and the "Regulation on the China (Guangdong) Pilot Free Trade Zone," among others. These zones are also subject to other laws, decrees, and related regulations governing customs, trade, and investment issues related to the zones.

[9] Standing Committee of the National People's Congress (NPC), Decision of the Standing Committee of the National People's Congress on Authorizing the State Council to Temporarily Adjust the Application of Relevant Legal Provisions in Pilot Free Trade Zones (2021)

During the development of SEZ policies, local legislative bodies and local governments were granted a high degree of autonomy as a testing ground for the application of new policies and approaches to support local economies.[10] Thus, the regulatory fragmentation in China is understandable and necessary because SEZ specialization in particular types of projects is suited to their individual resource endowments, while others, such as Shenzhen and Shanghai FTZ, are comprehensively open. These zones serve as social and economic laboratories where new approaches for a successful model can be tested, with far-reaching potential for future national emulation.

2.1.2 The Performance of China's SEZs

SEZs have played an instrumental role in driving China's export-led growth and economic success, as well as in integrating the country into the global economy and promoting broader economic development. Over the decades since the establishment of the first SEZs, China's total import and export value has experienced phenomenal growth. According to the National Bureau of Statistics of China, the ratio of total import and export value to GDP has risen dramatically, from less than 10% at the beginning of the country's reform and opening up to nearly 65% by 2006. This trajectory reflects the policy objectives of the first two phases of SEZ development, which leveraged SEZs as experimental laboratories and engines of export-led industrialization. The economic growth in SEZs in "the most likely to succeed" areas and later selected regions, forming "concentric circles," has led to spillover effects across the remaining parts of the country.

After the global economic crisis in 2008, China's foreign trade value continued to grow, but the degree of dependence on foreign trade dropped to approximately 30%. This is also consistent with the changing policy objectives of the new generation SEZs, which have shifted from the traditional export-oriented focus to a mix of diverse and comprehensive industrial, service, and urban amenity operations. This also suggests the significant positive spillover effects of SEZs on the country's economy as a whole, including FDI, manufacturing, and productivity.

Despite the economic success of SEZs in China, challenges to sustain SEZ success persist, including, but not limited to, the lack of horizontal linkages in SEZ governance and the absence of an overarching regulatory framework at a national level for SEZ regulation.

[10] See, for instance, Decision of the Standing Committee of the National People's Congress on Authorizing the People's Congress of Shenzhen City and its Standing Committee and People's Government of Shenzhen city to formulate regulations and Rules, respectively, for implementation in the Shenzhen Special Economic Zone, 26th Meeting of the 7th National People's Congress (July 1, 1992). See Madeleine Martinek, Special Economic Zones in China and WTO: Bleak or Bright Future?, 21(1) Zeitschrift für Chinesisches Recht 41, 41 (2014).

2.2 *Experience of India*

2.2.1 Evolving SEZ Policies in India

India's oldest SEZs were in the form of economic processing zones, the first of which was the Kandla EPZ in 1965, which became renowned as the first SEZ in Asia.[11] Several other export processing zones were set up in various parts of India in the subsequent years. The lack of a good economic policy from the government of India and inefficient management soon became detrimental factors for the success of these export processing zones. Thus, the performance of these export processing zones in India fell short of expectations.

While these EPZs had a similar structure to SEZs, the government began to establish SEZs in 2000 under the Foreign Trade Policy to address the infrastructural and bureaucratic challenges that were seen to have limited the success of EPZs. India's SEZs were structured closely to China's successful model. With a view to overcoming the shortcomings experienced due to the multiplicity of controls and clearances, absence of world-class infrastructure, and an unstable fiscal regime, and with the aim of attracting larger foreign investments in India, the Special Economic Zones (SEZs) Policy was announced in April 2000. This policy intended to make SEZs an engine for economic growth supported by quality infrastructure complemented by an attractive fiscal package, both at the center and the state levels, with the minimum possible regulations. SEZs in India functioned from November 2000 to February 2006 under the provisions of the Foreign Trade Policy, and fiscal incentives were made effective through the provisions of relevant statutes.

To instill confidence in investors and signal the government's commitment to a stable SEZ policy regime and with a view to imparting stability to the SEZ regime, thereby generating greater economic activity and employment through the establishment of SEZs, the Special Economic Zones Act was passed in 2005. The Act came into force along with the SEZ Rules in 2006, and this became one of the biggest pushes for industrial development in the history of India. The main objectives of the SEZ Act are:[12]

- Generation of additional economic activity
- Promotion of exports of goods and services
- Promotion of investment from domestic and foreign sources
- Creation of employment opportunities
- Development of infrastructure facilities

It is expected that this will trigger a large influx of foreign and domestic investment in SEZs, in infrastructure and productive capacity, leading to the generation of

---

[11] Kasturi Bhagat, Implementation of Labor Laws Inside SEZs in India: A Perfect Example of Economic Development Versus Social Security, 5(2) IUP Law Review 32, 32 (2015).

[12] See The Special Economic Zones Act, at https://www.indiacode.nic.in/bitstream/123456789/2042/3/a2005-28.pdf (Last visited on August 7, 2023).

additional economic activity and the creation of employment opportunities. A Single Window SEZ approval mechanism was also provided.

The SEZ Rules provide for different minimum land requirements for different classes of SEZs. Every SEZ is divided into a processing area where only the SEZ units would be established and the non-processing area where the supporting infrastructure is to be developed. The SEZ Rules provide for:[13]

- Simplified procedures for development, operation, and maintenance of the Special Economic Zones and for setting up units and conducting business in SEZs
- Single window clearance for setting up of an SEZ
- Single window clearance for setting up a unit in a Special Economic Zone
- Single window clearance on matters relating to central as well as state governments
- Simplified compliance procedures and documentation with an emphasis on self-certification

Indian SEZ policy provides for the development of these zones in the government, private, or joint sectors. Approximately 100% FDI is permitted for all investments in SEZs, except for activities included in the negative list. SEZ units are required to be net foreign-exchange earners. Goods flowing into the SEZ area from a domestic tariff area (DTA) are treated as exports, while goods coming from the SEZ into a DTA are treated as imports. Indian SEZs are exempt from paying any income tax. SEZ policy also provides enterprises and developers with a favorable and attractive range of incentives. It is worth noting that some of these incentives are not available to units that are set up in DTAs, and thus the SEZ policies, by definition, are discriminatory compared to the other local units set up in the country. However, in India, these exceptional treatments are allowed for SEZs as they undertake legally binding commitments that everything they produce in the zone shall be exported. In case some goods are supplied to the domestic market, appropriate duties with interest on the inputs used must be paid before the goods leave the SEZ.

Indian SEZs are also not without controversies and disputes. A major controversy surrounding the implementation of the Special Economic Zone scheme has been the manner in which the government acquired the land for developing SEZs. Since developing Special Economic Zones involves massive land procurement, which can lead to the displacement of farmers, it has created conflicts between industry, governments, farmers, and civil society. Therefore, state governments were advised that in land acquisition for Special Economic Zones, the first priority should be for the acquisition of waste and barren land and, if necessary, single-crop agricultural land. A new National Policy on Rehabilitation and Resettlement 2007 was introduced, which provided land-for-land compensation for the acquisition of land for development purposes, including Special Economic Zones, and employment for at least one person from each affected family. A National Rehabilitation Commission was set up by the central government, duly empowered to exercise

[13] Id.

independent oversight over the rehabilitation and resettlement of the affected families. Furthermore, wage employment would be provided to the willing affected persons in the construction work of the project. The policy also ensures housing benefits, including houses for landless affected families in both rural and urban areas. Adequate provisions have been made for financial support to the affected families for the construction of cattle sheds, shops, working sheds, transportation costs, temporary and transitional accommodation, comprehensive infrastructural facilities, and amenities in the resettlement area, including education, healthcare, drinking water, roads, electricity, sanitation, religious activities, cattle grazing, and other community resources. A robust grievance redressal mechanism has also been prescribed. This policy aims to strike a balance between the need for land for development purposes and protecting the interests of landowners and other displaced people.

2.2.2 The Performance of Indian SEZs

As of November 22, 2022, formal approval has been granted for 424 SEZs by the Board of Approval since the formulation of SEZ Rules in 2006. Currently, there are 270 operational SEZs as of the date of writing, with 5620 units operating within these SEZs, including those established before the SEZ Rules. These SEZs cover a variety of sectors, such as agro-based products, automobile manufacturing, mineral-based industries, biotechnology, electronic products, footwear, gems and jewelry, IT/ITES, textiles, multiproduct multiservices, pharmaceuticals, and power, among others.

In India, SEZs have attracted a cumulative investment of Rs. 6,457,852 million (equivalent to around US $100 million) as of November 22, 2022. SEZs have also generated employment opportunities for 2,807,256 individuals to date. During the fiscal year 2021–2022, SEZs contributed to a total export value of $133 billion, and from April to October 2022, the total exports reached $87.75 billion. Physical exports from SEZs witnessed a 30% growth in the 2021–2022 periods.[14]

3 Differences Between SEZ Policies in China and India

This section compares and analyzes the SEZ policies of China and India, exploring their legal frameworks, incentives, regulations, and overall effectiveness. One of the most important similarities between China and India's SEZ policies is that both countries offer tax breaks and other financial incentives to businesses that invest in SEZs. These incentives can include reduced corporate taxes, import duty

[14] See Department of Commerce, Annual Report, at https://commerce.gov.in/wp-content/uploads/2023/03/Annual-Report-FY-2022-23-DoC.pdf (Last visited on August 7, 2023).

exemptions, and accelerated depreciation allowances. It is worth noting that since China's accession to the WTO, the country has gradually and significantly reduced the number of subsidies that are contingent on export performance to comply with WTO norms,[15] particularly those set out in the Agreements on Subsidies and Countervailing Measures (SCM Agreement). The recent case brought against India regarding zone-specific subsidies provides a lesson for developing economies using SEZs to boost their economy. This will be elaborated in the later part of the article.

In addition, both China and India's SEZ policies allow for greater flexibility in terms of foreign investment regulations. For example, businesses operating in SEZs may be allowed to own 100% of their operations, which is not always the case in other parts of the country. The SEZ policies of both countries emphasize the importance of infrastructure development. SEZs are often located in areas with good transportation links and access to utilities. This helps ensure that businesses operating in SEZs have the resources they need to be successful.

Despite their respective economic performances and the common incentives offered to firms inside SEZs, the SEZ policies between the two emerging countries have striking differences, from overarching design to policy details.

The initial SEZs created by China were built in coastal regions with easy access to ports and transportation networks to ensure they are "most likely to succeed." Such models were only transplanted to inland cities after years of trial testing and when the overall transportation infrastructure networks of the entire country were significantly improved. In India, no restrictions on the geographic location have been imposed on SEZs. It is also noted that stimulating foreign investment was not a key objective for India's EPZs, unlike that of China. In the initial stage of SEZ development and before India liberalized its trade in 1991, EPZs were conceived more "as a means of providing relief to domestic exporters from the regulatory regime."[16] This could partially explain the geographic fragmentation of SEZs in India and their controversies with mixed results and challenges.[17]

China's SEZs are generally established in large open territories covering entire districts or cities and even spanning geographic units. SEZs in India vary in size, with some being fenced-in zones, the smallest being 1 ha. The fragmentation of SEZs in India is less likely to achieve social and economic spillover effects in neighboring districts not participating in the SEZ programs. In China, when local governments are assigned a given area SEZ status, they are credited with more discretion to design their own SEZ policies and preferential fiscal regulations based on their

[15] See WTO, India-Export Related Measures, at https://docs.wto.org/dol2fe/Pages/SS/directdoc.aspx?filename=q:/WT/DS/541-7.pdf&Open=True (Last visited on February 14, 2023).

[16] ASHOK KUNDRA, THE PERFORMANCE OF INDIA'S EXPORT ZONES: A COMPARISON WITH THE CHINESE APPROACH (2000), at http://opac.cshr.cmb.ac.lk:8080/jspui/handle/123456789/809 (Last visited on February 14, 2023).

[17] AKASH PODISHETTI, WHY HAVE SPECIAL ECONOMIC ZONES (SEZ) NOT TAKEN OFF IN INDIA? BUSINESS STANDARD, at https://www.business-standard.com/podcast/current-affairs/why-have-special-economic-zones-sez-not-taken-off-in-india-122070700036_1.html (Last visited Feb 14, 2023).

special needs to attract foreign investment and domestic firms. In contrast, in India, firms can submit an application to establish an SEZ, which is reviewed by state and local governments and must be approved by the Board of Approval.

The Indian government also allows private firms to develop an SEZ. In other words, the SEZ status can be assigned to a single firm in India. This has led to the establishment of SEZs in various regions across the country. In contrast, in China, the government is responsible for designating SEZ status and assigns it to specific areas. China's place-based policies, driven by overarching strategic designs, have demonstrated clear advantages for firms located within these zones, resulting in significant regional aggregation and spillover effects.

3.1 Legal Framework: Legislative Basis and Legal Provisions Governing SEZs in China

Regulations at the national level providing an overarching legal framework for the establishment, operation, and management of SEZs in the country include:

1. Law of the People's Republic of China on Foreign-Funded Enterprises (2000)[18]
2. Decision of the Standing Committee of the National People's Congress on Administrative Examination and Approval for Authorizing the State Council to Temporarily Adjust Relevant Legal Provisions in the China (Shanghai) Free Trade Zone (2013)
3. Decision of the Standing Committee of the National People's Congress on Authorizing the State Council to Temporarily Adjust the Relevant Administrative Approval Items as Prescribed in Laws in China (Guangdong) Pilot Free Trade Zone, China (Tianjin) Pilot Free Trade Zone, China (Fujian) Pilot Free Trade Zone, and the Extensions of China (Shanghai) Pilot Free Trade Zone (2015)
4. Catalogue of Industries Encouraged for Foreign Investment (2017, further expanded in 2019 and 2022)
5. Decision of the Standing Committee of the National People's Congress on Authorizing the State Council to Temporarily Adjust the Application of Relevant Legal Provisions in Pilot Free Trade Zones (2021)[19]

[18] This law was referred to in the subsequent decisions governing administrative measures of FTZs, including the Decision of the Standing Committee of the National People's Congress on Authorizing the State Council to Temporarily Adjust the Relevant Administrative Approval Items Prescribed in Laws in China (Guangdong) Pilot Free Trade Zone, China (Tianjin) Pilot Free Trade Zone, China (Fujian) Pilot Free Trade Zone, the Extensions of China (Shanghai) Pilot Free Trade Zone (2015), and many of the provisions set the basis for treatment of foreign investment in SEZs.

[19] Decision of the Standing Committee of the National People's Congress on Authorizing the State Council to Temporarily Adjust the Implementation of Relevant Provisions of Laws in Pilot Free Trade Zones (Adopted at the 28th Meeting of the Standing Committee of the Thirteenth National People's Congress on April 29, 2021) (China).

The Law on the Promotion of Foreign Investment also provides important provisions regarding Special Economic Zones (SEZs). It clarifies the legal status of SEZs and sets out the general rules and regulations that apply to foreign investment in SEZs. The Catalogue of Industries Encouraged for Foreign Investment identifies industries where FDI will be welcomed and treated with favorable policies in China. It also provides policies that promote foreign investment, particularly in SEZs. Several Decisions of the Standing Committee of the National People's Congress, authorizing the State Council to temporarily adjust the relevant administrative approval items prescribed in laws in different Free Trade Zones (FTZs) in recent years, provide test grounds for further optimizing the business environment, stimulating market vitality, and speeding up the transformation of government functions.

It is worth noting that instead of unified legislation on SEZs, China's SEZ legislations are zone specific, allowing for flexibility and autonomy for local governments of SEZs to make their own rules and policies in response to their respective needs. In fact, ordinary Chinese local regulations cannot contradict laws made by the national legislature or administrative regulations made by the State Council (the central government). The flexibility and legislative power delegated to each of the subnational legislatures under their respective authorization decisions of the NPC Standing Committee allow local legislatures to make adaptations to provisions of national laws and regulations and to local regulations. For instance, on June 10, 2021, the NPC Standing Committee issued an authorization decision granting the Shanghai Legislature the power to formulate regulations concerning the Pudong New Area. On the same day, the NPC Standing Committee also adopted the Law on Hainan Free Trade Port.[20]

The zone-specific SEZ regulations define the basic principles and policies of individual SEZs and set out the specific incentives and benefits available to businesses operating in SEZs.

India enacted the Special Economic Zones Act to regulate the establishment, operation, and management of SEZs. The Act provides legal provisions and guidelines for SEZ development in the country. The rules and articles of SEZ laws in India are governed by the following legislation:

1. Special Economic Zones Act, 2005
2. Special Economic Zones Rules, 2006
3. Special Economic Zones (Procedure for Approval and Development of) Rules, 2006
4. Special Economic Zones (Tax Exemption) Rules, 2006
5. Special Economic Zones (Deferment of Payment of Customs Duties) Rules, 2006

The Special Economic Zones Act, 2005, is the most important piece of legislation governing SEZs in India. It establishes the legal framework for SEZs and sets

[20] THE NATIONAL PEOPLE'S CONGRESS, CHINA'S TOP LEGISLATURE ADOPTS MULTIPLE LAWS AS STANDING COMMITTEE SESSION CONCLUDES, at http://www.npc.gov.cn/englishnpc/c23934/202106/778ecb5060334394a496cb56698814f0.shtml (Last visited on August 25, 2023)

out the specific incentives and benefits available to businesses operating in SEZs. The Special Economic Zones Rules, 2006, provide detailed procedures for the establishment and operation of SEZs. They specify the requirements that need to be met to establish an SEZ and the authorities responsible for approving SEZ proposals. The Special Economic Zones (Procedure for Approval and Development of) Rules, 2006, outline the procedures for the approval and development of SEZs. They specify the documents that must be submitted to obtain approval for an SEZ and set out the timeframes for the approval process. The Special Economic Zones (Tax Exemption) Rules, 2006, provide tax exemptions for businesses operating in SEZs in India. These exemptions include income tax exemption on profits and gains derived from authorized operations in SEZs for a period of 5 years, renewable for a further 5 years; customs duty exemption on the import of capital goods, raw materials, and consumables for authorized operations in SEZs; and excise duty exemption on goods produced or manufactured in SEZs for export. The Special Economic Zones (Deferment of Payment of Customs Duties) Rules, 2006 (SEZ Deferment of Payment Rules), allow businesses operating in SEZs to defer payment of customs duties on imported goods for up to 2 years. This deferment is available for goods used in the manufacture of goods for export. The SEZ Tax Exemption Rules and the SEZ Deferment of Payment Rules are important incentives designed to attract foreign investment and promote economic development in SEZs in India.

While both China and India have enacted legislation for SEZs, there are differences in their legal frameworks. China's SEZ laws are more comprehensive and address various aspects of SEZ operations in a piecemeal nature, whereas India's legal framework primarily focuses on the establishment and operation of SEZs.

3.2 *Objectives and Incentives Behind the Establishment of SEZs in China*

China aimed to attract FDI, promote exports, and foster economic development through the establishment of SEZs.[21] The objectives included the transfer of technology, the creation of jobs, and the development of industrial clusters. China offered a range of incentives to SEZs, including tax benefits, streamlined customs

[21] Resolution of the Standing Committee of the Fifth National People's Congress on Approving the "Regulations on the Special Economic Zones of Guangdong Province" (promulgated by the Standing Committee of the National People's Congress, Aug. 26, 1980, effective Aug. 26, 1980) (China); Resolution of the First Session of the Seventh National People's Congress on the Establishment of the Hainan Special Economic Zone (promulgated by the National People's Congress, Apr. 13, 1988, effective Apr. 13, 1988) (China); State Council's Instructions on "Minutes of the Meeting of Guangdong and Fujian Provinces" (promulgated by the State Council, May 16, 1980, effective May 16, 1980)(China); Interim Regulations of the State Council on Reducing and Exempting Enterprise Income Tax and Business Tax in Special Economic Zones and Fourteen Coastal Port Cities (promulgated by the State Council, Nov. 15, 1984, effective Dec. 1, 1984) (China).

procedures, preferential land policies, and infrastructure support. Additionally, SEZs in China enjoyed regulatory flexibility and a more business-friendly environment.

India's objectives for SEZs were similar to China's, emphasizing FDI attraction, export promotion, and employment generation. SEZs were seen as engines for economic growth, regional development, and the enhancement of manufacturing capabilities. India provided incentives such as tax exemptions, duty-free imports, simplified customs procedures, and infrastructure support to SEZs. Special fiscal and regulatory benefits were granted to attract investments and promote export-oriented industries.

3.3 Regulatory Framework: Administrative Bodies

In China, SEZs are governed by various administrative bodies, including the State Council, local governments, and specialized authorities like the China SEZ Authority. These bodies oversee the establishment, management, and coordination of SEZs with other government agencies. China's regulatory framework for setting up SEZs involves a comprehensive process, including feasibility studies, project approvals, land acquisition, and infrastructure development. The framework ensures coordination among government agencies and promotes a conducive environment for SEZ development. China's regulatory framework for SEZs is more streamlined and efficient, with a well-coordinated approach among various government agencies. In contrast, India's regulatory framework is perceived as complex, involving multiple approvals and compliance requirements.

India's SEZs are regulated by the Ministry of Commerce and Industry and implemented by the Development Commissioners in each SEZ. These administrative bodies monitor and facilitate SEZ operations, including approvals, clearances, and compliance. India's regulatory framework for establishing SEZs requires developers to submit proposals to the government for approval. The framework includes land acquisition, infrastructure development, and compliance with environmental and labor regulations.

3.4 Challenges Faced by SEZs and Suggestions

China's SEZs have encountered challenges related to rising labor costs, environmental concerns, industrial upgrading, and maintaining competitiveness in a changing global economic landscape.[22] Overreliance on export-oriented industries has

[22] XI JINPING, PRESIDENT, CHINA, SPEECH AT THE CELEBRATION OF THE 40TH ANNIVERSARY OF THE ESTABLISHMENT OF SHENZHEN SPECIAL ECONOMIC ZONE, PEOPLE'S DAILY (OCT. 14, 2020), at http://cpc.people.com.cn/n1/2020/1014/c64094-31892124.html (Last visited on August 9, 2022).

posed risks during economic downturns. China's SEZs face challenges related to sustaining competitiveness and adapting to changing market dynamics, while India's SEZs grapple with fundamental issues of infrastructure development and regulatory bottlenecks. SEZs in India encounter challenges such as land acquisition issues, slow infrastructure development, policy uncertainties, and complex regulatory processes. These challenges hinder the smooth functioning and overall performance of SEZs.

China's successful experiences with SEZs highlight the importance of comprehensive planning, strong infrastructure development, regulatory flexibility, and the need for continuous innovation and upgrading. India's experiences emphasize the significance of addressing infrastructure gaps, streamlining regulatory processes, and providing stable and predictable policies. To further enhance SEZ policies in China, it is recommended to focus on sustainable development, promoting innovation and technology-driven industries, addressing environmental concerns, and diversifying SEZs' economic base. Continued efforts to streamline regulations and provide a business-friendly environment would also be beneficial.

For India, key recommendations include addressing land acquisition challenges, accelerating infrastructure development, simplifying regulatory processes, and providing long-term policy stability. Additionally, fostering sector-specific SEZs, promoting skill development, and encouraging innovation-driven industries can contribute to the success of SEZs in India.

4 Conflicting Legal Implications of SEZs: With Domestic Policies and International Obligation

SEZs are areas where rules deviate from the rest of the country to promote strategic development and catalyze broader economic transformation. Although the impact of the SEZ policy has been positive in terms of stimulating the economy, SEZs often involve shifts in regulatory powers in the legislature and significant room for executive discretion. As a result, SEZs raise questions about their legal regime at both the domestic policy level and within international economic law, and the results have been mixed.

4.1 Potential Conflict with Domestic Industry Policies

In general, SEZs are geographical regions within the territory of a state that benefit from relaxed regulations compared to the rest of the country. The SEZ policy discriminates against domestic industries in favor of those that are set up in SEZs. As stated earlier, SEZ units receive the following facilities that are not available to domestic units:

Duty Concession and Exemption No duties (domestic or imported) are imposed on inputs, as well as other supplies, including construction materials, etc., for SEZ units. In some countries, such duty concessions are contingent upon exports. However, for domestic units, only the reimbursement of customs duties paid on actual inputs (raw materials, etc.) is allowed in the form of duty drawback or advance remission schemes. They do not receive any other duty benefits on capital goods, machinery, or other supplies for domestic units. Even if a domestic unit exports 100% of its production, it is not eligible for equivalent facilities as those provided to SEZs.

Tax Benefits As mentioned, to attract investment from the private sector to SEZs, governments may offer various tax incentives. This is especially the case in India, where certain tax exemptions are not available to domestic manufacturers. For example, India allows exemptions from customs/excise duties for the development of SEZs for authorized operations approved by the Board of Approvals (BOA); income tax exemption on income derived from the business of SEZ development for a period of 10 years out of 15 years under Section 80-IAB of the Income Tax Act (the Sunset Clause for Developers became effective from 01.04.2017); exemption from Central Sales Tax (CST); and exemption from Service Tax (as specified in Sections 7, 26, and the Second Schedule of the SEZ Act). Domestic producers do not receive income tax exemptions.

Land Acquisition and Land Use Rights The India SEZ Act of 2005 allows the government to transfer the land acquired for public purposes under the Land Acquisition Act to private companies for development. Preferential land use rights have also been granted in SEZs in China to attract investments. Land thus becomes the most significant incentive for being part of the SEZ scheme and for profit maximization. On the other hand, the operation of SEZs can affect land rights by transferring land for commercial activities without sufficient compensation. This has led to several unrests in the past by local landholders, after which the government decided not to intervene in procuring agricultural lands from farmers to be handed over to private SEZ developers. Now, developers have to negotiate with individual landholders to procure their lands.

4.2 Potential Conflict with International Trade and Investment Agreements

There is no internationally accepted legal framework to regulate SEZs. The Revised Kyoto Convention delineates SEZs as any area with "extraterritorial" elements that is deemed, for fiscal reasons, as being outside the customs territory.[23] This provides

[23] See Revised Kyoto Convention, supra note 2. See Sherzod Shadikhodjaev, International Regulation of Free Zones: An Analysis of Multilateral Customs and Trade Rules, 10(2) World Trade Review 189, 189 (2011).

a legal basis for specific national customs regulations to establish and operate SEZs, including their customs controls and the admission of goods. However, the incentives offered to recipients located within SEZs confer an advantageous position over other firms in the marketplace, thus creating potential tensions between domestic regulatory spaces and multilateral, as well as bilateral, trading rules.

4.2.1 SEZ in the Context of a Multilateral Trade Agreement

WTO disciplines relevant to SEZs include, but are not limited to, nondiscrimination, subsidies, trade-related investment measures, and trade-related intellectual property rights,[24] and the majority of discussions have centered on the application of the WTO SCM Agreement. Concerns have also been observed in the accession documents of most acceding members, explaining their SEZ policies, how their zone-based incentives are consistent with WTO Agreements, and their commitment to avoiding SEZ-related subsidies linked to local content and exportation requirements.[25]

As part of its Accession Protocol, China pledged to apply the provisions of the WTO Agreement and Protocol to "the entire customs territory of China, including border trade regions, and minority autonomous areas, SEZs, open coastal cities, economic technical development zones, and other areas where special regimes for tariffs, taxes, and regulations are established (collectively known as special economic areas)." China also committed to transparency requirements should some preferential arrangement for its SEZs be sustained.[26]

According to the SCM Agreement, a measure is defined to be a subsidy if (a) there is a financial contribution; (b) the contribution is provided by a government or any public body within the territory of a member; and (c) the contribution confers a benefit.[27] The SCM Agreement also provides a list that constitutes financial contributions, including (1) a direct transfer of funds; (2) the foregoing of revenue otherwise due (fiscal incentives); (3) the provision of goods or services other than for general infrastructure; and. finally, (4) if the entity is a private entity entrusted to or directed by a government or public body to make the above financial contribution.[28] Tax incentives and other preferential fiscal treatment, including land use rights applied to SEZs, may fall under any of the aforementioned categories of financial contributions. For instance, China's zone-specific governmental legislations,

---

[24] Id.; See Sherzod Shadikhodjaev, SEZs under the WTO's Scrutiny: Defining the Scope of Trade Issues, in International Economic Law and the Challenges of the Free Zones, at 213 (Alphen Aan Den Rijn (The Netherlands): Kluwer Law International, 2019); Julien Chaisse & Xueliang Ji, The Pervasive Problem of Special Economic Zones for International Economic Law: Tax, Investment, and Trade Issues, 19(4) World Trade Review 567, 567 (2020).

[25] Shadikhodjaev, supra note 19.

[26] Article 2 (A) of Protocol on the Accession of the People's Republic of China.

[27] Article1.1(a)(1) of Agreement on Subsidies and Countervailing Measures; Annex 1A of Marrakesh Agreement Establishing the World Trade Organization [hereinafter SCM Agreement].

[28] Id., Article 1.1(a)(1)(i)–(iv).

including tax incentives, low-cost loans, special land use rights, and discounted electricity rates, among others, were raised by Mexico as financial contributions that provide a preferential benefit.[29] Although the litigation ended during consultation, the matter raises a bell for SEZ-related incentives that will require examination under the SCM Agreement. It is worth noting that China's new generation of SEZs has shifted the focus from traditional export-oriented fiscal incentives to other incentives, including incentives linked to investment in research and development, a more favorable regulatory environment, greater flexibility to attract skilled labor, and streamlined administrative procedures. Most of the SEZ preferential policies that were inconsistent with the WTO rules have faded away after China's accession to the WTO and the improvement of the market system in the early 2000s.

The controversies surrounding India's SEZ incentives are more pronounced. In the October 2019 report, the WTO ruled against India in a dispute filed by the USA, claiming that five Indian export promotion initiatives for SEZs were in violation of certain provisions of the SCM Agreement. Among the fiscal provisions at stake in the dispute *India—Export Related Measures* at issue are the exemption of entrepreneurs from customs duties on imports into and exports from an SEZ; the exemption of goods imported into an SEZ by a unit or developer from India's Integrated Goods and Services Tax (IGST); and the deduction of the export earnings of an entrepreneur's SEZ unit from the corporate income tax base.[30] This further raises concerns over tensions between unilaterally provided incentives to SEZs and members' obligations under the SCM Agreement. With developing countries phasing out subsidies that are not WTO compatible, the SCM Agreement has become increasingly relevant to a great number of emerging countries, but the risk of SEZs falling victim to such disputes subsequently rises. Therefore, it is necessary to examine whether an SEZ scheme is inconsistent with multilateral trade rules. The Ministry of Commerce of India has already set up a committee tasked with formulating WTO-compliant alternatives to the existing disputed export subsidies under its SEZ scheme. India is actively considering introducing smart WTO-compliant subsidies rather than foreign exchange earnings.[31]

In summary, SEZs have unique configuration incentives that need to be compatible with WTO rules. They need to be administered in such a way for a diverse range of enterprises located within SEZs in India and China, as well as in other emerging economies that are export oriented. Subsidies could be potentially challenged as de facto export subsidies, if not de jure. There is no one-size-fits-all approach to SEZs

[29] See WTO, China–Measures Relating to the Production And Exportation of Apparel and Textile Products, WTO Doc. WT/DS451/1, at file:///C:/Users/LJ/Downloads/GEN103.pdf (Last visited on August 1, 2023)

[30] Supra note 13, ¶7.145.

[31] See ASIT RANJAN MISHRA, COMMERCE MINISTRY SETS UP PANEL TO MAKE SEZ POLICY COMPATIBLE WITH WTO RULES, MINT (2018), at https://www.livemint.com/Politics/LWcIXS4l3aQpEhCp8cdahJ/Commerce-ministry-sets-up-panel-to-make-SEZ-policy-compatibl.html (Last visited on August 1, 2023).

since their planning, development, and operations are highly contextualized,[32] so the support underlying SEZ programs needs to be examined on a case-by-case basis. It is important for members to devise a unilateral SEZ law consistent with multilateral trade values and norms while adopting a cautious approach to running their operations smoothly.

4.2.2 SEZs in the Context of Investment Treaties

SEZs are widely used as investment promotion tools. The experiences of both India and China have demonstrated how SEZs have successfully generated investment. The WTO Agreement on Trade-Related Investment Measures (TRIMs) does not mention SEZs either but is also relevant to a country's SEZ policy. Under TRIMs, local content requirements or import-export balancing requirements are not allowed, with a carve out for developing and least developed countries, which was phased out in 2020.[33] Since China's accession to the WTO, such requirements were gradually eliminated to meet the country's obligations. As a member of the WTO, India is also not eligible to apply such provisions to its SEZs.

It is worth noting that in order to promote cross-border investment, countries sign legally binding investment treaties to provide protection to each other's investors against adverse conduct by public authorities. Investment treaties primarily say little or nothing about SEZs. To date, international investors have initiated over 20 arbitrations over diverse aspects of SEZ-related investment.[34]

One issue that needs to be considered under investment treaties is expropriation. When governments establish zones to promote trade and investment with a "public purpose," expropriation may be inevitable. Landholders often have limited opportunities to negotiate over an overarching SEZ development plan. Expropriation could also occur between a host state and a foreign investor, and there have been a number of investor-state arbitration disputes (ISDS) on SEZs regarding expropriation. Professor Julien Chaisse reviewed a number of ISDS cases brought by foreign investors challenging SEZ-related measures and concluded that governments have the right to regulate in SEZs.[35] With that being said, governments should be careful in designing, implementing, modifying, and revoking regulations in SEZs to avoid triggering the expropriation clause.

[32] Douglas Z Zeng, The Past, Present, and Future of Special Economic Zones and Their Impact, 24(2) Journal of International Economic Law 259, 259 (2021).

[33] Article 5 of Agreement on Trade-Related Investment Measures [hereinafter TRIMs Agreement]; Annex 1A of Marrakesh Agreement Establishing the World Trade Organization.

[34] LORENZO COTULA & LILIANE MOUAN, SPECIAL ECONOMIC ZONES: DEVELOPMENT ENGINES OR SITES OF EXPLOITATION? (2018), at http://pubs.iied.org/17481IIED/ (Last visited on January 17, 2023).

[35] Chaisse and Ji, supra note 24.

4.2.3 SEZs in the Context of Regional Integration

The preceding decade witnessed the rapid development of SEZs, paralleled by the proliferation of free trade agreements (FTAs). Both are consequently important policy tools that promote trade and investment for countries and within regions. FTAs are reciprocal preferential trade agreements between two or more partners; they are derogations authorized under the WTO to boost trade and further economic integration among member states.[36] Despite their profound economic impacts, their overlapping geographic coverage, subject matter, and differing regulatory approaches inevitably trigger synergizing issues between them, with one representing unilateral instruments, while the other represents bilateral or multilateral instruments, respectively.

The nexus of SEZs and FTAs is complex. There is no one-size-fits-all to the synergetic mechanisms of these policy tools, and whether two tools can work positively toward a common objective depends on the context of each country and its partnered FTAs. Very few FTAs remain silent on issues encountered with and between SEZs, as most of the FTAs that have tried or raised concerns have found.

As of the current date of writing, China has signed and implemented a total of 16 FTAs, and the government deems FTAs to be an effective approach to integrating itself into the global economy and strengthening economic cooperation with other economies. Among all the FTAs signed by China, the Rules of Origin that were established serve as the de facto set of rules for the treatment of all SEZ-processed products within its territory. The China-Korea FTA is the only known exception, in addition to the Rule of Origin; a special clause has been set out for the treatment of certain goods from outward processing zones[37] as part of a continuous effort from Korean negotiators to introduce special provisions for their outward processing zones through nearly all of Korea's FTAs that have been agreed upon and adopted in force.[38] India also has a similar provision in its FTA with the Republic of Korea, as in the China-Korea FTA.

5 Conclusion

SEZs have proliferated over the past decade and are used as engines for development. While much debate has focused on their evolution and economic performance, laws sustaining and contesting SEZs should not be ignored. In many cases,

[36] Article XXIV of General Agreement on Tariffs and Trade [hereinafter GATT]; Paragraph 203 of Differential and More Favourable Treatment, Reciprocity and Fuller Participation of Developing Countries (L/4903) [hereinafter Enabling Clause for Developing Countries]; Article V of General Agreement on Trade in Services [hereinafter GATS].

[37] Article 3.3 of China-Korea Free Trade Agreement [hereinafter China-Korea FTA].

[38] Jeongjoon Park, The Evolution of Outward Processing Scheme in Korea's FTAs: The Case of the Gaeseong Industrial Complex in Korea-ASEAN and Korea-Vietnam FTA, 23(1) Journal of International and Area Studies 99, 99 (2016).

the regulation of SEZs is used as a laboratory for reform, contingent upon different political, institutional, and economic contexts.

The SEZ policies of China and India have played significant roles in attracting investments, promoting exports, and driving economic growth. While both countries share similar objectives, there are notable differences in their legal frameworks, incentives, and regulatory approaches. China's SEZ policies have demonstrated remarkable success, showcasing the importance of comprehensive planning, favorable business environments, and continuous innovation. India's SEZs have faced challenges but offer valuable lessons on the importance of addressing infrastructure gaps and streamlining regulatory processes. By understanding the similarities, differences, and lessons learned from the SEZ experiences of China and India, policymakers and stakeholders can develop effective strategies for fostering economic development in their respective countries.

China and India have different experiences in their SEZ development. Despite the differences in design, institutional characteristics, and economic outcomes, there are common concerns rooted in their legal regimes that underpin their conflicts with national policy and international obligations. While there are certain disputes in the WTO regarding incentives provided to the SEZs, there seems to be no judicial scrutiny about the conflict in domestic policies—one for the domestic producers who are also exporters and the SEZ units. However, it is evident that there is some level of differential treatment given through public policies.

If not properly contemplated, it could result in the state's liability before a dispute settlement body or an investment tribunal. In this regard, policymakers should properly consider the legal regimes governing SEZs and recognize their potential conflicting regimes with both national policy and international trade and investment agreements.

Chapter 6
Transformation of International Economic Law: Contours and Ways of the New Regulation

Igor A. Shulyatyev

Abstract The modern international economic legal order survives the changes and upheavals caused by the transition from one model of the international order to another political and economic structure of the international community of states. A liberal, cosmopolitan order with multilateral decision-making mechanisms does not allow reaching an interstate consent. A reflection of the crisis in multilateral economic decision-making is the political and jurisdictional paralysis of the World Trade Organization (WTO). The WTO rules and principles themselves have not lost their relevance but have actually lost the mechanisms for their implementation at the universal level. The response to the political crisis of multilateral economic associations was the regionalization of trade, investment, and financial cooperation. A paradoxical situation has emerged when the universal international legal values—equality and nondiscrimination—have found the potential for implementation at the mega-regional, regional, subregional, and bilateral levels. At the same time, regional cooperation makes it possible to form new international legal approaches that would reveal the needs of states with different socioeconomic levels of development. It is difficult to agree with ideas that criticize international law for inefficiency, since the problem is not in international law as a means of legally formalizing relations but in seeking the consent of states divided by questions about the goals and ways of further development of the international legal order. We are witnessing the collapse of the monopoly of Western states on international legal models of economic relations. For example, the idea of integration along the lines of the European Union does not stand up to criticism as a form of differentiation of powers between supranational bodies and member states of the association. The central point of division between developed and developing countries is on the issue of state support for economic development (market capitalist and state economic systems). And in this regard, we can say that the state is becoming a source of economic development (East), and the idea of market self-regulation (West) is being transformed and recedes into the past.

I. A. Shulyatyev (✉)
Center of International Law and Comparative Law Studies, The Institute of Legislation and Comparative Law under the Government of the Russian Federation, Moscow, Russian Federation

T. Du, X. Fei (eds.), *The BRICS Legal Cooperation and Perspectives*,
https://doi.org/10.1007/978-981-95-4356-4_6

Will this pattern find its place and formalization in the principles of international economic law? Maybe, yes. This, in particular, is evidenced by the experience of the USSR, which at the beginning of its historical path in bilateral trade agreements with European states consolidated the principle of the state monopoly of foreign trade. Another interesting trend is the politicization of international economic cooperation, which is reflected in the declining role of legal procedures in making economic decisions at the international level (e.g., G20). One of the consequences of such politicization is the growing role of the national legislation of states, which is clearly seen in the example of the regulation of investment legal relations. Thus, the modern transformation of international economic law is not just quantitative changes but precisely a qualitative transition to another international and national legal realities through acute interstate contradictions between developed and developing states.

Keywords International economic law · International organizations · Regionalization · National legislation · Eurasian Economic Union · "International economic law of the era of internationalization" · Dialectical principle · "General, special, and singular"

1 Introduction

The current international economic law is a branch of modern public international law, the norms and principles of which regulate international economic relations. The peculiarity of international economic law is that it is based on political interstate relations. It follows from this that the principles and norms of international economic law represent an interstate consensus. The presence of the consent of states is a distinctive feature of international economic law from other international regulatory systems in the field of economics.

The current international economic law in its structure and content is the result of the development of liberal economic ideas laid down in the works of such multilateral international institutions as the International Monetary Fund, the World Bank Group, the General Agreement on Tariffs and Trade, and World Trade Organization. The ideas of free convertibility of currencies, freedom of capital movement, and liberalization of international trade have found their consolidation and development in the norms of international agreements.

Having survived the economic crisis of the 1970s, the collapse of the Soviet Union, and the collapse of the European socialist bloc, international economic law in its liberal understanding reached its peak in the creation of the World Trade Organization (WTO) in 1995. The states have agreed on universal and global principles of international trade: the most favored nation and nondiscrimination. Unlike trade in the investment sphere, the international legal regime was built on the implementation of bilateral investment agreements. However, such an organization of regulation did not prevent the creation of a unified international investment legal order.

Another pattern of the current international economic law can be called the international legal regulation of the integration processes. The abovementioned characteristics allow us to call the current international economic law "the world economic law of the era of globalization," which has consolidated the hegemony of developed states in the world economy and ignores social and environmental aspects in favor of the commercial profits of transnational corporations.

However, the turbulence of the global political system and regular economic crises have shown that it is impossible to resolve the accumulated international and interstate contradictions within the framework of the paradigm of the "world economic law of the era of globalization."

Therefore, the task of the science of international law is to search for such knowledge about the models of international legal regulation of international economic processes that will allow us to find solutions to modern and real legal problems.

To solve such problems, the dialectical principle of cognition of the consideration of phenomena in three dimensions becomes relevant: general, special, and singular. The dialectical methodology reflects different levels of legal existence and allows us to find points of support for the formation of new international legal models of international economic relations that take into account the sovereign equality of states and social, environmental, and cultural aspects of economic development. And the result of such studies can be called "international economic law of the era of internationalization," when the legitimate rights and interests of the majority of states and peoples will be taken into account not only in the current regulation but also in its new formats and structures.

Internationalization of international economic relations is a new (or very well forgotten) interstate democratic consensus. An important aspect of this consensus is its acquisition of international legal and national legal forms.

Since there are serious interstate disagreements at the universal (general) level of international economic law, it is necessary to study regional and national dimensions that act as special and singular in legal reality.

2 Regionalization as a New Legal Institutionalization

One of the international legal forms of the institutional and organizational side of the international economic legal order is a regional integration economic association. The very formulation of this concept implies a fairly wide range of different formats of group cooperation of states in international economic relations. An association is not limited to an international organization, as an association created solely on the basis of international law and having an international legal personality. One thing is for sure, such associations are interstate in nature, since they serve as the political foundation of cross-border economic ties and a legal mechanism for coordinating the interests of states. An illustration of this combination at the bilateral level is the mechanism of regular meetings of the heads of government of Russia and China, created to coordinate cooperation between the two countries in trade, economic, military, scientific and technical, energy, transport, nuclear energy, and other areas, including large-scale projects and long-term cooperation programs that have the following objectives: strategic importance (Agreement between the Government of the Russian Federation and the People's Republic of China on the establishment and organizational basis of the mechanism for regular meetings of the Heads of Government of Russia and China, 1997).

For the current period of development of international relations in conditions of instability and turbulence, regional cooperation is a safety mechanism against attempts to isolate individual states from the world market and industrial cooperation. The prerequisites for cooperation between states of the same geographical region are much broader than at the universal level, including civilizational and cultural similarities between peoples, close legal traditions, and even a common language. The choice of forms of such cooperation is becoming wider due to the fact that globalization has created a single planetary space consisting of different legal systems and families. The means of communication provide almost instantaneous exchange of any information between regions of the world, so the cultural identity of individual states and regions becomes an important element influencing the legal forms and mechanisms of regional economic cooperation. If in the late twentieth and early twentieth centuries we witnessed the monopoly of the Western European model of regional cooperation, and many states sought to copy it, today there is an understanding that such a model cannot be universal, that is, it ignores the peculiarities and specifics of the cultural and historical development of Latin America, the Middle East, Africa, Asia, Eurasia, post-Soviet space, ASEAN, APEC, and subregional forums.

In this sense, the science of international law faces the problem of studying both the general concept of "regional integration economic association" and certain types of this concept on the example of various international economic organizations. The solution of this problem will make it possible to develop various legal means of regulating the processes of regional economic integration, select the most optimal forms and levels of regional cooperation for a particular region, propose optimal mechanisms for resolving international economic disputes, and formulate a position on the need to implement acts of regional integration economic associations in national legal systems. This scientific approach to studying the integration nature of the institutional and organizational side of the international economic order contains an element of balance between knowledge about universal and regional international organizations and a balance between an abstract understanding of globalization as a unification of regulation and regionalization as a manifestation of the identity and uniqueness of the international legal institutional creativity of peoples.

In the United Nations Framework Convention on Climate Change, 1992, there is the term "regional economic integration organization," which means an "organization established by the sovereign states of a given region, which has jurisdiction over matters governed by this Convention or its Protocols and which is duly authorized, in accordance with its internal procedures, to sign, ratify, adopt, and adopt international agreements and approve the relevant documents or join them." From this classical normative definition follows the main meaning of an international integration organization-expanded legal personality by delegating certain rights to member states of such an organization, in this case the right to sign, ratify, accept, and approve relevant documents or join them. In other words, the rights and obligations arise for the regional economic integration organization itself, and the member states are obliged to follow the agreements concluded by the international organization.

In the Russian international legal literature, a reasonable position is expressed that the specific features of subject competence, the pronounced supranational nature of international intergovernmental integration organizations, the preference for legal methods of regulation while maintaining political ones, the inclusion of the population of member states in the implementation of integration goals, and the creation of people's representation bodies (which can hardly be called supranational)—all this lends considerable originality to this type of international organization.[1] And in this case, regional integration economic associations take the most rigid legal form—an international intergovernmental organization with delegated powers from member states, a clear organizational structure, and procedures for making binding decisions. This is the Western European model of regional cooperation. It is characterized by extreme formal certainty, a coherent system of governing bodies with an international bureaucracy, prescribed procedures for decision-making, and dispute resolution. If we compare this model with Asian associations, we will see that the latter are based on the principle of interstate cooperation with the predominance of political and diplomatic means to achieve their goals.[2]

Theoretical approaches that identify the concepts of "regional integration economic associations" and "regional organization of economic integration" naturally come to the concept of integration law.[3] As a result, regional economic integration remains within the framework of ideas about the regulatory models created at the turn of the twentieth and twenty-first centuries borrowed by various regions of the world: MERCOSUR, the Eurasian Economic Community, and the African Economic Community.

And this model worked perfectly well until 2008, when the global financial and economic crisis first made itself felt. Under these conditions, states that were forced to collapse their national economies sought to maximize the use of their state power potential to stabilize domestic markets and socioeconomic systems. To do this, it was necessary to concentrate their powers and develop new mechanisms for

---

[1] Kapustin A.Ya. International organizations in the globalizing world: Monograph.—RUDN, 2010. p. 207.

[2] Taliya Khabriyeva et al., ASEAN IS A DRIVING FORCE OF REGIONAL INTEGRATION IN ASIA 256 (2016); APEC Summit: Legal Mechanisms of Regional Integration / I. I. Shuvalov, A. Ya. Kapustin, T. Ya. Khabrieva [et al.].—Moscow: Publishing House "Statute," 2012.—392 p.

[3] S. Yu. Kashkin. *Philosophy of Integration Law*, Actual Problems of Russian Law, Feb. 2019, at 43-50.

international cooperation in the economic sphere. At the same time, there was an awareness of the risks of globalization of economic processes and the collapse of consensus at the universal level. Organizational evidence of the strengthening of states and the departure from strict procedures for multilateral regulation of international economic relations was the functioning of the G20. This international conference of an interstate nature has a coordinating role and is not entitled to make legally binding decisions. Thus, states began to look for new forms of economic cooperation that would allow them to maintain control over the decision-making process and not bind themselves to international legal obligations. And this task was solved, first, by referring to the regional level of international relations and, secondly, by rethinking the content of the concept of "integration" in relation to interstate relations.

If earlier "integration" was considered as a delegation of decision-making rights to the bodies of an international organization, now "integration" is considered as such a delegation of rights to an international organization, which should at least take into account the state interests and the right of control over the organization's decisions by the state. In legal practice, this process has manifested itself through the strengthening of national bodies of constitutional control and supervision. For example, Article 79 of the Constitution of the Russian Federation was amended to state that "Decisions of interstate bodies adopted on the basis of provisions of international treaties of the Russian Federation in their interpretation contrary to the Constitution of the Russian Federation are not subject to execution in the Russian Federation."[4] In Germany, the Constitutional Court of the Federal Republic of Germany has put into practice the right of constitutional review of European Union regulations, which it reserved back in 1974, and has recognized a number of regulations of the European Central Bank (ECB) *ultra vires*, i.e., adopted with obvious excess of authority and therefore not applicable in Germany. In addition, he considered the preliminary opinion of the EU Court of Justice, which he received in response to his request, accepted with excess of authority and refused to follow it.[5] These are examples of changes in the content of the concept of "integration" at the national level. At the same time, national judicial authorities play an important role in this process.

The terms "integration" and "integrational" and their derivatives should be interpreted based on the text of the constituent documents. There is no and cannot be a common definition of these words, since modern international law is conciliatory in nature and does not imply the development of a single and universal definition of the

[4] Commentary to the Constitution of the Russian Federation (article by article): taking into account the amendments approved during the all-Russian vote on July 1, 2020 / T.Ya. Khabrieva, L.V. Andrichenko, S.B. Nanba, A.E. Pomazansky; edited by T.Ya. Khabrieva; appeal to readers of V.V. Putin.—Moscow: Institute of Legislation and Comparative Law under the Government of the Russian Federation: INFRA-M, 2021.—368 p.

[5] Casus belli, *how the request of the Constitutional Court of Germany to the EU Court turned into a war of courts*, Zakon.ru (Mar. 30, 2023), https://zakon.ru/blog/2020/5/14/casus_belli_kak_zapros_ks_frg_v_sud_es_pereros_v_vojnu_sudov.

concept of "integration." For example, the 1993 Charter of the Commonwealth of Independent States (CIS) defines the goals of the Commonwealth as "comprehensive and balanced economic and social development of the member states within the common economic space, interstate cooperation and integration" (Article 2). However, the spheres of joint activity of the CIS member states are implemented "...on an equal basis through common coordinating institutions in accordance with the with the obligations assumed by the member States within the framework of the Commonwealth" (Article 4). It turns out that in the CIS, integration is seen as a goal that is achieved through coordination. Thus, it can be stated that in the law of international organizations, "integration" can be implemented not only through granting state powers to interstate bodies but also through interstate coordination. This conclusion enriches the scientific understanding of the law of international organizations as a mechanism for implementing the principle of cooperation of states in an era of decision-making crisis at the multilateral level.

It can be argued that for the international legal discourse, the term "integration" can mean the balance of powers between the interstate association and the member states in the field of economic cooperation agreed by the states or, in other words, as a decision-making process. At the same time, "integration" can be considered both as a goal and as a process. In any case, the content of "integration" is always a product of the coordination of the will of states and cannot form an independent part of the legal regulation of international economic relations. The current trend can be called the transition of integration to an intergovernmental model from a supranational one. This is quite understandable because states are not yet ready to hand over to international organizations the right to make strategic decisions in shaping the general contours of the international economic system.

The classical international legal form of "integration" is an international organization. However, today you can also find such a concept as "integration of integrations."[6] The international legal concept of this political phenomenon is a promising scientific task. It is no coincidence that we are talking about a political phenomenon, since objective economic processes have not yet developed institutional approaches to the organizational design of such a process. Today, it is difficult to say what legal model the "integration of integrations" will adopt. At present, we are only talking about building political structures for such a grandiose association.

The Big Eurasian Partnership (unstable term) is an example of such an integration project. The main idea of the "Comprehensive Eurasian Partnership," announced in 2016, is to strengthen integration cooperation between the Eurasian Economic Union and the states of the Asia-Pacific region, relevant international organizations, and other integration associations in the region. As a result, a regional free trade zone and a free investment zone should be created with the participation of the Eurasian Economic Union (EAEU) and the EAEU member states. The main regulatory regulator of this process is international treaties and soft law, and the very

[6]Vladimir Putin, a video message at the plenary session of the 75th anniversary session of the United Nations General Assembly, President of Russia (Mar. 30, 2023), http://www.kremlin.ru/events/president/transcripts/statements/64074 (Date of access: 30.03.2023).

direction of such integration is explained by the matured international legal consciousness and the ongoing restructuring of the modern international legal order.[7]

It is obvious that the idea of "integration of integrations" involves much more regulatory regulators and process participants. And in this aspect, "integration" can already outgrow its international legal format. Thus, the activity of regional integration economic associations is no longer just an international legal regulation but an international legal regulation placed at the center of a whole system of norms, structures, and interests of a governmental and nongovernmental nature, at the bilateral, subregional, regional, mega-regional, and global levels. One can put forward the idea that the term "regional integration economic association" has not only a narrow understanding as an interstate organization but also a broad understanding as a complex of governmental and nongovernmental mechanisms and bodies. In the latter case, the scope of authority and content of competence of associations will receive a completely different institutional and legal model (of course, first of all, such a model should be economically effective, but in international relations, the relationship between politics and economics differs from national relations, so the criterion of economic efficiency will not be the only one for such a model).

We consider the concept of "regional integration economic association" to be a step forward in the scientific understanding of international legal forms of international economic relations. In our opinion, it adequately reflects the diversity of approaches to the institutionalization of the global economy. This concept acts as a generic one in relation to international organizations of an integration type, international economic conferences, para-organizations, and other formats for states to coordinate their economic interests and develop rights and obligations. A regional integration economic association can be developed as a political and legal framework (platform) for broader forms of international communication, including participants such as business circles and civil society. In this case, international law will act as a central regulatory system, interacting not only with the national legislation of the member states (participating states) but also with other regulatory complexes regulating international economic relations in the era of searching for new parameters of the international economic legal order. In any case, the word "integration" will always have a special meaning that states attach to it in the organizational structure of their political and economic dialogue.

Thus, new regional international legal forms of institutionalization of international economic relations can be considered as special characteristics of international economic law and one of the promising areas of its development. This view reflects the needs of most states and creates the political and legal conditions for new international obligations.

---

[7] Shumilov, V. M. The idea of a comprehensive (large) Eurasian partnership in the light of international law (Part 1) / V. M. Shumilov, M. R. Salia // Asia-Pacific region: Economics, Politics, Law.—2021.—Vol. 23, No. 2.—pp. 66-78.—DOI 10.24866/1813-3274/2021-2/66-78.; Shumilov, V. M. The idea of a comprehensive (large) Eurasian partnership in the light of international law (Part 2) / V. M. Shumilov, M. R. Salia // Asia-Pacific region: Economics, Politics, Law.—2021.—Vol. 23, No. 3.—pp. 111-123.—DOI 10.24866/1813-3274/2021-3/111-123.

3 National Legislation: A New Dimension of International Economic Order

Modern globalized international relations force states to enter into communication with each other and search for acceptable legal forms for this purpose. Relations that develop in the process of interaction between states are called interstate relations, which form the material basis of international law. International law and domestic law have much in common, since both normative systems are a set of formally defined, legally binding rules of conduct.

At the same time, the norms of law and legal relations in international law have their own specifics. This specificity is primarily manifested in the creation and application of legal norms, in the nature of their binding force. All this, in turn, manifests itself in the legal relations that arise as a result of the implementation of the norms of international law.[8]

When including international treaties in the national legal system as an integral part of it, it becomes necessary to determine the position that they occupy in this system. International law cannot itself exercise its supremacy at the domestic level. The operation of international law in national legal systems largely depends on how this issue is resolved in the law of various states. In most states, international treaties are considered hierarchically lower than constitutions, meaning that constitutions should prevail in the event of a conflict.[9]

Considering the interaction of international law and national legislation, some conditions for such interaction should be noted. First, a state has no right to invoke the provisions of its domestic law as justification for nonfulfillment of international legal obligations. Second, it is necessary to study the interaction of specific sources of international law and national legislation, since the combinations of such interaction can be different, for example, an international treaty and an ordinary law, an international legal custom, and a normative legal act of a national government, etc. Third, it is necessary to take into account the specifics of acts of international intergovernmental organizations as a source of international legal obligations. The lawmaking function of international organizations follows from the constituent treaty, and therefore the binding nature of the legal norms adopted by the organization for states follows from their obligations under this treaty.[10] The implementation of the act of such an organization in the national legal order is mediated by the provisions of the constituent treaty, that is, an international treaty. Fourth, the general norm of interaction between sources of public international law and domestic law is the

---

[8] V. M. Shurshalov. International legal relations. Publishing House "International Relations". Moscow: 1971. p. 16.

[9] Boris Osminin, *Priority Application of International Treaties in the National Legal System: Conditions and Consequences*, Journal of Russian Law, Dec. 2017, at 160–174.

[10] I. P. Blishchenko & A. H. Abashidze, THE LAW OF INTERNATIONAL ORGANIZATIONS 156 (2013).

coherent norm of states conscientious performance of their obligations under international law.

From these preliminary observations, the following general conclusions can be drawn:

- The national legislation of a state can be considered as a way of fulfilling the international legal obligations of a state while maintaining the autonomy of its national legal system.
- The state has autonomy in deciding on the choice of mechanisms for implementing sources of international law in national legislation.
- The principle of conscientious performance by states of their obligations under international law applies specifically to obligations arising from sources of public international law but not from acts of enforcement.

A separate aspect of the interaction between international law and domestic law is related to the consideration of constitutional prescriptions on this issue. By virtue of the principle of state sovereignty, each state, as a subject of international law and an equal participant in the international community, has the right to formulate its own constitutional ideas and principles, including those related to the external environment. These views, ideas, and concepts, which are reflected in the norms of the constitution, can be conditionally called the constitutional model of international law, which reflects the specifics of the state structure, the geopolitical position of the country, and legal traditions and views that have developed in each individual state. In this sense, the existence of such a model makes it possible to predict the development of international relations of a given state with a greater or lesser degree of confidence.[11]

In 2020, there were constitutional changes in Russia. The general rule remains in force: "The generally recognized principles and norms of international law and international treaties of the Russian Federation are an integral part of its legal system. If an international treaty of the Russian Federation establishes rules other than those provided for by law, the rules of the international treaty shall apply" (Part 4 of Article 15 of the Constitution of the Russian Federation).

According to Article 1 of the Law of the Russian Federation on the Amendment to the Constitution of the Russian Federation No. 1-FKZ of 14.03.2020 "On improving the regulation of certain issues of the organization and functioning of public power," the Constitution of the Russian Federation, adopted by popular vote on December 12, 1993, was amended in terms of international law as follows:

- Article 79 is set out in the following wording: "The Russian Federation may participate in interstate associations and transfer part of its powers to them in accordance with international treaties of the Russian Federation, if this does not entail restrictions on human and civil rights and freedoms and does not contradict the foundations of the constitutional system of the Russian Federation.

[11] A. Ya Kapustin Modern constitutional models of international law // Issues of economics and law. No. 2. 2015. p. 54.

Decisions of interstate bodies adopted on the basis of provisions of international treaties of the Russian Federation in their interpretation contrary to the Constitution of the Russian Federation are not subject to enforcement in the Russian Federation."

- Article 125 is supplemented by Part 5.1 with item (b) as follows: "in accordance with the procedure established by the federal constitutional law, it resolves the issue of the possibility of executing decisions of interstate bodies adopted on the basis of provisions of international treaties of the Russian Federation in their interpretation contrary to the Constitution of the Russian Federation, as well as the possibility of executing a decision of a foreign or international (interstate) body, a court, foreign or international arbitration court (arbitration) that imposes obligations on the Russian Federation, if this decision contradicts the fundamentals of the public legal order of the Russian Federation."

Such changes had their own ideology. Only a strong sovereign state can ensure a decent future for its citizens, so among the amendments is strengthening Russia's sovereignty by clarifying its relationship with the international legal order. While remaining committed to the generally recognized norms and principles of international law, the basic law of the country is supplemented by the provision that decisions of interstate bodies taken on the basis of international treaties of the Russian Federation in an interpretation that contradicts the Constitution of the Russian Federation are not subject to execution on the territory of Russia.[12]

Finally, we should also mention the legal position of the Constitutional Court of the Russian Federation, according to which "a decision of the European Court of Human Rights cannot be considered binding if, as a result of the interpretation of a specific provision of the Convention for the Protection of Human Rights and Fundamental Freedoms on which this decision is based, implemented in violation of the general rule of treaty interpretation, the meaning of this provision diverges with peremptory norms of general international law." This legal position is now included in Article 79 of the Russian Constitution.[13]

Without going into a detailed analysis of the constitutional amendments on the possibility of nonenforcement of decisions of international courts if they contradict the Constitution or the foundations of the public legal order of Russia, we note that they reflect the changes that have taken place in modern international relations due to the expansion of the powers of interstate bodies, including international courts. Articles 79 and 125 of the Constitution of the Russian Federation are aimed at

[12] Commentary to the Constitution of the Russian Federation (article by article): taking into account the amendments approved during the all-Russian vote on July 1, 2020 / T.Ya. Khabrieva, L.V. Andrichenko, S.B. Nanba, A.E. Pomazansky; edited by T.Ya. Khabrieva; appeal to readers of V.V. Putin.—Moscow: Institute of Legislation and Comparative Law under the Government of the Russian Federation: INFRA-M, 2021.— P. 17.—DOI 10.12737/1836403.

[13] Khabrieva T.Ya., Klishas A.A. Thematic commentary on the Law of the Russian Federation on the Amendment to the Constitution of the Russian Federation dated March 14, 2020 No. 1-FKZ "On improving the regulation of certain issues of the organization and functioning of public power" / T.Ya. Khabrieva, A.A. Klishas.—Moscow: Norma : INFRA-M, 2020. p. 21.

strengthening the supremacy of the Constitution in the Russian legal system, which is in full compliance with generally recognized principles and norms of international law.[14]

Consequently, the new version of the Constitution of the Russian Federation establishes the mechanism of interaction between the Constitution of the Russian Federation and "decisions of interstate bodies adopted on the basis of provisions of international treaties of the Russian Federation in their interpretation contrary to the Constitution of the Russian Federation." Article 125 of the new version of the Constitution of the Russian Federation supplements the list of institutions whose decisions may be deemed unenforceable on the territory of the Russian Federation: "a foreign or international (interstate) court, a foreign or international arbitration court (arbitration) that imposes obligations on the Russian Federation." But in this case, the decision of such an institution must contradict the principles of public policy of the Russian Federation. It is worth agreeing with Alexey S. Ispolinov that: "The situation with the constitutional control of decisions of interstate bodies, rather vaguely stated in the new version of Article 79 of the Constitution, was to some extent clarified in the updated Chapter XIII.1 of the Law on the Constitutional Court of the Russian Federation. Here we see already clearer formulations. The naked eye can see the difference between, on the one hand, decisions of interstate bodies and, on the other hand, decisions of courts (both international and national) and arbitrations (both foreign and international). Then everything falls into place. The decisions of interstate bodies hardly imply resolutions of the General Assembly of the United Nations or the Parliamentary Assembly of the Council of Europe, which, as a rule, are not binding. We are also not talking about binding resolutions of the UN Security Council, for example, the inclusion of a particular person in the sanctions lists. These resolutions are subject to mandatory implementation through the adoption of national legal acts and are subject to constitutional review at this stage. It is obvious that, within the meaning of Article 79, decisions of interstate bodies are binding and directly applicable in the national legal order decisions of the institutions of those interstate associations in which Russia participates, first of all, decisions of the EAEU institutions, вопросыwhose compliance with the Constitution, as well as their right to check these decisions for compliance with the Constitution, have already been independently resolved allowed by the Constitutional Court of the Russian Federation in the Definition of 03.03.2015 N 417-O. Now this right is enshrined in the Constitution and then reproduced in the Law on the Constitutional Court of the Russian Federation.[15]"

From the text of changes (amendments) according to the Constitution, it can be concluded that we are talking about a specific type of acts of interstate bodies—acts of law enforcement practice or decisions taken during the peaceful settlement of a

[14] A. Ya. Kapustin, *International Judicial Interpretation of an International Treaty: Modern Trends*, Journal of Russian Law, Jul. 2022, at 1.

[15] A. S. Ispolinov New powers of the Constitutional Court of the Russian Federation to verify the constitutionality of decisions of international courts and arbitrations // Law. № 12. 2020. Access: SPS "Consultant Plus".

dispute. This interpretation of the term "Decisions of interstate bodies" (Article 79) is also indicated by the wording "adopted on the basis of the provisions of international treaties of the Russian Federation in their interpretation."

If we return to the systematic interpretation of the provisions of the current Article 79 of the Constitution of the Russian Federation, we can argue that we are not talking about all interstate bodies but only about those to which the Russian Federation transferred part of its powers in accordance with international treaties, if this did not entail restrictions on human and civil rights and freedoms and the constitutional order of the Russian Federation. The Constitutional Court of the Russian Federation clarified that the Constitution of the state has the supremacy, and therefore decisions of the European Court of Human Rights (ECHR) that contradict it cannot be enforced in Russia. This is not a contradiction between the Convention for the Protection of Human Rights and Fundamental Freedoms as such and the national constitutions but a conflict of interpretation of the convention provision given by the ECHR in its judgment and the provisions of national constitutions as interpreted by the constitutional courts. The Constitutional Court of the Russian Federation considers that a dialogue with the ECHR is necessary and seeks to avoid complications as much as possible.[16]

Another meaningful question is what is the term "interstate body." The concept of "interstate body" is close to, but not identical to, the concept of "international organization" (according to Professor A. Ya. Kapustin, "an international organization is usually defined as a voluntary association of independent states, created on the basis of an international agreement that defines the goals and principles of the association, gives it independent, permanent bodies (organizational structure), intended for the development of international relations, defend collective interests and are able to express the will of the association, which is legally different from the will of its members, or, in other words, have and exercise independent rights and obligations that differ from the rights and obligations of States". This concept of an international organization refers primarily to international intergovernmental organizations and is used with some variations in educational literature),[17] since an international legal personality is a mandatory feature of the latter, and an interstate body, having competence in the field of international law enforcement practice, is not always endowed with the rights of an independent subject of international law.

At the same time, the bodies can be interstate or supranational, as well as relate to the bodies of international justice. In addition, modernity is distinguished by the presence of a large number of weakly institutionalized structures—BRICS, G20, or simply international forums and conferences. And the question arises as to what significance these structures have on Russian legislation and the legal system, from the point of view of lawmaking and law enforcement practice. In addition, there are global international bodies, such as the UN Security Council, which makes binding

[16] Boris Osminin, *National and International Courts: a Dialogue is Needed*, Journal of Russian Law, Sep. 2018, at 131.

[17] Kapustin A. Ya. International organizations in a globalizing world: Monograph.—M.: RUDN, 2010. pp. 302–303.

decisions for states. Here it is necessary to divide the word "solutions" into two parts: acts of bodies of international organizations and decisions of interstate and international courts. It should be emphasized that these decisions can be recognized as unenforceable only in the Russian legal order, at the international level and in other jurisdictions, such decisions remain valid.

Another category of acts of international organizations is the so-called soft law, which formally and legally does not have binding legal force. Of course, international advisory acts themselves do not pose a political and legal danger without their introduction into the legal system of the state. At the same time, the practice of individual international organizations and the emerging attitude to the recommendations adopted by their bodies can sometimes have a certain destructive impact on the legal system of a particular country or a number of states. Such a negative impact can be expressed in individual cases in violation of sovereign powers and inconsistency with the national interests of the country, serious contradictions with legislation, legal traditions, and law enforcement practice.[18] An example is the work of the Committee on Social, Economic and Cultural Rights. Acts adopted by the Committee are not legally binding; they are recommendations in nature. Not all states have formally adopted them. At the same time, all these acts of the Committee are striking in their similarity, and they are based on international law and best practices of states. Taken together, they strongly support trends toward greater uniformity and certainty in human rights obligations related to environmental protection. These trends are further confirmed by state practice, as reflected in the universal periodic review (UPR) process and reports on international environmental agreements.[19]

From the above, it follows that in the context of constitutional changes in the Russian Federation, "decisions of an interstate body" should be understood as law enforcement acts of judicial or quasi-judicial bodies of interstate organizations/associations, to which the Russian Federation has delegated powers to consider and resolve disputes, in accordance with the provisions of its international treaties.

The World Trade Organization (WTO) and the Eurasian Economic Union are among the international intergovernmental organizations that have the right to consider and resolve disputes involving the Russian Federation in the economic sphere.

The specifics of the WTO consist in the dialectical unity of its legal essence as the main international intergovernmental organization regulating the multilateral trading system and its understanding as an international forum with institutional characteristics, which "… provides for negotiations between its Members regarding their trade relations on issues settled by agreements that make up the annexes to this Agreement…can provide for negotiations between its Members on other issues, as well as create an organizational mechanism for the legal implementation of such negotiations." The above provision determines the features of the organizational

[18] A. A. Kashirkina & A. N. Morozov, *International Advisory Acts in the Russian Legal System: Limits and Possibilities of Use*, Journal of Russian Law, Feb. 2015, at 142.

[19] A. M. Solntsev, *Environmental human rights under the International Covenant on Economic, Social and Cultural Rights,* Issues of Economics and Law, 2016, at 43.

structure and system of governing bodies of the World Trade Organization.[20] It follows that the WTO is intergovernmental in nature and has not received any sovereign powers from the Russian Federation. The main link in the WTO's enforcement practice is the dispute resolution body (DSB). The function of the panels of arbitrators is to assist the DSB in fulfilling its responsibilities under this Agreement and the covered Agreements. Accordingly, the panel should make an objective assessment of the issue before it, including an objective assessment of the factual circumstances of the case and the applicability and compliance of the relevant covered Agreements, and draw such other conclusions as will assist the DSB in making recommendations or making a decision, as provided for in the covered Agreements. Arbitration panels should regularly consult with the parties to the dispute and provide them with adequate opportunities to reach a mutually satisfactory solution. If the panel or appellate body finds that a measure does not comply with the covered Agreement, it recommends that the member concerned bring the measure into compliance with the Agreement. In addition to its recommendations, the panel of arbitrators or the appellate body may suggest ways for the member concerned to implement the recommendations. Thus, the acts of the WTO dispute resolution body are aimed at changing national legislation in the event of its noncompliance with the international legal obligations of the state. Theoretically, one can imagine that the DSB made a decision "contrary to the Constitution of the Russian Federation, not subject to implement in the Russian Federation." In this case, the Constitutional Court of the Russian Federation could consider the question of the unenforceability of the DSB decision. However, in its Decision No. 17-P of 09.07.2012,[21] the Constitutional Court ruled that:

- An international treaty of the Russian Federation that has not entered into force—the Protocol on the Accession of the Russian Federation to the Marrakesh Agreement on the Establishment of the World Trade Organization in accordance with the Constitution of the Russian Federation in the order of adoption—at the stage of its signing and approval by the Government of the Russian Federation.
- An international treaty of the Russian Federation that has not entered into force—the Protocol on the Accession of the Russian Federation to the Marrakesh Agreement on the Establishment of the World Trade Organization is consistent with the Constitution of the Russian Federation in terms of the content of the norms to the extent that its provisions entail the extension to the Russian Federation of the Agreement attached to the Marrakesh Agreement and being an integral part of it on the Rules and Procedures Governing the Settlement of Disputes, which provides for the establishment and activity within the frame-

[20] Shulyatyev I.A, *To the issue on the international legal status of the World Trade Organization*, RUDN Journal of Law, 2009, at 130–136.

[21] Resolution of the Constitutional Court of the Russian Federation dated 09.07.2012 N 17-P "On the case of checking the constitutionality of an international treaty of the Russian Federation that has not entered into force - the Protocol on the Accession of the Russian Federation to the Marrakesh Agreement on the Establishment of the World Trade Organization." Access: SPS "Consultant Plus".

work of the World Trade Organization dispute resolution body, as well as in that part, to what extent they establish specific obligations of the Russian Federation with respect to the admission of persons to the provision of legal services on the territory of the Russian Federation.

In addition, Russian judicial practice and doctrine[22] have established uniformity in the approach that disputes in the WTO are exclusively interstate in nature and should be resolved at the international level.

Another interstate body—the Court of the Eurasian Economic Union (EAEU Court), which is a judicial body of the Eurasian Economic Union—is formed and operates on a permanent basis in accordance with the Treaty on the Eurasian Economic Union and the Statute of the Court of the Eurasian Economic Union. The purpose of the Court's activities is to ensure, in accordance with the provisions of this statute, the uniform application by the member states and the Union bodies of the treaty, international treaties within the Union, international treaties of the Union with a third party, and decisions of the Union bodies.

The Court considers disputes arising on the implementation of the treaty, international treaties within the Union, and (or) decisions of the Union's bodies:

1. At the request of a member state:

   On the compliance of an international treaty within the Union or its individual provisions with the treaty

   On compliance by another member state (other member states) Agreements, international agreements within the Union, and (or) decisions of the Union's bodies, as well as individual provisions of these international agreements and (or) decisions

   On compliance of the Commission's decision or its individual provisions with the treaty, international treaties within the Union, and (or) decisions of the Union's bodies

   On challenging an action (omission) Commission fees
2. At the request of an economic entity:

   On compliance of the Commission's decision or its individual provisions directly affecting the rights and legitimate interests of an economic entity in the field of business and other economic activities with the treaty and/or international treaties within the Union, if such a decision or its individual provisions resulted in a violation of the rights and legitimate interests granted by the treaty and/or international treaties within the Union an economic entity

   On challenging an action (omission) Commission, directly affecting the rights and legitimate interests of an economic entity in the field of entrepreneurial and other economic activities, if such an action (inaction) resulted in a violation of the rights and legitimate interests of the economic entity granted by the Agreement and/or international treaties within the Union

[22] A. S. Ispolinov, *Application of WTO Agreements by National Courts: Theory and Practice*, State and Law, 2014, at 75–85.

The competence of the EAEU Court is interstate in nature. It follows that the decisions and advisory opinions of the EAEU Court are aimed at forming an international legal order within the framework of an international integration association. Despite the fact that the Russian Federation has delegated the right to consider and resolve disputes to the EAEU Court, the acts of the EAEU Court are not aimed at changing national legislation. Thus, in the sphere of Eurasian integration, the acts of the EAEU Court cannot form new international legal obligations for the Russian Federation.

It should be recognized that the current version of Article 79 of the Constitution of the Russian Federation does not create direct prerequisites for Russia's failure to fulfill its international legal obligations in the economic sphere. Interstate economic disputes have their own procedures and international legal framework. Law enforcement acts of international economic organizations should be based on the norms of existing international economic treaties of the Russian Federation, thereby maintaining a balance between the necessary behavior of Russia in the world economy and the constitutional identity of the Russian state.

Thus, national legislation (on the example of the Russian Federation) reflects individual characteristics (singular) of an element of legal regulation that has a significant impact on the forms and content of international economic law. National legislation becomes an essential part of the mechanism for implementing international legal obligations in the economic sphere.

4 Justice in the EAEU: Regional Content of Universal Principles

Along with regional regulation and national legislation, it is necessary to recognize the law enforcement practice of mechanisms for resolving international economic disputes as a new direction for the transformation of international economic law. Universal peaceful means of dispute resolution are losing their relevance due to global political instability and ideological confrontation. This steady trend requires careful consideration of the practice of international regional courts, since it is necessary to take into account the peculiarities of the regional level of international economic law.

Established in 2014 in accordance with the Treaty on the Eurasian Economic Union (EAEU Treaty), the Court of the Eurasian Economic Union (EAEU Court) is currently at the stage of initial active accumulation of judicial material on the development of the Eurasian economic integration. The EAEU Court, as a body of an interstate organization, resolves issues on the basis of public international law and interprets and formulates legal positions on international legal obligations. It follows that the results of the EAEU Court's activities are primarily of interest to the member states of the Eurasian Economic Union (EAEU).

The number of reviews of individual issues related to the application of the provisions of the EAEU Treaty allows us to proceed cautiously with some generalizations of the practice of the EAEU Court. One of these issues is the creation by the EAEU member states of equal legal conditions for the functioning of the customs union and the single economic space. The current text of the EAEU Treaty establishes a variety of linguistic constructions related to the legal consolidation of discrimination/nondiscrimination: unjustified discrimination or hidden restriction in trade (Article 29), creation of discriminatory conditions (Article 76), random or unjustified discrimination (Annex 8), on the basis of the principles of transparency and nondiscrimination (Article 46), ensuring nondiscriminatory access (Article 70), ensuring nondiscriminatory conditions (Article 79), nondiscrimination (Article 92), etc. The international legal interpretation of such constructions is complicated by the interstate nature of obligations under the EAEU Treaty and the presence of various economic forms of integration: "common economic space," "common (single) market," and "customs union."

According to the existing ideas in the scientific literature, the forms of concretization of the legal provisions of the principle of nondiscrimination are "most favored nation treatment" and "national treatment." However, the principle of nondiscrimination itself has an independent meaning and should not be reduced to these two regimes, since its content is not "favorable conditions" and "equal legal status of individuals and legal entities" but general equal conditions, deviation from which threatens to reduce the benefits obtained as a result of agreements. The principle of nondiscrimination means that "you cannot get any worse, you can only get better."

Each specific provision of the EAEU Treaty provides an idea of the content of the principle of nondiscrimination in relation to a specific type of interstate economic legal relations. The principle of nondiscrimination in international trade is a variation of the principle of mutual benefit and hence a manifestation of the principle of equality directly in the regulation of international trade relations.[23]

According to Professor V. M. Shumilov: "The principle of economic nondiscrimination has the character of a generally binding legal norm. It stems from the principle of the sovereign equality of States and is confirmed in a number of important multilateral international instruments related to international economic relations: in the documents of UNCTAD, in the Declaration and Programme of Action for the Establishment of a New International Economic Order (1974), the Charter of

[23] Genovsky M. Legal principles of international trade // International trade law. Some questions of theory and practice. Collection of articles. Edited by V. Lisovsky. 1979. M., "International Relations". p.60. According to M. Genovsky: "… a typical form of discrimination is the unilateral granting of rights and privileges, which violates the principles of equality and reciprocity" (p. 65). "The requirement of reciprocity in international relations is often attributed to rights, obligations, concessions, advantages, advantages, benefits, etc., and the presence of reciprocity is judged, depending on the case, by such qualitative and quantitative characteristics as symmetry, equivalence, equivalence, identity, uniformity, equivalence, reciprocity, etc. With such a multiplicity of approaches to achieving reciprocity, it may seem that the principle of reciprocity does not have any meaning at all."—V. M. Shumilov. The Institute of the Most favored Nation in modern international law: monograph / Edited by E. N. Puzankova. M.: VAVT-MMA, 2021. p. 61.

Economic Rights and Obligations (1974), etc."[24] We believe that the principle of nondiscrimination should have a conventional form of consolidation, since the requirement of nondiscrimination in modern international economic relations does not in itself formulate the scope and content of nondiscrimination obligations. Indirect proof of the treaty nature of the principle of nondiscrimination can be seen in the provisions of the Draft Articles of the United Nations International Law Commission" On most favored nation clauses: "A most-favoured-nation clause is a contractual provision by virtue of which one State undertakes to grant most-favoured-nation treatment to another State in an agreed sphere of relations."[25]

The principle of nondiscrimination (as a special norm) is a form of implementation of the principle of sovereign equality of states (as a general norm), which is the basis of the legal system of the Eurasian Economic Union. According to Article 3 of the Treaty on the Eurasian Economic Union, "The Union carries out its activities within the competence granted to it by the Member States in accordance with this Treaty, on the basis of the following principles: respect for generally recognized principles of international law, including the principles of sovereign equality of the Member States and their territorial integrity; respect for the peculiarities of the political structure of the Member States; ensuring mutually beneficial cooperation, equality and consideration of national interests of the Parties; compliance with the principles of market economy and fair competition; functioning of the customs union without exceptions and restrictions after the end of transition periods." The principles of functioning of the Union set out in Article 3 of the treaty can be called international legal norms with political and ideological content, aimed at creating common conditions for cooperation between the EAEU member states and the activities of the EAEU bodies.

A concise description of the principle of the sovereign equality of states is laid down in the Declaration on Principles of International Law concerning Friendly Relations and Cooperation among States in Accordance with the Charter of the United Nations (Adopted on 24.10.1970 by Resolution 2625 (XXV) at the 1883rd plenary session of the UN General Assembly): "All States enjoy sovereign equality. They have the same rights and obligations and are equal members of the international community, regardless of economic, social, political or other differences."

The principle of sovereign equality of the member states of the EAEU correlates with the general provisions on the competence of the EAEU provided for in Article 5 of the EAEU Treaty: "The Union is vested with competence within the limits and volumes established by this Treaty and international treaties within the Union."

Thus, the EAEU's bodies are responsible for creating such legal conditions that create mechanisms for implementing the principles of functioning of the EAEU provided for in Article 3 of the EAEU Treaty.

---

[24] Shumilov V. M. Institute of the Most favored nation in modern international law: monograph / Edited by E. N. Puzankova. M.: VAVT-MMA, 2021. p. 68.

[25] Report of the Commission to the General Assembly on the work of its thirtieth session, 1978 Yearbook of the International Law Commission, A/CN.4/SER.A/1978/Add.l (Part 2).

The legal status of the Court of the Eurasian Economic Union is disclosed in Appendix No. 2 to the EAEU Treaty. The purpose of the Court's activities is to ensure, in accordance with the provisions of this statute, the uniform application by the member states and the Union bodies of the treaty, international treaties within the Union, international treaties of the Union with a third party, and decisions of the Union bodies. The court in the administration of justice applies (1) generally recognized principles and norms of international law; (2) the treaty, international treaties within the Union, and other international treaties to which the state parties to the dispute are parties; (3) decisions and orders of the Union's bodies; and (4) international custom as evidence of universal practice recognized as a legal norm.

Taking into account that "the absence of a unified system of international justice creates a high degree of autonomy in the activities of specific international judicial bodies, including in matters of interpretation of international treaties,"[26] the normative content of the principle of nondiscrimination, as a normative requirement for creating common conditions for cooperation between member states in the law of the EAEU, should be derived from the provisions of the sources of the EAEU law itself. General ideas about the content of this principle, borrowed from other international legal regimes, primarily the WTO[27] or UNCTAD,[28] should be taken into account only as a last resort, when applying the provisions of the EAEU law rules will make a reasonable conclusion about the lack of necessary regulation. An important international legal element that distinguishes the principle of nondiscrimination in the law of the EAEU from universal international legal regimes is the international legal personality of the EAEU as an "international organization of regional economic integration" (Article 1, paragraph 2, of the Treaty on the EAEU). It follows from this that the principle of nondiscrimination operates in international economic law as a rule of the most general order and cannot directly settle a disputed legal relationship by itself without using specific obligations of states

[26] A. Ya. Kapustin, *International Judicial Interpretation of an International Treaty: Modern Trends*, Journal of Russian Law, Jul. 2022, at 106.

[27] In the preamble of the General Agreement on Tariffs and Trade of 1947, the contracting parties expressed their intention to contribute to improving living standards, ensuring full employment and a significant and continuous increase in real income and effective demand, ensuring the full use of world resources, and expanding production and exchange of goods by concluding mutual and mutually beneficial agreements aimed at significantly reducing tariffs and other barriers to trade and the elimination of discriminatory treatment in international trade. The specification of the GATT provision "elimination of discriminatory treatment in international trade" is carried out through the consolidation of the "general regime of the most favored nation" (Article I) and the "national regime of internal taxation and regulation" (Article III).

[28] "The first session of UNCTAD was convened by decision of the UN General Assembly after lengthy preparations and was held in Geneva on March 23—April 16, 1964. In the final act of the session, basically two groups of principles were formulated—general and special, which define trade policies that promote development. In addition, principles on transit trade of landlocked countries have been developed and adopted. All the principles recommended by the first session of UNCTAD, which guide States in their foreign economic relations, were also summarized." International trade law. Some questions of theory and practice. Collection of articles. Edited by V. Lisovsky. 1979. M., "International Relations." p. 51.

expressed in certain sources of international law. Consequently, the principle of nondiscrimination in the EAEU is, firstly, a legal principle; secondly, it has a contractual basis; and thirdly, it contains specific rights and obligations.

The Court of the Eurasian Economic Union in its acts has repeatedly decided on the content of the principle of nondiscrimination in the law of the EAEU: Advisory Opinion of 30.10.2017 on clarification of the provisions of paragraphs 1 and 3 of Article 29 of the Treaty on the Eurasian Economic Union of May 29, 2014,[29] Advisory Opinion of 07.12.2017 on clarification of paragraph 2 of Article 97 of the treaty regarding the employment of professional athletes who are citizens of the Union member states and the possibility of establishing quantitative restrictions in national legislation on professional athletes engaged in employment in the member states of the Union,[30] Advisory Opinion of 11.01.2021 on clarification of the provisions of paragraphs 11 and 31 of the Protocol on the Procedure for Regulating Procurement (Annex No. 25 to the Treaty on the Eurasian Economic Union of May 29, 2014),[31] and Advisory Opinion of 23.11.2021 on clarification of Article 92 of the Treaty on the Eurasian Economic Union.[32] It follows that the EAEU Court is looking for its legal position on the normative content and forms of implementation of the principle of nondiscrimination between the EAEU member states. Nondiscrimination (equal conditions) acts as an interstate legal obligation and an interstate legal relationship. Individuals and businesses cannot influence the content and nature of this obligation, nor can they use Court procedures to assess states' compliance with nondiscrimination norms. In this approach, the EAEU Court resembles in its functional characteristics the dispute resolution body of the World Trade Organization. Decisions of the EAEU Court in this case become the basis for adjusting the national legislation of the EAEU member states.

In its Advisory Opinion of 30.10.2017 on clarifying the provisions of paragraphs 1 and 3 of Article 29 of the Treaty on the Eurasian Economic Union of May 29, 2014, the Grand Panel of the Court draws attention to the fact that in order to ensure the fulfillment of the conditions for the free movement of goods and the functioning of the internal market, the member states of the Union must create favorable conditions for the performance of its functions by the Union and refrain from measures that could jeopardize the achievement of the Union's objectives, while avoiding as much as possible the introduction of unilateral restrictions in mutual trade, based on the principles of transparency, adequacy, proportionality, and objective conditionality arising from the content of paragraph 2 of Article 3 of the treaty. The Eurasian Economic Commission monitors the restrictions applied by the member states of

[29] Case card R-3/17, Court of the Eurasian Economic Union (Feb. 8, 2023), https://courteurasian.org/court_cases/eaeu/P-3.17/.

[30] Case card R-3/18, Court of the Eurasian Economic Union (Feb. 8, 2023), https://courteurasian.org/court_cases/eaeu/P-3.18/.

[31] Case card R-3/20, Court of the Eurasian Economic Union (Feb. 8, 2023), https://courteurasian.org/court_cases/eaeu/P-3.20/.

[32] Case card R-2/21, Court of the Eurasian Economic Union (Feb. 8, 2023), https://courteurasian.org/court_cases/eaeu/P-2.21/.

the Union in mutual trade in goods. In case of disputes, the parties have the right to apply to the Court of the Eurasian Economic Union. Thus, the Grand Collegium stated that the mechanism for violating the principle of nondiscrimination may consist in unilateral acts of states. A further development of this position could be to assess the legal forms that these “unilateral restrictions on trade” take.

In Advisory Opinion of 07.12.2017 on clarification of paragraph 2 of Article 97 of the treaty regarding the employment of professional athletes who are citizens of the Union member states and the possibility of establishing quantitative restrictions in national legislation on professional athletes when performing their work in the Union member states, the Grand Panel of the Court concluded that it is not allowed to establish in the legislation of the member states and local acts of physical culture and sports organizations, as well as the application of existing quantitative restrictions to professional athletes who are citizens of the member states of the Union, in relation to their employment, occupation, and territory of stay. This position is interesting because in order to assess the legality of establishing discriminatory quantitative restrictions, the EAEU Court considers not only the legislation of the member states but also local acts of organizations.

In Advisory Opinion of 11.01.2021 on clarification of the provisions of paragraphs 11 and 31 of the Protocol on the Procedure for Regulating Procurement (Annex No. 25 to the Treaty on the Eurasian Economic Union of May 29, 2014), the Grand Board considered that the proportionality test includes two components: whether the proposed measure will actually contribute to solving one of the tasks set in a particular situation: the limits proportionality of the specified measure to achieve the stated goal. The second component of the proportionality test involves confirming that there are no less restrictive ways to achieve the same goal. In this legal position of the EAEU Court, attention should be paid to the approach to the choice by the EAEU member states of ways of national regulation of relations, which may be unbalanced by the principle of nondiscrimination. “Less restrictive ways to achieve the same goal” presuppose such an implementation of the right of the EAEU member states that allows them to deviate from their obligations under the EAEU Treaty but only within specified borders that ensure equal conditions.

In Advisory Opinion of 23.11.2021 on clarification of Article 92 of the Treaty on the Eurasian Economic Union, the Grand Collegium came to the following conclusions. The Grand Panel of the Court concludes that the Union should create equal conditions for fair competition and mutual trade, based on the principle of nondiscrimination, when regulating economic relations stipulated by the treaty. Thus, the possibility of applying restrictive measures by member states is conditioned on compliance with the principle of nondiscrimination. The adoption by the member states of measures aimed at creating more favorable conditions for goods originating from third countries compared to those of the member states is not consistent with the basic principles of functioning and objectives of the Union. The principle of nondiscrimination, enshrined in subparagraph 4 of paragraph 2 of Article 92 of the treaty, provides for the existence of obligations of the member states of the Union to ensure the most-favored-nation treatment for industrial goods of both member states and third countries. In this Advisory Opinion, the EAEU Court, in fact, identified the principle of nondiscrimination as a principle of law and as a principle of national policy. The reduction of the principle of nondiscrimination to the most-favored-nation regime can be explained by the abstract nature of the issue under consideration. It can be assumed that the interpretation of Article 92 of the EAEU Treaty would be different if the EAEU Court considered an interstate dispute and did not clarify the provisions of the EAEU Treaty.

Finally, the principle of nondiscrimination is the most important general principle of law and an important layer of legal awareness of the law enforcer. It contains both an ideological component that reflects the objective patterns of development of interstate relations at this historical stage and a normative core that is important for the legal regulation of these relations. In the Russian international legal literature, there is already a point of view that the principle of nondiscrimination deserves to be qualified as a general principle of Union law.[33] While agreeing with this characteristic for the purposes of choosing sources of law in dispute resolution, let us add that the principle of nondiscrimination has a contractual nature in its content, so first of all, the law enforcement focus should be on the provisions and articles of the treaty on the EAEU as the core of the legal system of the EAEU.[34] It is through this principle that the national legislation of the EAEU member states is evaluated for compliance with their obligations, the possibility of its application by national courts, as well as balancing international legal obligations in mutual trade and trade of the EAEU with third states and associations.

An important legal element in achieving a clear legal position of the EAEU Court on the principle of nondiscrimination, which will allow the development and development of the EAEU law, is the procedure for reviewing the case itself: substantive proceedings or issuing an advisory opinion. The procedure for resolving an interstate dispute, rather than explaining the provisions of the EAEU Treaty, is crucial for the authority of interpretation and allows establishing specific relationships between the provisions of the EAEU law and the national legislation of the EAEU member state in the field of free movement of goods, services, capital, and labor.

Thus, regional international courts (as can be seen from the example of the EAEU court) form their views on the content of universal principles of international economic law. This indicates the existence of its own legal content of the nondiscrimination regime, due to the composition of the subjects of the regional association and the specific of international legal obligations in the economic sphere.

---

[33] Entin K. V, *General principles of the law of integration associations as a secret weapon of the Court of the EU and the Court of the EAEU*, International Justice, 2022, at.

[34] Kapustin A. Ya, *The law of Eurasian economic integration in the focus of international law*, State and Law, 2017, at 79–88.

5 Conclusions

The transformation of modern international law can be considered from the point of view of a dialectical principle—general, special, and singular—where the general is the universal level of regulation, the special is the regional level of regulation, and the singular is national legislation.

Such a scientific paradigm makes it possible to form a legitimate and effective system of international legal regulation of international economic relations, which reflects a fair consideration of the interests and needs of most states of the international community.

Problems on one of these levels can be balanced by two other levels. Such a balance will ensure the stability and predictability of the development of international economic law in the field of regulation, institutions, and dispute resolution and will allow for the formation of a truly fair and democratic new international economic legal order.

Chapter 7
The Arbitrability of International Commercial Disputes Involving Economic Sanctions

Shanshan Ye

Abstract As intervention in private legal relations, economic sanctions have led to a large number of international commercial disputes. Economic sanctions also pose a challenge to the arbitrability of such disputes, resulting in significant divergence of views among states as to the arbitrability of international commercial disputes involving economic sanctions. The prevailing view is that a dispute will not become inarbitrable because it involves the application of economic sanctions norms. A few countries, such as Italy, take the opposite view, arguing that economic sanctions will result in the parties' inability to freely dispose of their contractual rights, thereby rendering such disputes inarbitrable. The divergence stems from different criteria for arbitrability adopted by states and the arbitrability of disputes involving mandatory rules under such criteria. Given that economic sanction norms fall within the category of mandatory rules, the divergence also extends to the arbitrability of international commercial disputes involving economic sanctions. In light of the provisions concerning arbitrability and the notion of encouraging and supporting arbitration of China, it is recommended to be prudent to deny the arbitrability of disputes due to the involvement of economic sanctions.

Keywords Economic sanctions · International commercial arbitration · Arbitrability · Mandatory rules · Public policy

---

This article was previously published in Law Science—Selected Papers Volume 3, Issue 1 (2024).

S. Ye (✉)
Law School of Guangdong University of Finance and Economics, Guangzhou, China

T. Du, X. Fei (eds.), *The BRICS Legal Cooperation and Perspectives*,
https://doi.org/10.1007/978-981-95-4356-4_7

1 Introduction

In international law, sanctions can be divided into military and nonmilitary sanction, depending on whether military measures are taken.[1] As a non-forceful sanction, economic sanction is "a discriminatory restriction, including an outright prohibition, of economic interaction with an international actor by one or more international actors to achieve certain foreign policy objectives."[2] After World War II, national rethink on war led to the establishment of the United Nations and the principle of prohibition on the use of force.[3] Since then, forceful sanctions have been prohibited by international law, and some states have turned to economic sanctions as a tool for the realization of their foreign policy. With the rapid development of economic globalization, the interdependence and close interconnectedness of the modern global economy have resulted in the fact that economic sanctions are no less effective than forceful sanctions.[4] Since 1966, the United Nations Security Council (hereinafter referred to as "UNSC") has adopted 31 economic sanctions regimes, 15 of which are still in force.[5] In addition, Western countries, led by the United States (hereinafter referred to as "USA"), have been imposing unilateral economic sanctions more frequently. Since the outbreak of the Russian-Ukraine conflict, the USA, the European Union (hereinafter referred to as "EU"), and other states and international organizations have imposed historically the harshest economic sanctions against Russia. Relevant statistics have shown that Russia has become the country with the largest number of subjects included in the USA's list of Specially Designated Nationals.[6] To date, the EU has adopted 17 packages of economic sanctions against

---

[1] *See* DU TAO (杜涛), Guoji Jingji Zhicai Falv Wenti Yanjiu (国际经济制裁法律问题研究) [INTERNATIONAL LAW OF ECONOMIC SANCTIONS] 24-26 (1st. ed., 2023).

[2] Zhou Fangyin (周方银), *Guoji Guanxi zhong de jingji zhicai (*国际关系中的经济制裁*) [Economic Sanctions in International Relations]*, XIANDAI GUOJI GUANXI (现代国际关系) [CONTEMPORARY INTERNATIONAL RELATIONS], no. 10, 1997, at 40; Qiu Zhi (邱芝), *Lun Lengzhan hou Guoji Guanxi zhong de jingji zhicai (*论冷战后国际关系中的经济制裁*) [On Economic Sanctions in Post-Cold War International Relations],* SHEHUI KEXUE (社会科学) [JOURNAL OF SOCIAL SCIENCES], no. 10, 1999, at 24.

[3] The principle of prohibition on the use of force is stipulated in Article 2(1)(4) of the *Charter of the United Nations*, which stipulates that "All Members shall refrain in their international relations from the threat or use of force against the territorial integrity or political independence of any state, or in any other manner inconsistent with the Purposes of the United Nations."

[4] *See* DU, *supra* note 1, at 1.

[5] *See Sanctions*, United Nations Security Council (Jul. 13, 2023, 11:40 AM), https://www.un.org/securitycouncil/sanctions/information.

[6] *See* Xiong Qiyue (熊启跃) & Zhao Xueqing (赵雪情), *Meiou dui Eluosi Jingji Zhicai de Luoji, Yingxiang ji Qishi (*美欧对俄罗斯经济制裁的逻辑、影响及启示*) [The Logic, Impact, and Implications of U.S. and EU Economic Sanctions against Russia]*, ELUOSI YANJIU (俄罗斯研究) [RUSSIAN STUDIES], no. 6, 2022, at 133.

Russia.[7] Arguably, economic sanctions have become the most frequently used method of non-forceful sanctions in international law.[8]

Interference in private legal relations is an important method in which economic sanctions can be implemented.[9] In this sense, economic sanctions constitute intervention in private legal relations.[10] Therefore, although originating from public law, economic sanctions affect private legal relations significantly.[11] Specifically, economic sanctions usually prohibit relevant subjects from concluding or performing contracts with the sanctioned. After relevant subjects stop performing contractual obligations due to economic sanctions, the counterparty of the contract will often claim default and seek legal remedies.[12] As a result, numbers of international commercial disputes involving the application of economic sanctions norms (hereinafter referred to as "international commercial disputes involving economic sanctions") have arisen.

Given that international commercial arbitration is the most popular dispute resolution mechanism among international commercial entities,[13] most international commercial disputes involving economic sanctions are resolved through international commercial arbitration. In such cases, the arbitrability of disputes is the first issue that the arbitral tribunal needs to consider. In practice, one party often argues that such disputes are inarbitrable due to the application of economic sanctions norms. As states adopt different criteria for arbitrability, the application of the laws of different states may cause different determinations on the issue by arbitral tribunals or courts.

In international commercial arbitration, the arbitrability of disputes is a prerequisite for a legally effective arbitration agreement, for an arbitral tribunal with jurisdiction, and for enforcement of an arbitral award.[14] In an era of intensifying

[7] *See EU Agrees 17th Package of Sanctions Against Russia*, European Commission (Jun. 25, 2025, 1:30PM),https://finance.ec.europa.eu/news/eu-adopts-17th-package-sanctions-against-russia-2025-05-20_en.

[8] *See* DU, *supra* note 1, at 26.

[9] *See* TAMÁS SZABADOS, ECONOMIC SANCTIONS IN EU PRIVATE INTERNATIONAL LAW 34 (1st. ed., 2019); *See* Mercédeh Azeredo da Silveira, *Economic Sanctions and Contractual Disputes between Private Operators*, *in* RESEARCH HANDBOOK ON UN SANCTIONS AND INTERNATIONAL LAW 330, 332 (Larissa van den Herik ed., 2017).

[10] *See* SZABADOS, *supra* note 10, at 32.

[11] *Id.*, at 33.

[12] *See* Mercédeh Azeredo da Silveira, *Economic Sanctions, Force Majeure and Hardship*, *in* HARDSHIP AND FORCE MAJEURE IN INTERNATIONAL COMMERCIAL CONTRACTS: DEALING WITH UNFORESEEN EVENTS IN A CHANGING WORLD 161, 162 (Fabio Bortolotti & Dorothy Ufot eds., 2018); *See* Silveira, *supra* note 10, at 333.

[13] According to the 2021 International Arbitration Survey jointly released by Queen Mary University of London and White & Case, 90% of respondents chose international arbitration to resolve transnational disputes.

[14] *See* Guoji Shangshi Zhongcai Zhuanti Yanjiu (国际商事仲裁专题研究) [A MONOGRAPHIC STUDY ON INTERNATIONAL COMMERCIAL ARBITRATION LAW] 4 (Liu Xiaohong (刘晓红) ed., 2009); *See* OU MINGSHENG (欧明生), Minshangshi Jiufen Kezhongcaixing Wenti

economic sanctions, studying the arbitrability of international commercial disputes involving economic sanctions is of great practical value. Firstly, Chinese enterprises in international commercial transactions often face enormous legal risks brought about by economic sanctions. When choosing the seat of arbitration, the applicable law of the arbitration agreement, and the place where the recognition and enforcement of the arbitral award are sought, Chinese enterprises need to consider the legislation and judicial practice of different states concerning the arbitrability of international commercial disputes involving economic sanctions. Secondly, in international commercial arbitrations involving economic sanctions, arbitrators shall determine their jurisdiction, including the arbitrability of such disputes. Thirdly, when conducting judicial review on international commercial arbitrations involving economic sanctions, including the confirmation of the validity of arbitration agreements, the revocation of arbitral awards, and the recognition and enforcement of foreign arbitral awards, Chinese courts may also be required to determine the arbitrability of such disputes.

However, this issue has not yet attracted sufficient attention from scholars in China. Currently, only one paper briefly discussed the arbitrability of international commercial disputes involving economic sanctions when elaborating on the impact of economic sanctions on international commercial arbitration.[15] In addition, some scholars have also paid attention to the judicial application of blocking statutes[16]

Yanjiu (民商事纠纷可仲裁性问题研究) [RESEARCH ON ARBITRABILITY OF THE CIVIL AND COMMERCIAL DISPUTE] 35 (1st. ed., 2013); *See* Ma Decai (马德才), *Lun Guoji Shangshi Zhongcai zhong Zhengyi Shixiang de Kezhongcaixing Wenti (论国际商事仲裁中争议事项的可仲裁性问题) [On the Arbitrability of Disputes in International Commercial Arbitration]*, JIANGXI CAIJING DAXUE XUEBAO (江西财经大学学报) [JOURNAL OF JIANGXI UNIVERSITY OF FINANCE AND ECONOMICS], no. 3, 2000, at 57–58; *See* Yu Xifu (于喜富), *Lun Zhengyi Kezhongcaixing Sifa Shencha zhi Qidong Chengxu (论争议可仲裁性司法审查之启动程序) [On the Starting Procedure of Judicial Review on the Arbitrability of Disputes]*, FAXUE PINGLUN (法学评论) [LAW REVIEW], no. 3, 2016, at 50; *See* Chen Zhidong (陈治东), *Lun Woguo Shewai Zhongcai de Kezhongcaixing Wenti (论我国涉外仲裁的可仲裁性问题) [On the Arbitrability of Foreign-related Arbitration in China]*, FAXUE (法学) [LAW SCIENCE], no. 6, 1997, at 60; *See* Zhou Yanbo (周艳波) & Pang Yushi (庞玉石), *Lun Waizi Zhengyi Shixiang de Bukezhongcaixing yu Woguo Zhongcai Guanxiaquan Zhidu de Wanshan—yi Wahaha yu Daneng GongsiQianggouAnweiLizheng(论外资争议事项的不可仲裁性与我国仲裁管辖权制度的完善—以娃哈哈与达能公司抢购案为例证) [Non-arbitration of the Foreign Capital Dispute Items and the Perfection of China's Arbitration Jurisdiction System—Taking Wahaha's Purchased by Danone Case as an Example]*, SHANGYE YANJIU (商业研究) [COMMERCIAL RESEARCH], no. 7, 2013, at 207.

[15] *See* Du Tao (杜涛) & Ye Ziwen (叶子雯), *Lun Jingji Zhicai dui Guoji Shangshi Zhongcai de Yingxiang (论经济制裁对国际商事仲裁的影响) [The Impact of Economic Sanctions on International Commercial Arbitration]*, WUDA GUOJIFA PINGLUN (武大国际法评论) [WUHAN UNIVERSITY INTERNATIONAL LAW REVIEW], no. 3, 2023, at 69-84.

[16] *See* Huo Zhengxin (霍政欣) & Chen Ruida (陈锐达), *Fan Waiguo Zhicai de Sifa Weidu Zhankai (反外国制裁的司法维度展开) [A Study on the System of Anti-foreign Sanctions: From the Judicial Perspective]*, SHIJIE SHEHUI KEXUE (世界社会科学) [SOCIAL SCIENCES INTERNATIONAL], no. 2, 2023, at 165–193; *See* Qian Zhenqiu (钱振球), *Lun Zuduanfa de Sifa Shiyong (论阻断法的司法适用) [On the Judicial Application of Blocking Statutes]*, ZHONGGUO

and the impact of economic sanctions on international investment arbitration.[17] In view of this, this paper will first clarify the connotation and criteria for arbitrability and then present the divergence of views regarding the arbitrability of international commercial disputes involving economic sanctions based on existing arbitral and judicial practice. After that, this paper will conduct a jurisprudential analysis on the reasons for the divergence and make a rational determination on the arbitrability of international commercial disputes involving economic sanctions in accordance with current legislation and judicial practice of China.

2 The Connotation and Criteria for Arbitrability

Arbitrability involves the question of whether a dispute may be resolved by arbitration.[18] A dispute is arbitrable if it can be settled through arbitration; conversely, it is inarbitrable if it can only be settled by litigation.[19] Arbitrability is essentially a matter of domestic law and is generally left to each state to determine. Consequently, the *UNCITRAL Model Law on International Commercial Arbitration* (hereinafter referred to as "*Model Law*") only lists the non-arbitrability as a ground for setting

---

YINGYONG FAXUE (中国应用法学) [CHINA JOURNAL OF APPLIED JURISPRUDENCE], no. 2, 2022, at 197–208; *See* Shen Wei (沈伟) & Shao Hui (邵辉), *Lun Zuduan Susong de Falv Fengxian jiqi Sifa Kongzhi (论阻断诉讼的法律风险及其司法控制) [On the Legal Risks of Blocking Litigation and Its Judicial Control]*, ZHONGGUO YINGYONG FAXUE (中国应用法学) [CHINA JOURNAL OF APPLIED JURISPRUDENCE], no. 2, 2022, at 168–182; *See* Xiao Kai (肖凯) & Xu Jiayun (徐佳云), *Lun Woguo Fan Waiguo Zhicai de Sifa Jiuji Jizhi zhi Wanshan (论我国反外国制裁司法救济机制之完善) [On the Perfection of China's Judicial Remedy Mechanism for Anti-Foreign Sanctions]*, WUDA GUOJIFA PINGLUN (武大国际法评论) [WUHAN UNIVERSITY INTERNATIONAL LAW REVIEW], no. 3, 2023, at 85–102; *See* Liu Guiqiang (刘桂强), *Woguo Fanzhicai Zhuichang Susong Zhidu Mianlin de Tiaozhan yu Yingdui (我国反制裁追偿诉讼制度面临的挑战与应对) [Challenges and Responses to China's Anti-sanctions Clawback Mechanism]*, HUANQIU FALV PINGLUN (环球法律评论) [GLOBAL LAW REVIEW], no. 3, 2023, at 211–224.

[17] *See* Fan Xiaoyu (范晓宇) & Qi Tong (漆彤), *Jingji Zhicai dui Guoji Touzi Zhongcai de Yingxiang—jiyu ISDS Shijian de Fenxi (经济制裁对国际投资仲裁的影响—基于ISDS实践的分析) [The Impact of Economic Sanctions on Investor-State Arbitration: Based on Analysis of the ISDS Practice]*, GUOJIFA YANJIU (国际法研究) [CHINESE REVIEW OF INTERNATIONAL LAW], no. 5, 2022, at 69–86; *See* Zhao Deming (赵德铭) et al., *Guoji Touzi Zhongcai zhong de Jingji Zhicai Wenti Yanjiu (国际投资仲裁中的经济制裁问题研究) [Economic Sanctions in International Investment Arbitration]*, GUOJI JINGJIFA XUEKAN (国际经济法学刊) [JOURNAL OF INTERNATIONAL ECONOMIC LAW], no. 2, 2023, at 70–86.

[18] *See* Loukas A. Mistelis, *Part I Fundamental Observations and Applicable Law, Chapter 1 - Arbitrability -International and Comparative Perspectives*, in ARBITRABILITY: INTERNATIONAL AND COMPARATIVE PERSPECTIVES 1, 3–4 (Loukas A. Mistelis & Stavros L. Brekoulakis eds., 2009); *See* NIGEL BLACKABY et al., REDFERN AND HUNTER ON INTERNATIONAL ARBITRATION 80 (6th. ed., 2015).

[19] *See* Liu, *supra* note 15, at 3.

aside[20] and refusing to recognize or enforce[21] arbitral awards but does not clarify what types of disputes are arbitrable.[22] Instead, Article 1(5) of the *Model Law* provides that it shall not affect any other law of the state concerning the arbitrability of certain disputes.

Because "states' limitations on party autonomy extend to arbitration with contractual nature" and "states are inherently skeptical and wary of arbitration with a private character,"[23] states make explicit stipulations on arbitrability of disputes based on their political, social, and economic policies, leaving specific types of disputes to be subject to the exclusive jurisdiction of domestic courts.[24] States have thus drawn a dividing line between the scope of arbitration and the exclusive jurisdiction of courts and "determines the point at which the exercise of contractual freedom ends and the public mission of adjudication begins."[25]

Generally speaking, the criteria for arbitrability mainly include the criteria of "disposability," "commercial dispute," "economic interest," and "public order."[26] Firstly, the criterion of "disposability" may also be referred to as the criterion of "reconcilability" or "autonomy of rights."[27] The criterion of "disposability," which derives from the principles of the autonomy of private law and contractual freedom, holds that the parties are entitled to choose a dispute resolution method, including arbitration, for matters that are freely disposable and amenable to settlement by them. In other words, under the criterion of "disposability," matters that the parties can freely dispose of and reach a settlement are arbitrable. Several states have

---

[20] Article 34(2)(b)(i) of the *UNCITRAL Model Law on International Commercial Arbitration*stipulates that "An arbitral award may be set aside by the court specified in article 6only if: …(b) the court finds that: (i) the subject-matter of the dispute is not capable of settlement by arbitration under the law of this State…"

[21] Article 36(1)(b)(i) of the *UNCITRAL Model Law on International Commercial Arbitration* stipulates that "Recognition or enforcement of an arbitral award, irrespective of the country in which it was made, may be refused only: …if the court finds that: (i) the subject-matter of the dispute is not capable of settlement by arbitration under the law of this State…"

[22] *See* Mistelis, *supra* note 19, at 11.

[23] *Id.*, at 18.

[24] *See* NIGEL BLACKABY et al., *supra* note 19, at 111; *See* Guoji Sifa (国际私法) [PRIVATE INTERNATIONAL LAW] 481 (Du Tao (杜涛) & Chen Li (陈力) eds., 2008).

[25] Thomas E. Carbonneau & Francois Janson, *Cartesian Logic and Frontier Politics: French and American Concepts of Arbitrability*, 2 TUL. J. INT'l & COMP. L. 193, 194 (1994).

[26] *See* Liu, *supra* note 15, at 7–8; *See* Yu, *supra* note 15, at 49–50; *See* Zhao Xueqing (赵学清) & Wang Junjie (王军杰), *Guoji Shangshi Zhongcai Kezhongcaixing Wenti de Lishi Yanjin ji Fazhan Qushi (国际商事仲裁可仲裁性问题的历史演进及发展趋势) [The Historical Evolution and Development Trend of Arbitrability Issue in International Commercial Arbitration]*, GUOJI JINGJIFA XUEKAN (国际经济法学刊) [JOURNAL OF INTERNATIONAL ECONOMIC LAW], no. 4, 2008, at 323–326.

[27] *See* Chen Zhidong (陈治东) & Shen Wei (沈伟), *Guoji Shangshi Zhongcai Chengren yu Zhixing de Guojihua Qushi (国际商事仲裁裁决承认与执行的国际化趋势) [The Internationalization Trend of Recognition and Enforcement of International Commercial Arbitral Awards]*, ZHONGGUO FAXUE (中国法学) [CHINA LEGAL SCIENCE], no. 2, 1998, at 114.

adopted the criterion of "disposability" for the determination of arbitrability.[28] For example, Article 2059 of the 1804 *Civil Code* of France provides that "All persons may agree to arbitration in relation to rights which they are free to dispose of."[29] Additionally, the existing laws of Sweden,[30] Spain,[31] the Netherlands,[32] Italy,[33] Japan,[34] and other countries have also explicitly applied the criterion of "disposability" when stipulating the arbitrability of disputes.

Secondly, the criterion of "commercial dispute" is based on whether the dispute is commercial, and it excludes noncommercial disputes from the scope of arbitration. For example, although Section 2 of the *Federal Arbitration Act* of the USA[35] does not directly provide for the arbitrability of disputes, it affirms the legal effect of the agreement to submit disputes arising out of commercial contracts to arbitration, thus indirectly affirming the arbitrability of commercial disputes.

Thirdly, the criterion of "economic interest" grants arbitrability to any dispute involving an economic interest. For instance, Article 177(1) of the 1987 *Swiss Federal Act of Private International Law* provides that "Any dispute involving an economic interest may be the subject matter of an arbitration."

Fourthly, unlike the previous criteria, which directly define arbitrable disputes, the criterion of "public order" reversely excludes specific disputes relating to public

---

[28] *See id.*, at 114; *See* Zhao & Wang, *supra* note 27, at 323.

[29] JEAN ROUCHE et al., FRENCH ARBITRATION LAW AND PRACTICE: A DYNAMIC CIVIL LAW APPROACH TO INTERNATIONAL ARBITRATION 291 (2rd. ed., 2009).

[30] Article 1(1) of the 1929 *Swedish Arbitration Act* stipulates that "Disputes concerning matters in respect of which the parties may reach a settlement may, by agreement, be referred to one or several arbitrators for resolution. Such an agreement may relate to future disputes pertaining to a legal relationship specified in the agreement. The dispute may concern the existence of a particular fact."

[31] Article 2(1) of the 2003 *Arbitration Act* of Spain stipulates that "All disputes relating to matters within the free disposition of the parties according to law are capable of arbitration."

[32] Article 1020(3) of the 1986 *Dutch Code of Civil Procedure* stipulates that "The arbitration agreement shall not serve to determine legal consequences that may not be freely determined by the parties."

[33] Article 806(1) of the 2015*Italian Code of Civil Procedure* stipulates that "The parties may refer to arbitrators the settlement of disputes arisen between them when their subject matter does not concern rights which may not be disposed of, unless arbitration is expressly prohibited by law." *See* MASSIMO BENEDETTELLI, INTERNATIONAL ARBITRATION IN ITALY 501 (1st. ed., 2020).

[34] Article 13(1) of the 2003*Arbitration Law* of Japan stipulates that "Except as otherwise provided for in laws and regulations, an Arbitration Agreement shall be effective only when the subject thereof is a civil dispute (excluding disputes of divorce or dissolution of adoptive relation) which can be settled between the parties." *See* ICCA INTERNATIONAL HANDBOOK ON COMMERCIAL ARBITRATION 4 (Lise Bosman ed., 2019).

[35] Section 2 of the *Federal Arbitration Act* of the United States stipulates that "A written provision in any maritime transaction or a contract evidencing a transaction involving commerce to settle by arbitration a controversy thereafter arising out of such contract or transaction, or the refusal to perform the whole or any part thereof, or an agreement in writing to submit to arbitration an existing controversy arising out of such a contract, transaction, or refusal, shall be valid, irrevocable, and enforceable, save upon such grounds as exist at law or in equity for the revocation of any contract."

order from the scope of arbitration.[36] For example, Article 2060(1) of the 1804*Civil Code* of France states that "It is not permissible to submit to arbitration matters of civil status and capacity of individuals, or relating to divorce or judicial separation of spouses or disputes concerning public communities and public establishments and more generally all matters which concern public policy."[37] Similarly, Article 11(1) of the1994 *International Arbitration Act* of Singapore[38] considers a breach of public policy as an exception to the arbitrability of disputes. Article 1649 of the 2014 *National Civil and Commercial Code* of Argentina[39] also restricts arbitrable disputes to those that do not impact public order.

In essence, the criteria for arbitrability reflect the degree of confidence that a state places in arbitration as a dispute resolution mechanism.[40] Among the aforementioned criteria, the criteria of "disposability," "commercial dispute," and "economic interest" are progressively more lenient in determining arbitrability. Specifically, the criterion of "disposability" limits arbitrable disputes to matters that the parties are free to dispose of and reach a settlement, while the criterion of "commercial dispute" extends the scope to commercial disputes, and the criterion of "economic interest" further extends that scope to all disputes with an economic interest.

It is noteworthy that the aforementioned criteria may be applied alone or in combination.[41] For instance, Switzerland adopts the criterion of "economic interest" alone, while in France, the criteria of "disposability," "commercial dispute," and "public order" are used simultaneously. In addition, Article 1030(1) of the 1998 *German Code of Civil Procedure* stipulates that "Any claim involving an economic interest can be subject to an arbitration agreement. An arbitration agreement concerning claims not involving an economic interest shall have legal effect to the

[36] *See* Liu, *supra* note 15, at 11; *See* Hu Chenhang (胡程航), *Lun Fanlongduan Jiufen de Kezhongcaixing Panduan ji Shishi Jizhi (论反垄断纠纷的可仲裁性判断及实施机制) [Criterion for the Arbitrability of Antitrust Disputes and Its Implementation Mechanism]*, GUOJI JINGJIFA XUEKAN (国际经济法学刊) [JOURNAL OF INTERNATIONAL ECONOMIC LAW], no. 1, 2023, at 131.

[37] *See* ROUCHE, *supra* note 30, at 291.

[38] Article 11(1) of the 1994 *International Arbitration Act* of Singapore stipulates that "Any dispute which the parties have agreed to submit to arbitration under an arbitration agreement may be determined by arbitration unless it is contrary to public policy to do so."

[39] Article 1649 of the 2014 *National of Civil and Commercial Code* of Argentina stipulates that "There is an arbitration agreement when the parties decide to submit to the decision of one or more arbitrators all or some of the disputes that have arisen or could arise between them with respect to a specific legal relationship of private law, contractual or non-contractual, which does not affect public order." *See* ICCA INTERNATIONAL HANDBOOK ON COMMERCIAL ARBITRATION 1 (Lise Bosman ed., 2023).

[40] *See* FOUCHARD GAILLARD GOLDMAN ON INTERNATIONAL COMMERCIAL ARBITRATION 331 (Emmanuel Gaillard & John Savage eds., 1999).

[41] *See* Yu, *supra* note 15, at 50.

extent that the parties are entitled to conclude a settlement on the issue in dispute."[42] Thus, with regard to the arbitrability of disputes, Germany has also adopted a composite criterion based on the criterion of "economic interest," supplemented by the criterion of "disposability."

3 Differences in the Determination of Arbitrability of International Commercial Disputes Involving Economic Sanctions

As mentioned earlier, the interference of economic sanctions in private relations has given rise to a large number of international commercial disputes. In the adjudication of such disputes, one of the disputed issues necessarily involves the application of economic sanctions norms. In practice, the issue of arbitrability of international commercial disputes involving economic sanctions often arises in two situations. The first situation is where one party initiates arbitration pursuant to an arbitration agreement after disputes arise, while the other party raises a jurisdictional objection or files an application to set aside the arbitral award or resist its recognition and enforcement, arguing for the inarbitrability of such dispute due to economic sanctions. The other situation is where a party files a lawsuit with the courts of a state (usually in the state where the party is located) after disputes arise, and the other party raises a jurisdictional objection, lodges an appeal, or makes defenses against the recognition and enforcement of a judgment based on the arbitration agreement between the parties.

In light of existing practice, there are divergent views on the arbitrability of international commercial disputes involving economic sanctions. Among them, the prevailing view and practice are that a dispute will not become inarbitrable just because it involves the application of economic sanctions norms.[43] A few countries, such as

[42] *See* ICCA INTERNATIONAL HANDBOOK ON COMMERCIAL ARBITRATION 2 (Lise Bosman ed., 2018).

[43] *See* SZABADOS, *supra* note 10, at 174; *See* Tamás Szabados, *EU Economic Sanctions in Arbitration*, 35 J. Int'l Arb. 439, 445 (2018); *See* Silveira, *supra* note 13, at 162; *See* Gaillard & Savage, *supra* note 41, at 358–359; *See* Eric De Brabandere & David Holloway, *Sanctions and International Arbitration*, *in* RESEARCH HANDBOOK ON UN SANCTIONS AND INTERNATIONAL LAW 304, 306 (Larissa van den Herik ed., 2016); *See* Eric De Brabandere & David Holloway, *Unilateral Sanctions through an International Arbitration Lens: Procedural and Substantive Issues*, *in* RESEARCH HANDBOOK ON UNILATERAL AND EXTRATERRITORIAL SANCTIONS 342, 345 (Charlotte Beaucillon ed., 2021); *See* Eric De Brabandere & David Holloway, *Overriding Mandatory Provisions and Arbitrability in International Arbitration: The Case of Multilateral and Unilateral Sanctions*, *in* OVERRIDING MANDATORY RULES AND COMPLIANCE IN INTERNATIONAL ARBITRATION 153, 155 (Georges Affaki & Vladimir Khvalei eds., 2022); *See* Joséphine Hage Chahine, *UN and EU Sanctions versus US Sanctions: Two Different Yardsticks Commentary on the Decision of the Paris Court of Appeal (International Commercial Chamber) of 3 June 2020, No. 21/2020*, 38 J. Int'l Arb. 71, 76 (2021); *See* Tom

Italy, take the opposite view, arguing that economic sanctions will result in the parties' inability to freely dispose of their contractual rights, thereby rendering such disputes inarbitrable.[44] The following cases may illustrate these two conflicting views.

3.1 The Prevailing View: The Application of Economic Sanctions Norms Does Not Affect Arbitrability

Both of the respondents in *Fincantieri-Cantieri navali italiani SpA v. Oto Melara SpA, M. and others*[45] and *La Compagnie Nationale Air France v. Libyan Arab Airlines*[46] raised defenses of arbitrability and jurisdictional objections based on economic sanctions, neither of which were upheld by the arbitral tribunals or the courts at the seat of arbitration.

3.1.1 Fincantieri-Cantieri navali italiani SpA v. Oto Melara SpA, M. and Others

In this case, two Italian shipbuilders, Fincantieri-Cantieri Navali Italiani SpA and Oto Melara SpA, entered into two Agency Contracts in 1979 and 1980, with a Syrian citizen, M., under which M. agreed to act as an agent for the Italian shipbuilders in their sale of warships and other war materials to the government of Iraq. Following the suspension of payments by the government of Iraq in 1987, M. initiated arbitration on December 4, 1989, before the International Court of Arbitration of the International Chamber of Commerce (hereinafter referred to as "ICC") pursuant to the arbitration clauses in the Agency Contracts, claiming agency fees from the Italian shipbuilders.[47] In August 1990, due to Iraq's invasion of Kuwait, the UNSC adopted a sanction resolution against Iraq. The EU and Italy then enacted corresponding sanction legislation in accordance with that resolution.

During the arbitration, the Italian shipbuilders raised jurisdictional objection, arguing that the dispute was inarbitrable due to the UNSC embargo resolution against Iraq, which had been incorporated into Italian and Swiss laws. In an interim award rendered on November 25, 1991, the arbitral tribunal confirmed its

Cornell, *Sanctions and Arbitration: The Impact of Sanctions on English Law-Governed Contracts and English-Seated Arbitrations*, *in* INTERNATIONAL ARBITRATION IN ENGLAND: PERSPECTIVES IN TIMES OF CHANGE 267, 278 (Gregory Roy Fullelove et al., eds., 2022).

[44] *See* SZABADOS, *supra* note 10, at 178; *See* Szabados, *supra* note 44, at 450.

[45] *Switzerland No. 24, Fincantieri-Cantieri navali italiani SpA v. Oto Melara SpA, M. and others, Tribunal fédéral [Supreme Court], Not Indicated, 23 June 1992*, *in* ICCA YEARBOOK COMMERCIAL ARBITRATION 766 (Albert Jan van den Berg ed., 1995).

[46] CanLII 35834 (2003).

[47] ICC Case No. 6719.

jurisdiction and dismissed the objection. The interim award stated that "*the Tribunal is convinced that in so far as they may apply to the dispute, the international and legislative provisions [organizing the sanctions against Iraq] are matters of international public policy. However, the Tribunal is also convinced, in common with legal authors and recent case law, that one should not confuse the application by international arbitrators of public policy provisions, on the one hand, and the non-arbitrability of a dispute on the other. The mere fact that the nature of the dispute may lead to the arbitrator to apply various rules of law implicating public policy does not mean that the dispute becomes non-arbitrable as a result. The arbitrator must comply with the rules of international public policy, but he need not decline jurisdiction.*"[48] Subsequently, the Italian shipbuilders appealed to the Federal Supreme Court of Switzerland.

In its judgment of June 23, 1992, the Federal Supreme Court of Switzerland first elaborated on the provisions of Swiss law concerning the arbitrability of disputes and then concluded that the involved dispute was arbitrable under Swiss law. In particular, the Federal Supreme Court of Switzerland stated that, in order to avoid the difficulties in determining the applicable law for arbitrability and to make it easier for the parties to resort to international arbitration, the Swiss laws adopts the objective criterion of "economic interest" for arbitrability. It was emphasized that there is a significant difference between the criterion of "economic interest" and the criterion of "disposability," and thus they should not be equated. Hence, the Federal Supreme Court of Switzerland held that the involved dispute was arbitrable in accordance with article 177(1) of the 1987 *Swiss Federal Act of Private International Law*.

Secondly, the Federal Supreme Court of Switzerland rejected all arguments raised by the Italian shipbuilders. Firstly, the Italian shipbuilders argued that the international embargo against Iraq barred the possibility of relying upon claims arising out of contracts concluded with Iraq and of submitting such claims to an arbitral tribunal and that the arbitrability of the involved dispute should be denied, so as not to violate public policy.

In response to this argument, the Federal Supreme Court of Switzerland stated that "*The fact that the said claim affects public policy would not suffice, in itself, to rule out the arbitrability of the dispute...Hence, the arbitrability of the dispute does not depend on the material existence of the claim. Thus, it cannot be denied for the only reason that mandatory provisions of law or a given material public policy render the claim null and void or its execution impossible; it could be denied only as far as the claims are concerned which should have been heard exclusively by a State court, according to provisions of law which were to be taken into consideration for reasons of public policy. This is not at all the case here. The commercial measures taken against the Republic of Iraq raise indeed the issue of the validity of the contracts concluded before these measures were taken, or the issue of the subsequent impossibility to perform under said contracts. It does not seem, however, and*

[48] Gaillard & Savage, *supra* note 41, at 358–359.

[Fincantieri and Oto Melara] in any case do not prove, that all this must lead us to find that the claims arising out of these contracts are not arbitrable, and even more that the claims arising out of related contracts, like the agency contract on which M. bases his claims, are not arbitrable. We do not see, in particular, which fundamental legal principles would establish a State courts monopoly over disputes concerning claims of a private law nature influenced by provisions of public international law. Similarly, it is in fact the material existence of the claim, and not its arbitrability, which these provisions concern."

Thirdly, the Italian shipbuilders also based their objection on the impossibility of enforcing an award eventually rendered against them, invoking Article 5(2) of the 1958 *Convention on the Recognition and Enforcement of Foreign Arbitral Awards* (hereinafter referred to as the "*New York Convention*"). In response, the Federal Supreme Court of Switzerland held that "*By opting for a material regulation of arbitrability, the federal legislator chose a solution which undoubtedly does not rule out that enforcement of awards rendered in Switzerland be denied in this or that State. However, [the legislator] made this choice in all awareness, leaving it to the parties alone to evaluate the risk of the arbitral award not being recognized, so that the existence of such risk does not justify a restrictive approach toward arbitrability.*"

For the reasons above, the Federal Supreme Court of Switzerland affirmed the arbitral tribunal's decision on jurisdiction and dismissed the appeal of the Italian shipbuilders.

3.1.2 La Compagnie Nationale Air France v. Libyan Arab Airlines

La Compagnie Nationale Air France (hereinafter referred to as "Air France") and Libyan Arab Airlines (hereinafter referred to as "LAA") reached an agreement on February 2, 1972, under which Air France undertook to provide LAA with aircraft maintenance services, flight crews, and customized air transportation services. Article 23 of the agreement stipulated that disputes arising out of the agreement should be submitted to arbitration by the International Air Transport Association (hereinafter referred to as "IATA").

Following the Lockerbie Bombing in December 1988, the UNSC adopted Resolution 748 on March 31, 1992, declaring an embargo against Libya, which included a ban on the supply of any aircraft or aircraft components to Libya and the provision of maintenance services of Libyan aircraft or aircraft components. In order to implement the resolution, the EU and Canada issued *Regulation No. 945/92* and the *United Nations Libya Regulations* on April 14, 1992, and April 15, 1992, respectively. On November 11, 1993, the UNSC adopted Resolution 883, which extended the embargo to all financial and commercial relations with Libya and its nationals and decreed the freezing of all Libyan assets in all countries. Specifically, Article 8 of Resolution 883 required that "all States, and the Government of Libya, shall take the necessary measures to ensure that no claim shall lie at the instance of the Government or public authorities of Libya, or of any Libyan national, or of any

Libyan undertaking as defined in paragraph 3 of this resolution, or of any person claiming through or for the benefit of any such person or undertaking, in connection with any contractor other transaction or commercial operation where its performance was affected by reason of the measures imposed by or pursuant to this resolution or related resolutions." On November 30, 1993, Canada incorporated the new measures into its *United Nations Libya Regulations*.

After Air France unilaterally terminated the agreement due to the embargo, LAA submitted a request for arbitration to IATA on October 23, 1995, alleging Air France's breach of contract. Air France argued that the dispute was inarbitrable because the UNSC embargo resolutions and the EU sanctions regulations prevented it from taking part in any procedure related to a request formulated by a Libyan company in connection with a contract whose performance has been affected, directly or indirectly, by the aforementioned international rules.

In the partial award No. 1 rendered on July 10, 1998, the arbitral tribunal held that the dispute was arbitrable under French law, Canadian law, and transnational public order and thus confirmed its jurisdiction and dismissed Air France's jurisdictional objection. On August 12, 1998, Air France filed proceedings with the Quebec Superior Court, requesting to declare the dispute inarbitrable and to set aside the partial award.

The Quebec Superior Court, by judgment rendered on February 15, 2000, dismissed Air France's application. It first pointed out that, pursuant to Article 26(3) of the 1976 *UNCITRAL Arbitration Rules*[49] chosen by the parties, state courts could not be involved in the arbitration process except for requests for interim measures. Therefore, the arbitral tribunal had the competence to rule on its jurisdiction. Further, the Quebec Superior Court held that the dispute was arbitrable and that the question raised by Air France concerned the inadmissibility of LAA' requests and not the non-arbitrability of the dispute. Air France appealed to the Quebec Court of Appeal, which dismissed its appeal by judgment of March 31, 2003.

The Quebec Court of Appeal held as follows. Firstly, Article 21 of the 1976 *UNCITRAL Arbitration Rules*[50] and Article 943 of the *Code of Civil Procedure* of Canada[51] authorized the arbitral tribunal to rule on objections on jurisdictional grounds.

Secondly, inspired by Article 5 of the *Model Law*,[52] Article 940(3) of the *Code of Civil Procedure* of Canada stipulated that "In all matters governed by this Title, no

[49] Article 26(3) of the 1976 *UNCITRAL Arbitration Rules* stipulates that "A request for interim measures addressed by any party to a judicial authority shall not be deemed incompatible with the agreement to arbitrate, or as a waiver of that agreement."

[50] Article 21(4) of the 1976*UNCITRAL Arbitration Rules* stipulates that "In general, the arbitral tribunal should rule on a plea concerning its jurisdiction as a preliminary question. However, the arbitral tribunal may proceed with the arbitration and rule on such a plea in their final award."

[51] Article 943 of the *Code of Civil Procedure* of Canada stipulates that "The arbitrators may decide the matter of their own competence."

[52] Article 5 of the *UNCITRALModel Law on International Commercial Arbitration* stipulates that "In matters governed by this Law, no court shall intervene except where so provided in this Law."

judge or court may intervene except as provided by this Title." Meanwhile, Article 26(3) of the 1976 *UNCITRAL Arbitration Rules* and Article 940(4) of the *Code of Civil Procedure* of Canada only provided for interim measures that could be taken by the court. The present affair was clearly not a case of interim measures. Therefore, the court should not interfere with the jurisdictional decision made by the arbitral tribunal. In fact, the present case was about jurisdictional objection, and in such cases, the court may intervene only after subsequent to the final award.

Lastly, in line with the Superior Court of Quebec, the Quebec Court of Appeal agreed with the expert witnesses that the argument raised by Air France was not a matter of arbitrability but of admissibility, which should be left to the arbitral tribunal to decide on the merits. The opinion of the expert witnesses read that "*Security Council Resolution 883 and the European Union Council Regulations institute no objective, nor even any subjective, non-arbitrability in assigning exclusive jurisdiction to the State jurisdictions of the European Convention countries to hear disputes that are not the consequence of the embargo against Libya, unlike the dispute between LAA and Air France. These documents are intended solely to render provisionally inadmissible only those requests that are aimed at obtaining compensation for damage that is the direct or indirect consequence of the embargo, which is consistent with the objective set by the United Nations Security Council and the Council of the European Union. To interpret the letter and the spirit of these texts otherwise would result in the institution of absolute, retroactive jurisdictional immunity to the benefit of the Libyan parties and their co-contractors, which would be contrary not only to law and to fairness, but to plain common sense.*" Therefore, the Quebec Court of Appeal held that it was not contrary to international public policy for the arbitral tribunal to affirm its competence to hear the case.

3.2 The Minority View: Disputes Involving Economic Sanctions Are Inarbitrable

Unlike the situation in the previous cases, the argument that economic sanctions would render a dispute inarbitrable was upheld by the Court of Appeal of Genoa and the Supreme Court of Cassation of Italy in *Fincantieri-Cantieri Navali Italiani SpA and Oto Melara SpA v. Ministry of Defence, Armament and Supply Directorate of Iraq, and others*[53] and *Government and Ministries of the Republic of Iraq v. Armamenti e Aerospazio SpA et al.*,[54] respectively.

---

[53] *Italy No. 138, Fincantieri-Cantieri Navali Italiani SpA and Oto Melara SpA v. Ministry of Defence, Armament and Supply Directorate of Iraq and others, Corte di Appello [Court of Appeal], Geona, Not Indicated, 7 May 1994, in* ICCA YEARBOOK COMMERCIAL ARBITRATION 594 (Albert Jan van den Berg ed., 1996).

[54] *Italy No. 189, Government and Ministries of the Republic of Iraq v. Armamenti e Aerospazio SpA et al., Supreme Court of Cassation of Italy, Case No. 23893, 24 November 2015, in* ICCA YEARBOOK COMMERCIAL ARBITRATION 503 (Albert Jan van den Berg ed., 2016).

3.2.1 Fincantieri-Cantieri Navali Italiani SpA and Oto Melara SpA v. Ministry of Defence, Armament and Supply Directorate of Iraq, and Others

This case was a related case to the aforementioned *Fincantieri-Cantieri navali italiani SpA v. Oto Melara SpA, M., and others*. In this case, two Italian shipbuilders, Fincantieri-Cantieri Navali Italiani SpA and Oto Melara SpA, concluded three contracts with the government of Iraq for the supply of corvettes to the Iraqi Navy. All contracts contained an arbitration clause referring disputes to ICC arbitration in Paris. The government of Iraq stopped making payments in 1987.

Following the adoption of the resolutions by the UNSC imposing sanctions against Iraq in August 1990, the Italian shipbuilders filed a lawsuit against the government of Iraq with the Court of First Instance of Genoa, alleging frustration of contract and seeking termination of the contracts and damages. The government of Iraq objected to the court's jurisdiction and maintained that the dispute should be referred to arbitration as provided for in the contracts.

On December 9, 1992, the Court of First Instance of Genoa granted the Iraqi parties' objection and found that it had no jurisdiction over the case. It held that arbitration was excluded under Article 806 of the *Italian Code of Civil Procedure* only when it directly affected the rights of which the parties may not freely dispose by bringing about a result which was forbidden by the law, in this case, delivery of the corvettes. It found that in the present case the dispute did not directly affect such rights, as the Italian parties were only seeking termination of the contracts and damages. The Italian shipbuilders appealed against this decision to the Court of Appeal of Genoa.

On May 7, 1994, the Court of Appeal of Genoa reversed the first instance decision and confirmed the jurisdiction of the Italian courts. First of all, the Court of Appeal of Genoa stated that the validity of the arbitration clauses must be ascertained in accordance with Article 2(3) of the *New York Convention*.[55] Pursuant to Article 2(3) of the *New York Convention*, when the parties have made an arbitration agreement, a court of a contracting state should, at the request of a party, refer the parties to arbitration, unless it finds that the said agreement was null and void, inoperative, or incapable of being performed. In other words, if a court of a contracting state finds that the arbitration agreement was null and void or incapable of being performed, it could exercise jurisdiction over the dispute.

Secondly, the Court of Appeal of Genoa held that, according to jurisprudential principle and the principles set forth in Articles 2 and 5 of the *New York Convention*, the *lex fori*, i.e., the Italian law, should be applied for the determination on whether the involved arbitration agreement was null and void, inoperative, or incapable of

[55] Although Italy was a party to the *New York Convention* while Iraq was not, the Court of Appeal of Genoa held that the contracting states' obligations under the *New York Convention* were generally considered to be independent of reciprocity and that the obligations still existed when the party of a non-contracting state relies upon the arbitration clause, and thus the *New York Convention* could be applied in this case.

being performed. The Court of Appeal of Genoa further also held that the dispute was inarbitrable under Italian law. Specifically, pursuant to Article 806 of the *Italian Code of Civil Procedure*, disputes that could not be the subject of a compromise were inarbitrable. As per Article 1966 of the *Civil Code* of Italy, a compromise was null and void when the parties could not freely dispose of the rights which were the subject matter of the dispute, either by the nature of these rights or by express provisions of the law. These two provisions showed that the Italian law prohibited the parties from initiating arbitration in respect of rights that were not freely disposable by them. The Court of Appeal of Genoa considered that "*It is beyond doubt that the rights deriving from the contracts between [the parties] could be freely disposed of at the time when the arbitral clause was stipulated. It is equally beyond doubt that they could not when this action was commenced, as a consequence of the international measures sanctioning Iraq's aggression of Kuwait and of the legislative measures implementing them in our country.*" Therefore, pursuant to the Italian law, the dispute was inarbitrable due to Italian embargo legislation,[56] the arbitration agreement was null and void, and the Italian court had jurisdiction over the case.

In addition, the Court of Appeal of Genoa noted that, although the main claim of the Italian parties aimed at terminating the contracts, referral of the dispute to arbitration could still have affected the rights that the parties could not freely dispose due to the embargo legislations. To be specific, if the claim had been accepted and the contract terminated, a restitution after termination, including the return of advance payments made by the Iraqi party, would have been prohibited by the embargo legislations. On the contrary, if the arbitral tribunal did not uphold the Italian parties' claim and denied termination of the contract, the performance of the involved contract would affect the rights that parties could not dispose of in a contrary but similar manner. The Court of Appeal of Genoa considered that the Court of First Instance had wrongly held the arbitration clause to be valid because it ignored such possibility.

It is worth mentioning that, after obtaining the decision in favor of it, the Italian shipbuilders sought recognition in France of the decision rendered by the Court of Appeal of Genoa. By an order of October 19, 2004, the Court of First Instance of Paris granted recognition under the 1968 *Brussels Convention on Jurisdiction and the Enforcement of Judgments in Civil and Commercial Matters* (hereinafter referred to as "*Brussels Convention*"). Upon Iraqi parties' appeal, on June 15, 2006, the Paris Court of Appeal annulled the order and denied the request of recognition and enforcement of the decision.[57]

---

[56] Such legislation included both Italian legislation on embargo against Iraq and *EC Rule no. 3541/1992*. Specifically, Article 21 of the latter forbade [parties] to meet or take any measure to meet Iraqi requests to perform in any way under contracts or transactions falling under Resolution no. 686/1990 and following of the UN Security Council [the UN embargo legislation].

[57] *France No. 37, Legal Department of the Ministry of Justice of the Republic of Iraq v. Fincantieri – Cantieri Navali Italiani (Italy), Finmeccanica (Italy) and others, Court of appeal, Paris, Not Indicated, 15 June 2006, in* ICCA YEARBOOK COMMERCIAL ARBITRATION 635 (Albert Jan van den Berg ed., 2006).

First, the Paris Court of Appeal held that the *Brussels Convention* should not apply to the case because Article 1(2)(4) of the *Brussels Convention*[58] excludes its application to arbitration, and the decision whose recognition and enforcement were sought had found the arbitration agreement to be null and void.

Second, the Paris Court of Appeal held that the 1930 *Treaty between Italy and France on the Enforcement of Judgment in Civil and Commercial Matters* could not serve as a basis for the recognition and enforcement of the involved decision. Article 1 of the treaty provided that the court rendering the decision should have jurisdiction over the case in accordance with the laws of the state in which recognition is sought, i.e., France. The Paris Court of Appeal held that "*When there is an arbitration agreement, even when the arbitral tribunal has not been seized, the state court must find that it lacks jurisdiction unless a summary examination allows it to hold that the clause is null and void or manifestly inapplicable. The arbitrator has priority and may decide on his own competence to decide on the validity and efficacy of the arbitration clause. [Hence,] the decision [at issue], which held after a substantial examination that the arbitration agreements in the contracts between the Government of the Republic of Iraq and [the Italian parties] were inoperative because of the UN embargo provisions in Resolution no. 661 of 1990, was rendered by a court lacking jurisdiction, whose decision may not be recognized in France.*"

Obviously, the Paris Court of Appeal did not agree with the Genoa Court of Appeal's practice of denying the validity of the arbitration agreement by declaring the involved dispute inarbitrable due to economic sanctions.

3.2.2 Government and Ministries of the Republic of Iraq v. Armamenti e Aerospazio SpA et al.

The dispute in this case arose out of a sale and purchase contract dated November 12, 1983, between an Italian company, Agusta SpA (hereinafter referred to as "Agusta"), and the Government and the Ministry of Defense of Iraq (hereinafter collectively referred to as "Iraq"), under which Agusta sold helicopters to Iraq. The contract stipulated that the governing law should be French law and disputes should be settled in accordance with the rules of the ICC in Paris. During the performance of the contract, Agusta suspended delivery of the helicopters due to Iraq's failure to pay an installment. In August 1990, the UNSC and EU imposed an embargo against Iraq as a result of Iraq's invasion of Kuwait.

On November 28, 1991, Agusta filed an action against Iraq with the Court of First Instance of Busto Arsizio, seeking a declaration that the sale and purchase contract was terminated for Iraq's breach and damages. On November 18, 2003, the Court of First Instance of Busto Arsizio held that it lacked jurisdiction because of the arbitration clause contained in the sale and purchase contract.

---

[58] Article 1(2)(4) of the 1968 *Brussels Convention on Jurisdiction and the Enforcement of Judgments in Civil and Commercial Matters* stipulates that "The Convention shall not apply to: (4) arbitration."

On December 27, 2012, the Court of Appeal of Milan reversed the first instance decision, holding that the Italian courts had jurisdiction over the dispute because the arbitration clause had become inoperative at the time the claim was filed with the Court of First Instance due to the embargo declared against Iraq and had not been revived when the embargo was lifted. The Court of Appeal of Milan then decided on the merits in favor of the Italian party. On March 25, 2013, Iraq filed an appeal with the Supreme Court of Cassation of Italy.

On November 24, 2015, the Supreme Court of Cassation of Italy affirmed the second instance judgment and denied Iraq's appeal. According to the Supreme Court of Cassation of Italy, "*The core of the grounds for the decision [of the court below] is that the arbitration clause, which was originally valid, became null and void because the parties could no longer freely dispose of the disputed right as a consequence of the embargo deliberated by the UN and the European Union: a factum principis that imposed an external ban on contractual performance.*" In addition, it emphasized that "*The supranational character of this act—whose non-application would have led to sanctions for the state that had the obligation to make sure that it was complied with—leads to the conclusion that the ascertainment of whether the arbitration agreement was still or no longer valid could not be entrusted to private judges, who are not part of the state's jurisdictional organization.*"

In response to Iraq's argument that the arbitration clause should be evaluated under French law, the Supreme Court of Cassation of Italy held that the supranational character of the embargo prevailed over the general substantive and procedural rules provided for in the contract, including the agreement on dispute resolution methods. Given that the embargo pertained to international public policy, its effects "*had to be assessed by the Italian court—whose territorial competence was belatedly disputed ... only before us—in accordance with the lex fori.*" It emphasized that Articles 2(1) and 2(3) of the *New York Convention* authorized the courts of the contracting states not to apply the arbitration clause if they found that it was null and void and to conduct *ex ante* judicial evaluation of the arbitrability of the dispute. Therefore, the conclusion it reached conforms with the *New York Convention*.

In addition, the Supreme Court of Cassation of Italy considered Iraq's argument that the dispute became arbitrable again when the embargo was lifted unfounded. On the one hand, "*As a general premise, the [Italian] legal system recognizes the supervening invalidity of juridical acts and transactions but not their supervening validity.*" On the other hand, "*the embargo did not affect commercial relations with Iraq in an interim, suspensive manner, as a temporarily limited measure to be lifted following the end of the international violation imputed to Iraq, so that the procedural means agreed by the parties could subsequently resume. On the contrary, this was a sanction that made referral to arbitration directly inadmissible and the civil action commenced before the court competent under the lex fori irreversible.*"

4 Jurisprudential Analysis on Arbitrability of International Commercial Disputes Involving Economic Sanctions

It can be observed from the above cases that the reason why different countries hold different attitudes toward the arbitrability of international commercial disputes involving economic sanctions lies in the fact that they adopt different criteria for arbitrability. Italy and Switzerland are the most typical examples.

As mentioned earlier, Italy has adopted the criterion of "disposability" to determine whether a dispute is arbitrable, and Article 806(1) of its *Code of Civil Procedure* expressly limits the scope of arbitrable disputes to those arising from the parties' disposable rights. Therefore, the Court of Appeal of Genoa and the Supreme Court of Cassation of Italy, in *Fincantieri-Cantieri Navali Italiani SpA and Oto Melara SpA v. Ministry of Defence, Armament and Supply Directorate of Iraq, and others* and *Government and Ministries of the Republic of Iraq v. Armamenti e Aerospazio SpA et al.*, both held that economic sanctions would result in the parties' inability to freely dispose of their contractual rights, thereby rendering such disputes inarbitrable.

In contrast, Switzerland adopts the criterion of "economic interest" for arbitrability, and Article 177(1) of its *Federal Code of Private International Law* explicitly grants arbitrability to any dispute involving an economic interest. Obviously, international commercial disputes involving economic sanctions involve economic interests. Therefore, international commercial disputes involving economic sanctions are arbitrable under the criterion of "economic interest."

Indeed, the disagreement over the arbitrability of international commercial disputes involving economic sanctions is rooted in the arbitrability of disputes involving mandatory rules. Given that economic sanction norms fall within the category of mandatory rules, this disagreement also extends to the arbitrability of international commercial disputes involving economic sanctions.

4.1 Definition and Characteristics of Mandatory Rules

Mandatory rules, also known as overriding mandatory provisions, intervention rules, *lois d'application immediate*, and *lois de police*, are national or transnational substantive legal norms that must be applied to a transnational legal relation, irrespective of the law that governs the legal relation.[59] The following characteristics of mandatory rules can be summarized from this definition.

---

[59] *See* Pierre Mayer, *Mandatory Rules of Law in International Arbitration*, 2 Arb. Int'l 274, 275 (1986); *See* HOSSEIN FAZILATFAR, OVERRIDING MANDATORY RULES IN INTERNATIONAL COMMERCIAL ARBITRATION 21 (1st. ed., 2019); *See* Sang Yuanke (桑远棵), *Guoji Shangshi Zhongcai zhong Qiangzhixingguifan de Shiyong Yanjiu (国际商事仲裁中强制性规范的适用研究) [Study on the Application of Mandatory Rule of Law in International*

Firstly, they are characterized as mandatory in their application, and they can be directly applied to specific transnational legal relations without the need to be guided by rules of conflict of laws.[60] It is because their application does not depend on rules of conflict of laws that mandatory rules are referred to as *lois d'application immediate*.[61]

Secondly, the mandatory character of mandatory rules is conferred by themselves. In particular, mandatory rules usually provide for their application in all circumstances falling within their scope of application, irrespective of the applicable law.[62]

Thirdly, the reason why mandatory rules confer on themselves mandatory force lies in their purpose to protect the public interest of the state or the community that enacts them. In other words, mandatory rules are aimed at protecting the public interest.[63] This is also reflected in the definition of "overriding mandatory provisions" stipulated in Article 9(1) of the *EU Regulation No. 593/2008 on the Law Applicable to Contractual Obligations* (hereinafter referred to as "*Rome I Regulation*")[64] and in the definition of "mandatory rules" stipulated in Article 8 of the *Interpretation of the Supreme People's Court on Several Issues Concerning the Application of the Law of the People's Republic of China on the Law Applicable to Foreign-Related Civil Relationships (I) (2020 Amendment)*.[65]

Commercial Arbitration], GUOJIFA YANJIU (国际法研究) [CHINESE REVIEW OF INTERNATIONAL LAW], no. 4, 2020, at 94.

60 *See* Mayer, *supra* note 60, at 275.

61 *See* MERCÉDEH AZEREDO DA SILVEIRA, TRADE SANCTIONS AND INTERNATIONAL SALES: AN INQUIRY INTO INTERNATIONAL ARBITRATION AND COMMERCIAL LITIGATION 51 (1st. ed., 2014).

62 See *id.*, at 50–51.

63 *See* Mayer, *supra* note 60, at 275; *See id.*, at 56; *See* Sang, *supra* note 60, at 94.

64 Article 9(1) of the *EU Regulation No. 593/2008 on the Law Applicable to Contractual Obligations* stipulates that "Overriding mandatory provisions are provisions the respect for which is regarded as crucial by a country for safeguarding its public interests, such as its political, social or economic organisation, to such an extent that they are applicable to any situation falling within their scope, irrespective of the law otherwise applicable to the contract under this Regulation."

65 Article 8 of the *Interpretation of the Supreme People's Court on Several Issues Concerning the Application of the Law of the People's Republic of China on the Law Applicable to Foreign-Related Civil Relationships (I) (2020 Amendment)* stipulates that "Under any of the following circumstances, the provisions of the laws and administrative regulations in connection with the social public interests of the People's Republic of China, the application of which the parties cannot preclude by agreement, and that can be directly applicable to the foreign-related civil relationship without guidelines on conflict rules, may be determined by the people's courts as the mandatory provisions as set forth in Article 4 of the Law of the PRC on the Law Applicable to Foreign-Related Civil Relationships: (1) where they relate to the protection of the rights and interests of the laborers; (2) where they relate to food or public health safety; (3) where they relate to environmental safety; (4) where they relate to foreign exchange control and other financial safety; (5) where they relate to anti-monopoly and anti-dumping; or (6) other circumstances under which they shall be determined as mandatory provisions."

Fourthly, generally speaking, the public interest served by mandatory rules can only be achieved by exerting influence on the legal relations between private actors. In other words, in order to achieve their purpose, mandatory rules usually need to intervene in the legal relations between private actors. The public interest served by mandatory rules is considered to prevail over private interests under such circumstances.[66] This is why mandatory rules are referred as "overriding mandatory provisions" by *Rome Regulation I.*

Fifthly, mandatory rules are substantive, as opposed to rules of conflict of laws.[67] Mandatory rules in international commerce are commonly found in competition laws, securities laws, antitrust laws, foreign exchange control laws and regulations, import and export control laws and regulations, tax laws, environmental protection laws, embargoes, blockades and boycotts, as well as in legislation enacted to protect the weaker party in a commercial transaction.[68]

4.2 Relationship Between Mandatory Rules and Economic Sanctions Norms

It is generally recognized that economic sanction norms fall within the category of mandatory rules.[69] When listing the various types of mandatory rules, many scholars, including Professor Pierre Mayer, referred to embargoes, blockades, and boycotts,[70] which are specific measures of economic sanctions.[71] The reason is that

---

[66] *See* SILVEIRA, *supra* note 62, at 56.

[67] *See id.*, at 50.

[68] *See* Mayer, *supra* note 60, at 275; *See* Liu, *supra* note 15, at 124; *See* Sang, *supra* note 60, at 94.

[69] *See* SZABADOS, *supra* note 10, at 36; *See* Szabados, *supra* note 44, at 440; *See* Silveira, *supra* note 13, at 164; *See* Silveira, *supra* note 10, at 338; *See* SILVEIRA, *supra* note 62, at 61; *See* Brabandere & Holloway, *Unilateral Sanctions through an International Arbitration Lens: Procedural and Substantive Issues*, *supra* note 44, at 343; *See* Garima Shahani, *Impact of Sanctions under the CISG*, 33 ASA Bulletin 849, 854-856 (2015); *See* Chahine, *supra* note 44, at 76; *See* Taejoon Ahn, *The Applicability of Economic Sanctions to the Merits in International Arbitration Proceedings: With a Focus on the Dynamics between Public International Law Principles, Private International Law Rules and International Arbitration Theories*, 18 PEPP. Disp. Resol. L.J. 299, 303 (2018); *See* Mercédeh Azeredo da Silveira, *Economic Sanctions, Exchange Control Regulations and the Like: Black Sheep Among the Provisions of the Lex Contractus?* Kluwer Arbitration Blog (Jul. 18, 2023, 11:10 AM), https://arbitrationblog.kluwerarbitration.com/2015/07/14/economic-sanctions-exchange-control-regulations-and-the-like-black-sheep-among-the-provisions-of-the-lex-contractus/.

[70] *See* Mayer, *supra* note 60, at 275; *See* Daniel Hochstrasser, *Choice of Law and Foreign Mandatory Rules in International Arbitration*, 11 J. Int'l Arb. 57, 68 (1994); *See* Abdul F. Munir Maniruzzaman, *International Arbitrator and Mandatory Public Law Rules in the Context of State Contracts*, 7 J. Int'l Arb. 53, 57-58 (1990).

[71] *See* YUAN JIANPING (阮建平), Zhanhou Meiguo Duiwai Jingji Zhicai (战后美国对外经济制裁) [POST-WAR U.S. FOREIGN ECONOMIC SANCTIONS] 7 (1st. ed., 2009).

economic sanction norms fit into the aforementioned definition and characteristics of mandatory rules.[72]

"Trade sanctions strive to apply to all contractual relationships that involve the performance of an action prohibited by the sanction or subject to a regime of authorization, irrespective of the law applicable to these contractual relationships whether selected by the parties or identified through mechanisms of conflict of laws. Trade sanctions strive to be given effect in the context of all contracts the performance of which could defeat their purpose." For example, an economic sanction prohibits a party from performing the contract concluded with the sanctioned individual, thereby influencing the contractual relationship between the parties. In this sense, the contractual relationship falls within the scope of application of the economic sanction because the performance of the contract is prohibited by the sanctions. It follows that economic sanctions also achieve their purpose by intervening in private legal relations.[73] Therefore, in the private international law perspective, economic sanction norms fall with the category of mandatory rules.[74]

[72] *See* SILVEIRA, *supra* note 62, at 61; *See* Ahn, *supra* note 70, at 303.

[73] *See* SZABADOS, *supra* note 10, at 34; *See* Silveira, *supra* note 10, at 332.

[74] *See* SZABADOS, *supra* note 10, at 36; *See* SILVEIRA, *supra* note 62, at 61.

4.3 *Historical Evolution of Arbitrability of Disputes Involving Mandatory Rules*

There is a close link between arbitrability of disputes and public policy.[75] As mentioned above, states' stipulation on arbitrability of disputes stems primarily from considerations of public policy.[76] In other words, protection of public policy is the key objective of the limitations imposed by states on the scope of arbitration.[77] Arguably, the concept of arbitrability is essentially a public policy limitation imposed by states on the statutory scope of arbitration.[78] On the other hand, public policy is a fundamental criterion for determining arbitrability.[79]

---

[75] *See* Anne-Sophie Papeil, *Conflict of Overriding Mandatory Rules in Arbitration*, *in* CONFLICT OF LAWS IN INTERNATIONAL ARBITRATION 341, 350 (Franco Ferrari & Stefan Kröll eds., 2019); *See* Liu, *supra* note 15, at 53; *See* XIAO YONGPING (肖永平), Xiao Yongping Lun Chongtufa (肖永平论冲突法) [XIAO YONGPING ON CONFLICT OF LAWS] 233 (1st. ed., 2002); *See* Xiao Yongping (肖永平) & Zhu Kepeng (朱克鹏), *Lun Qiangzhixing Guize yu Gonggong Zhengce dui Guoji Shangshi Zhongcai de Yingxiang (*论强制性规则与公共政策对国际商事仲裁的影响*) [On the Impact of Mandatory Rules and Public Policy on International Commercial Arbitration]*, GUOJI MAOYI WENTI (国际贸易问题) [JOURNAL OF INTERNATIONAL TRADE], no. 9, 1997, at 58; *See* KOU LI (寇丽), Xiandai Guoji Shangshi Zhongcai Falv Shiyong Wenti Yanjiu (现代国际商事仲裁法律适用问题研究) [STUDY ON THE APPLICATION OF LAW IN MODERN INTERNATIONAL COMMERCIAL ARBITRATION] 79 (1st. ed., 2013); *See* Zhang Aiqing (张艾清), *Guoji Shangshi Zhongcai zhong Gonggong Zhengce Shixiang de Kezhongcaixing Wenti Yanjiu (*国际商事仲裁中公共政策事项的可仲裁性问题研究*) [Study on Arbitrability of Public Policy Matters in International Commercial Arbitration]*, FAXUE PINGLUN (法学评论) [LAW REVIEW], no. 6, 2007, at 94; *See* Zhang Aiqing (张艾清), *Fanlongduan Zhengyi de Kezhongcaixing Yanjiu—Jianlun Oumei Guojia de Lifa yu Sifa Shijian jiqi dui Woguo de Qishi (*反垄断争议的可仲裁性研究—兼论欧美国家的立法与司法实践及其对我国的启示*) [Study on the Arbitrability of Antitrust Disputes--An Introduction to the Legislative and Judicial Practices of European Countries and America and Their Implications for China]*, FASHANG YANJIU (法商研究) [STUDIES IN LAW AND BUSINESS], no. 4, 2006, at 146; *See* Zhang Xiaoling (张晓玲) & Wang Wenkui (王文奎), *Guoji Shangshi Kezhongcaixing yu Gonggong Zhengce de guanxi jiqi Yanbian (*国际商事仲裁可仲裁性与公共政策的关系及其演变*) [The Relationship between Arbitrability and Public Policy in International Commercial Arbitration and Its Evolution]*, QIUSUO (求索) [SEEKER], no. 3, 2007, at 110; *See* Ma, *supra* note 15, at 58.

[76] *See* XIAO, *supra* note 76, at 233; *See* Xiao & Zhu, *supra* note 76, at 58; *See* Du & Chen, *supra* note 25, at 481; *See* KOU, *supra* note 76, at 79.

[77] *See* Yu, *supra* note 15, at 50.

[78] *See* ALAN REDFERN et al., LAW AND PRACTICE OF INTERNATIONAL COMMERCIAL ARBITRATION 137 (2nd. ed., 1991); See Brabandere & Holloway, *Sanctions and International Arbitration*, *supra* note 44, at 306; *See* Liu, *supra* note 15, at 4; *See* Zhang & Wang, *supra* note 76, at 110; *See* Zhao & Wang, *supra* note 27, at 322–323.

[79] *See* Liu, *supra* note 15, at 12; *See* 1958 nian <Chengren yu Zhixing Waiguo Zhongcai Caijue Gongyue> (<Niuyue Gongyue>) Lilun yu Shiyong (1958年《承认与执行外国仲裁裁决公约》(《纽约公约》)理论与适用) [CONVENTION ON THE RECOGNITION AND ENFORCEMENT OF FOREIGN ARBITRAL AWARDS (1958 NEW YORK CONVENTION) THEORY AND PRACTICE] 200 (Zhongguo Guoji Zhongcai 30 Ren (中国国际仲裁30人) eds., 2020); *See* Li Shanshan (李姗姗), *Guoji Shangshi Zhongcai Kezhongcai Shixiang de Kuozhang yu*

In view of the close link between mandatory rules and public policy, states tended to consider disputes involving the application and interpretation of mandatory rules inarbitrable in early practice. Taking France as an example, French courts in the nineteenth and early twentieth centuries did not recognize the arbitrability of any dispute involving public policy.[80] For instance, the Court of Appeal of Paris stated in *Société anonyme agricole v. Torris*in 1954 that an arbitral tribunal could not hear a dispute relating to contracts concerning taxable goods because "the legal or regulatory provisions relating to the taxation of goods are a matter of public policy."[81] Similarly, the US courts had once denied the arbitrability of disputes involving the interpretation and application of mandatory rules, such as antitrust laws and securities laws.[82] For example, the US Supreme Court held in *Wilko v. Swan*[83] in 1953 that security disputes were inarbitrable and invalidated the agreement to submit securities disputes to arbitration.

With the increasing sophistication of the arbitration system and the growing caseload of courts in the context of "litigation explosion," states' attitude toward arbitration has gradually shifted from skepticism and hostility to encouragement and support.[84] An important manifestation of this is the expansion of arbitrable disputes.[85] On one side, the criterion for arbitrability has gradually evolved from the criterion of "disposability" to the more lenient criteria of "commercial dispute" or "economic interest."[86] For example, in its reform of arbitration legislation in 1998,

Zhongguo de Celue Xuanze (国际商事仲裁可仲裁事项的扩张与中国的策略选择) [Expansion of Arbitrable Disputes in International Commercial Arbitration and China's Strategic Choices], YUNNAN MINZU DAXUE XUEBAO (ZHEXUE SHEHUI KEXUE BAN) (云南民族大学学报(哲学社会科学版)) [JOURNAL OF YUNNAN MINZU UNIVERSITY (PHILOSOPHY AND SOCIAL SCIENCES EDITION)], no. 4, 2023, at 159.

80 *See* Gaillard & Savage, *supra* note 41, at 333; *See* Antoine Kirry, *Arbitrability: Current Trends in Europe*, 12 Arb. Int'l 373, 375 (1996).

81 *See* Gaillard & Savage, *supra* note 41, at 333.

82 *See* William W. Park, *National Law and Commercial Justice: Safeguarding Procedural Integrity in International Arbitration*, 63 TUL. L. REV. 647, 700 (1988–1989).

83 346 U.S. 427 (1953).

84 *See* Liu, *supra* note 15, at 62; *See* Li, *supra* note 80, at 154.

85 See Zhang, *Guoji Shangshi Zhongcai zhong Gonggong Zhengce Shixiang de Kezhongcaixing Wenti Yanjiu (国际商事仲裁中公共政策事项的可仲裁性问题研究) [Study on Arbitrability of Public Policy Matters in International Commercial Arbitration]*, *supra* note 76, at 97; *See* Zhao & Wang, *supra* note 27, at 328; *See* Chen, *supra* note 15, at 61; *See* Huang Jin (黄进) & Ma Decai (马德才), *Guoji Shangshi Zhengyi Kezhongcai Fanwei de Kuozhan Qushi zhi Tanxi—Jianping Woguo Youguan Guiding (国际商事争议可仲裁范围的扩展趋势之探析—兼评我国有关规定) [Exploration of the Trend of Expansion of the Scope of Arbitrability of International Commercial Disputes—An Analysis of China's Relevant Provisions]*, FAXUE PINGLUN (法学评论) [LAW REVIEW], no. 3, 2007, at 54; *See* Zhang Jie (张洁), *Dui Guoji Shangshi Zhengyi Kezhongcai Fanwei de Tantao (对国际商事争议可仲裁范围的探讨) [Exploration of the Scope of Arbitrability of International Commercial Disputes]*, FAXUE ZAZHI (法学杂志) [LAW SCIENCE MAGAZINE], no. 2, 2002, at 53; *See* Li, *supra* note 80, at 152.

86 *See* Zhao & Wang, *supra* note 27, at 326.

Germany modified the old criterion of "disposability"[87] to the criterion of "economic interest" while maintaining the criterion of "disposability" only for disputes not involving economic interest.[88] Austria,[89] Portugal,[90] Belgium,[91] and the Republic of Korea[92] have also drawn on this German approach and have modified their criteria for arbitrability correspondingly.

On the other side, the role of the criterion of "public order" in precluding arbitrability of disputes is diminishing. Many states have adopted a stricter and more cautious approach to the interpretation of public policy, distinguishing between the public policy nature of a particular dispute itself and the public policy nature of a

---

[87] Article 1025(1) of the *Code of Civil Procedure* of Germany prior to 1998 stipulated that "The agreement by which the settlement of a dispute is submitted to one or more arbitrators is legally valid when the parties have the right to enter into a settlement on the subject matter of the dispute." *See* ARBITRATION IN GERMANY: THE MODEL LAW IN PRACTICE 1109 (Patricia Nacimiento et al. eds., 2015).

[88] *See* Sun Jun (孙珺), Deguo Zhongcai Lifa Gaige (德国仲裁立法改革) [Reform of German Arbitration Legislation], WAIGUOFA YIPING (外国法译评) [GLOBAL LAW REVIEW], no. 1, 1999, at 84.

[89] Article 577 (1) of the 1983 *Code of Civil Procedure* of Austria stipulates that "An agreement that a legal dispute shall be settled by one or more arbitrators (an arbitration agreement) is valid insofar as the parties are entitled to conclude a settlement concerning the subject matter of the dispute." Article 582 (1) of the 2006 *Code of Civil Procedure* of Austria stipulates that "Any pecuniary claim within the jurisdiction of the courts of law may be made the subject of an arbitration agreement. An arbitration agreement as to non-pecuniary claims shall be legally effective insofar as the parties are capable of concluding a settlement upon the matter in dispute."

[90] Article 1(1) of the 1986 *Portuguese Law on Voluntary Arbitration* stipulates that "Any dispute relating to disposable rights which has not been exclusively submitted by a special act to a court or to compulsory arbitration may be submitted by the parties for decision by arbitrators." Articles 1(1) and 1(2) of the 2011 *Portuguese Law on Voluntary Arbitration* stipulates that "Any dispute involving economic interests may be referred by the parties to arbitration, by means of an arbitration agreement, provided that it is not exclusively submitted by a special law to the State courts or to compulsory arbitration," and "An arbitration agreement concerning disputes that do not involve economic interests is also valid provided that the parties are entitled to conclude a settlement on the right in dispute," respectively.

[91] Article 1676 (1) of the 1985 *Judicial Code* of Belgium stipulates that "Any dispute already existing or that may arise from a given legal situation, and which can be the object of a settlement, may by agreement be submitted to arbitration." The 2013 *Judicial Code* of Belgium amends this provision to "Any pecuniary claim may be submitted to arbitration. Non-pecuniary claims with regard to which a settlement agreement may be made may also be submitted to arbitration."

[92] Article 2 (1) of the 1973 *Arbitration Act* of the Republic of Korea stipulates that "An arbitration agreement shall take effect under an agreement between the parties concerned to settle through an arbitration the whole or part of any dispute which has arisen or will arise in the future between them with respect to any legal relationship under the private law (hereinafter referred to as an "arbitration agreement"): Provided, That this shall not apply to those legal relations which the parties concerned shall not change." Article 3 of the 2016 *Arbitration Act* of the Republic of Korea defines "arbitration" as "a procedure to resolve a dispute over a property right or a dispute over a non-property right which can be resolved by the parties' settlement, by the arbitrators' award as opposed to the court's judgment, as per an agreement between parties." Therefore, pursuant to the 2016*Arbitration Act* of the Republic of Korea, a dispute over a property right or a dispute over a non-property right which can be resolved by the parties' settlement is arbitrable.

particular rule of law and no longer readily denying arbitrability of disputes on the basis of the latter but precluding it on the basis of the former alone.[93]

In France, for example, since the late twentieth century, arbitrators' power to apply and interpret mandatory rules has been recognized, and the link between the application of mandatory rules and arbitrability of disputes has been denied.[94] Specifically, in 1991, the Paris Court of Appeal held in *Ganz* Case that "*in international arbitration, an arbitrator...is entitled to apply the principles and rules of [international] public policy and to grant redress in the event that those principles and rules have been disregarded...except in cases where the non-arbitrability is a consequence of the subject-matter.*"[95] In 1993, the Paris Court of Appeal also noted in the *Labinal* Case, which involved the application of the antitrust law in EU, that "*if the character of the law of economic policy of the Community rule in competition law prohibits arbitrators from pronouncing injunctions or levying fines, they may nonetheless draw the civil conclusions of behavior judged to be illicit with respect to public order rules that can be directly applied to the relations of the parties in the action, even if these are not all drawn together to the arbitration proceedings.*"[96]

Similarly, the USA has progressively brought disputes involving mandatory rules, which had previously been held to be non-arbitrable, into the scope of arbitration through case law. To be specific, the arbitrability of international securities disputes involving the application of securities laws was first affirmed by the US Supreme Court in 1974 in *Scherk v. Alberto-Culver Co.*[97] In 1985, the US Supreme Court further stated in *Mitsubishi Motors Corp. v. Soler Chrysler - Plymouth, Inc.*[98] that the application of the antitrust laws as mandatory rules did not preclude the arbitrability of a dispute.[99]

Nowadays, the prevailing view and judicial and arbitral practice are that a dispute will not lose its arbitrability merely because it involves the application of mandatory rules, including economic sanctions norms.[100] In this regard, it has been summarized by a scholar that "Supporting the submission of disputes involving public policy to arbitration has become a growing trend in modern international commercial arbitration."[101]

---

[93] *See* Kirry, *supra* note 81, at 375; *See* Zhao & Wang, *supra* note 27, at 333; *See* Zhang & Wang, *supra* note 76, at 112.

[94] *See* Kirry, *supra* note 81, at 376-377.

[95] *See* Gaillard & Savage, *supra* note 41, at 336.

[96] *See id.*, at 337.

[97] 417 U. S. 506 (1974).

[98] 473 U. S. 614 (1985).

[99] *See* SZABADOS, *supra* note 10, at 174.

[100] *See id.*, at 174; *See* SILVEIRA, *supra* note 62, at 86.

[101] *See* Zhang, *Guoji Shangshi Zhongcai zhong Gonggong Zhengce Shixiang de Kezhongcaixing Wenti Yanjiu (国际商事仲裁中公共政策事项的可仲裁性问题研究) [Study on Arbitrability of Public Policy Matters in International Commercial Arbitration]*, *supra* note 76, at 97.

5 Rational Determination on Arbitrability of International Commercial Disputes Involving Economic Sanctions

In an era of intensifying economic sanctions, China[102] will inevitably encounter many international commercial arbitration cases involving economic sanctions and new issues raised by economic sanctions on international commercial arbitration, which include the issue of arbitrability of international commercial arbitration involving economic sanctions. Therefore, it is necessary for China to make a rational determination on the arbitrability of international commercial disputes involving economic sanctions.

5.1 The Practical Need to Determine Arbitrability of International Commercial Disputes Involving Economic Sanctions

To date, there is no publicly available judicial or arbitral practice in China concerning the arbitrability of international commercial disputes involving economic sanctions. This may result from the following two reasons. First, owing to the confidential nature of arbitration, relevant arbitration cases are not publicly available except cases of judicial review. Second, China is not traditionally the most favored seat of arbitration for international commercial subjects. In terms of the choice of substantive governing law and arbitration institutions, the laws and arbitration institutions of China are also not the first choice of international commercial subjects.

However, China will inevitably encounter more and more international commercial arbitration cases involving economic sanctions in the near future. First of all, with the increased participation of Chinese enterprises in international commercial transactions and their increased voice in international commercial transactions, the number of international commercial arbitrations seated in China or administered by Chinese arbitration institutions has been growing. The International Arbitration Survey 2021, jointly published by Queen Mary University of London and White & Case, showed that Beijing and Shanghai ranked sixth and eighth, respectively, in the list of most popular seats of arbitration, selected by 12% and 8% of respondents. Meanwhile, Shenzhen is also among the seats selected by 2–4% of respondents.[103] Also, according to the report, for the first time, CIETAC made it into the top five of the most popular arbitration institutions, with 17% of respondents choosing it.[104] In

---

[102] The term "China" used in this paper does not include the Hong Kong Special Administrative Region, the Macao Special Administrative Region, and the Taiwan Region.

[103] *See 2021 International Arbitration Survey: Adapting arbitration to a Changing World*, White & Case (Jul. 19, 2023, 3:52PM), https://www.whitecase.com/sites/default/files/2023-05/qmul-international-arbitration-survey-2021-web-single-final-v3.pdf, at 6-7.

[104] *See id.*, at 9–10.

international commercial arbitration involving economic sanctions seated in China, arbitrators are required to make a determination as to their jurisdiction and arbitrability of the dispute. Accordingly, Chinese courts may also need to determine the arbitrability of the dispute in cases concerning confirmation of the validity of the arbitration agreement and revocation of the arbitral award.

Secondly, Chinese courts will be confronted with an increasing number of application for the recognition and enforcement of international commercial arbitral awards involving economic sanctions. In fact, relevant practice already exists in China, such as *Macquarie Bank Ltd. v. Wanda Holding Group Ltd.*,[105] which was accepted by the Shanghai Financial Court in 2021. Although this case did not involve the issue of arbitrability of international commercial disputes involving economic sanctions, Chinese courts will inevitably need to make a determination on this issue in other cases of application for recognition and enforcement of foreign arbitral awards in the future.

5.2 Arbitrability of International Commercial Disputes Involving Economic Sanctions Under Chinese Law

Similar to France and Germany, China has constructed a composite criterion in defining arbitrability of disputes, adopting the criteria of "equal subjects," "economic interest," and "disposability."[106]

On the one hand, Article 2 of the *Arbitration Law of the People's Republic of China* (hereinafter referred to as "*Arbitration Law*")[107] limits the parties to arbitration to "citizens, legal persons and other organizations that are equal subjects." It can be observed that China has adopted the criterion of "equal subject" regarding subjective arbitrability.

On the other hand, regarding objective arbitrability, the *Arbitration Law* clarifies arbitrable and inarbitrable matters, respectively. Specifically, Article 2 of the *Arbitration Law* confines arbitrable matters to "contractual disputes and other disputes over rights and interests in property." Thus, the *Arbitration Law* adopts the standard of "economic interest" when determining arbitrable matters. At the same time, Article 3 of the *Arbitration Law*[108] excludes disputes that are not disposable, including marital, adoption, guardianship, support and succession disputes, as well

---

[105] [2021] Hu 74 Xie Wai Ren No. 1 ([2021]沪74协外认1号).

[106] *See* Huang & Ma, *supra* note 86, at 57–58.

[107] Article 2 of the *Arbitration Law of the People's Republic of China* stipulates that "Contractual disputes and other disputes over rights and interests in property between citizens, legal persons and other organizations that are equal subjects may be arbitrated."

[108] Article 3 of the *Arbitration Law of the People's Republic of China* stipulates that "The following disputes may not be arbitrated: (1) marital, adoption, guardianship, support and succession disputes; (2) administrative disputes that shall be handled by administrative organs as prescribed by law."

as administrative disputes, from the scope of arbitration. China's determination of non-arbitrable matters is plainly based on the criterion of "disposability."

According to the aforementioned provisions on arbitrability of China, international commercial disputes involving economic sanctions are arbitrable. On one side, such disputes in essence are international commercial disputes but involve the application of economic sanction norms due to the intervention of economic sanctions. Thus, like other international commercial disputes, the disputes arise between equal commercial subjects and involve economic interests, which meet the aforementioned criteria of "equal subjects" and "economic interest." On the other side, such disputes do not fall into the category of inarbitrable matters enumerated in Article 3 of the *Arbitration Law*. Therefore, international commercial disputes involving economic sanctions are arbitrable under Chinese law.

Moreover, recognizing the arbitrability of international commercial disputes involving economic sanctions is also in line with the long-standing notion of encouraging and supporting arbitration of China. In terms of arbitrability, this notion is reflected in the following aspects. On the one hand, it is clear from the above provisions on arbitrability of China that China imposes fewer restrictions on the scope of arbitration, which is consistent with the international trend of expanding arbitrable matters.[109]

On the other hand, China also explicitly allows disputes involving public interests, such as securities disputes and copyright disputes, to be resolved through arbitration.[110] For instance, Articles 79[111] and 80[112] of the *Interim Provisions on the Management of the Issuing and Trading of Stocks* explicitly affirm the arbitrability of disputes relating to the issuance and trading of stocks. Article 60(1) of the *Copyright Law of the People's Republic of China (2020 Amendment)*[113] also expressly grants parties the right to submit copyright disputes to arbitration. It can

---

[109] *See* Liu, *supra* note 15, at 76; *See* Huang & Ma, *supra* note 86, at 58; See Zhang, *Fanlongduan Zhengyi de Kezhongcaixing Yanjiu—Jianlun Oumei Guojia de Lifa yu Sifa Shijian jiqi dui Woguo de Qishi (反垄断争议的可仲裁性研究—兼论欧美国家的立法与司法实践及其对我国的启示) [Study on the Arbitrability of Antitrust Disputes—An Introduction to the Legislative and Judicial Practices of European Countries and America and Their Implications for China]*, *supra* note 76, at 152.

[110] *See* Liu, *supra* note 15, at 76.

[111] Article 79 of the *Interim Provisions on the Management of the Issuing and Trading of Stocks* stipulates that "For disputes concerning the issuing and trading of stocks, the parties concerned may apply for mediation or arbitration with the arbitration organizations according to their agreements."

[112] Article 80 of the *Interim Provisions on the Management of the Issuing and Trading of Stocks* stipulates that "Disputes involving the issuing and trading of stocks among securities managing organizations or between a securities managing organization and a stock exchange shall be mediated or arbitrated by arbitration organizations set up with the approval of or designated by the Securities Committee of the State Council."

[113] Article 60(1) of the *Copyright Law of the People's Republic of China (2020 Amendment)* stipulates that "A dispute over copyright may be settled by mediation or be submitted for arbitration to a copyright arbitration institution under a written arbitration agreement concluded between the parties concerned, or under the arbitration clause in the copyright contract."

thus be concluded that China does not deny the arbitrability of disputes merely because of the application of mandatory rules, which is consistent with the international trend of strictly applying the criterion of "public order" to exclude arbitrability and distinguishing between disputes and rules of law in terms of their natures of public policy.

Since the outbreak of the economic crisis at the end of the nineteenth century, in order to safeguard public interests such as the maintenance of economic order and the protection of the weaker party, many states have strengthened their intervention in the economy and intervened in private legal relations through various mandatory rules.[114] As a result, the boundary between private and public law has become increasingly blurred, and public interests have gradually penetrated into the dispute resolution between private subjects.[115] Consequently, there are few international commercial disputes that do not involve any legal norms with a public policy nature entirely.[116] Since international commercial arbitration is the most popular international commercial dispute resolution mechanism, most international commercial arbitrations involve mandatory rules more or less.[117] Therefore, if all disputes involving mandatory rules are excluded from the scope of arbitration based on the criterion of "public order," there will be few arbitrable matters.[118] Such an approach of interpreting public policy broadly will greatly narrow the scope of international commercial arbitration, undermine the predictability of arbitration clauses, and thereby hinder normal international commercial transactions. On the contrary, the approach of strictly limiting the application of the criterion of "public order" to the public policy nature of the dispute itself is conducive to encouraging the development of international commercial arbitration, enhancing the predictability of arbitration clauses, and thus promoting international commercial transactions.

Therefore, when applying Chinese law to determine the arbitrability of international commercial disputes involving economic sanctions, the prevailing view should be adopted, i.e., the arbitrability of a dispute shall not be denied due to the application of economic sanctions norms, in accordance with China's provisions regarding arbitrability as well as the notion of encouraging and supporting arbitration.

---

114 *See* DU, *supra* note 1, at 268; *See* Xu Junke (许军珂), *Lun Gongsifa de Huafen dui Chongtufa de Yingxiang—Waiguo Gongfa zuowei Zhunjufa de Kexingxing Fenxi (论公私法的划分对冲突法的影响—外国公法作为准据法的可行性分析) [On the Influence of the Division of Public and Private Law on Conflict of Laws—Feasibility Analysis of Foreign Public Law as Applicable Law]*, DANGDAI FAXUE (当代法学) [CONTEMPORARY LAW REVIEW], no. 3, 2007, at 32–33.

115 *See* ALEC STONE SWEET & FLORIAN GRISEL, THE EVOLUTION OF INTERNATIONAL ARBITRATION: JUDICIALIZATION, GOVERNANCE, LEGITIMACY 171 (1st ed., 2017).

116 *See* Liu, *supra* note 15, at 54.

117 *See id.*, at 124.

118 *See id.*, at 54.

6 Conclusion

As an intervention in private legal relationships, economic sanctions have led to numbers of international commercial disputes, which in turn have had an undeniable impact on international commercial arbitration. Among them, economic sanctions pose a challenge to the arbitrability of disputes, resulting in the divergence of views among states regarding the arbitrability of international commercial disputes involving economic sanctions. The divergence stems from the different criteria for arbitrability adopted by states and the arbitrability of disputes involving mandatory rules under the criteria. Given that economic sanction norms fall within the category of mandatory rules, the divergence also extends to the arbitrability of international commercial disputes involving economic sanctions norms. Under the international trend of expanding arbitrable matters and narrowing scope of public policy, China should be cautious in denying the arbitrability of disputes due to the intervention of economic sanctions in private legal relations, so as to encourage and support international commercial arbitration to play its due role in international commercial dispute resolution and to promote China's construction of "arbitration-friendly" jurisdiction.

Chapter 8
Concurrent Criminal Jurisdiction: A Challenge to the Concept of Traditional Jurisdictional Rule

Pooja Devi and Diksha Munjal-Shankar

Abstract International law strives to promote and maintain peaceful relations among States. The concept of sovereignty which helps in maintaining equality among States is enshrined in the United Nations Charter under the principle of non-interference and the prohibition on the threat or use of force against each other. The traditional jurisdictional rules of international law were developed on these above values and aim to lessen regulatory conflict and maintain the peaceful coexistence of States. But from late twentieth century, there has been a dramatic rise in the criminal activities such as terrorism, child trafficking, etc., and when the preparation, commission and presence of accused do not limit at one place. Therefore, territoriality principle is no more suitable to deal with the crimes having extraterritorial reach. Hence, increased assertion of extraterritorial jurisdiction on different grounds—such as territoriality, nationality, protective and universality—has emerged as the preferred approach to bring perpetrator of crime to justice. However, this approach pulls jurisdictional conflicts among the States. The conflict of extraterritorial criminal jurisdiction is an emerging area of concern. These conflicts lead to challenges in collection of evidence, extradition of accused and violation of ne bis in idem and ultimately cause delay in justice to victim as well as accused. Hence, resolving or preventing the jurisdictional conflict that becomes a major concern of international community is an emerging area of concern. The conflict of jurisdiction is competency conflict, as to which State has adjudicative authority to try the crime. It is not deniable that international law is dominated by international relations and politics. There have been many instances of competing jurisdictional claims turned into internal or international politics. The international cooperation is

This article was previously published in Law Science—Selected Papers Volume 3, Issue 4 (2024).

P. Devi (✉) · D. Munjal-Shankar
Law Centre 1, Faculty of Law, University of Delhi, New Delhi, India

T. Du, X. Fei (eds.), *The BRICS Legal Cooperation and Perspectives*,
https://doi.org/10.1007/978-981-95-4356-4_8

guided by political, economic and social affinity, which ideally should not be the case especially in respect of criminal conduct. This research work will address the ambiguity in the law of jurisdiction and the conflicts/constraints in asserting the extraterritorial jurisdiction and provide suggestions to resolve the problems identified in exercise of extraterritorial jurisdiction.

Keywords Jurisdiction · Territorial principle · Extraterritorial · Sovereignty · Immunity · Concurrent criminal jurisdiction

1 Introduction

Every sovereign State is entitled to shape its sovereignty or *imperium* by adopting laws and "*juris-dicere*",[1] to state what the law is relating to persons, activities or legal interests.[2] The term jurisdiction can be understood in terms of the three branches of government which exercise it, and they are legislature, executive and judicial.[3] These three branches of government have to exercise their power within their respective territory.

Jurisdiction has become a concern of international law due to expansion of interest of States, movement of people, international and transnational crime and more particularly due to the extraterritorial reach of the States, etc.[4] The public international law guarantees that every State is equal and every State enjoys the sovereignty which means no State will interfere with its sovereign rights.[5] It means that the State has to exercise its powers within the State or under the principles which

[1] Cedric Ryngaert, *Jurisdiction in International Law,* 5 (2015) quoted H.E. Yntema, "The Comity Doctrine," 65 MICHIGAN L.R. (1966); GBENGA ODUNTAN, SOVEREIGNTY AND JURISDICTION IN AIRSPACE AND OUTER SPACE, 31 (2011).

[2] J H Beale, *The Jurisdiction of a Sovereign State*, 36 HARVARD L.R. 241–252 (1923); C.L. Blakesley, *United States Jurisdiction over Extraterritorial Crime*, 73 THE JOURNAL OF CRIMINAL LAW & CRIMINOLOGY, 1109-1145 (1982).

[3] IAN BROWNLIE, PRINCIPLES OF PUBLIC INTERNATIONAL LAW, 299 (1990).

[4] Dr. Jennifer A. Zerk, *Extraterritorial Jurisdiction: Lessons for the Business and Human Rights Sphere from Six Regulatory Areas, CORPORATE* SOCIAL RESPONSIBILITY INITIATIVE WORKING PAPER 59, (2013); Alex Mills, *Rethinking Jurisdiction in International Law*, 84 BRITISH YEARBOOK OF INTERNATIONAL LAW, 187–239 (2014); Hiroshi Fukuda, *Jurisdiction in International Application of United States Antitrust Laws*, 12 CLEVELAND-MARSHALL L.R., 125–145 (1963), also *available at: https://engagedscholarship.csuohio.edu/cgi/viewcontent.cgi?article=3208&context=clevstlrev* (accessed on 24 July 2018).

[5] Hans Kelsen, *The Principle of Sovereign Equality of States as A basis for International-Organisation*, 53 YALE L.J. 207–220 (1944); Ryngaert, *supra note* 1, at 6; B. Moslemi, *Principle of Sovereign Equality of States in the Light of the Doctrine of Responsibility to Protect*, INTERNATIONAL JOURNAL OF HUMANITIES AND CULTURAL STUDIES, 687–697 (2015).

international law considers proper. If there is any protest over the jurisdiction, then the matter will be submitted to International Court.[6]

Under international law, every State is equal, for being sovereign. That means they have no power to regulate each other. Hence law of jurisdiction has become important because it regulates and delimits the competence of the States and may help in limiting the risk of overlapping of jurisdiction,[7] when two or more States claim jurisdiction on legitimate grounds or principles recognised in international law.[8]

2 Understanding Jurisdiction

The word jurisdiction can be literally understood as power or competence. It is made up of two Latin words, i.e. *juris* and *dicere* meaning "law" and "to speak", respectively, and translating as "speaking the law".[9] The term jurisdiction gives legality to the power or authority of the sovereign State to affect the rights of an individual or entity.[10] But in legal terms it indicates some form of competence or authority of a legal body or State "to tell what the law is, what law or rule applies to whom, in what place, and in regard to whom, in what place, and in regard to what acts or events".[11]

For the purpose of this article the term jurisdiction is understood in two contexts. First is State relations with individuals, i.e. their power to regulate conduct of individuals, and this may be done in number of ways, and State's criminal jurisdiction is one aspect of such power. The second species of jurisdiction is State's legal relationship with another State and the dynamics at play when there is overlap or conflict between such jurisdictions.

Under international law, every State is equal, for being sovereign. Hence they have no power to regulate each other. So in the context of State's criminal jurisdiction, which State can exercise or is entitled to exercise the jurisdiction over the criminal conduct which started in one State and consummated in another State? And when one State maintains to establish its criminal jurisdiction over a certain

[6] For example, *Case between France and Turkey (called Lotus Case).*

[7] Ryngaert, *supra note* 1 at 8 (he asserted that "law of jurisdiction determines how far, *ratione loci*, a state's laws might reach").

[8] DANIELLE IRELAND-PIPER, ACCOUNTABILITY IN EXTRATERRITORIALITY, 17 (2017).

[9] Joseph H. Beale, *The Jurisdiction of a Sovereign State*, HARVARD L.R,, 221–264 (1923).

[10] Harvard Law School, *Draft Convention on Jurisdiction with respect to Crime*, Article 1 (b) 439 29 AMERICAN JOURNAL OF INTERNATIONAL LAW (1935).

[11] Philip C. Jessup, *Jurisdiction*, 61 INTERNATIONAL LEGAL STUDIES SERIES, U.S. NAVAL WAR COLLEGE, 303–318 (1980).

criminal act, it is simultaneously stating that it has the extensive right *vis-a-vis* all other States to penalise and punish this act.[12]

The concept of jurisdiction acts as a link between the relationship of the sovereign State and the individual. It provides legality to such relationship and is the foundation of the State authority over the individuals.[13] Therefore, the territorial jurisdiction has been widely accepted as a State's authority to legislate, enforce and adjudicate legal rules.[14]

Legislative jurisdiction or prescriptive jurisdiction refers to making of laws via the legislature or chosen representatives or framing of rules, regulation, etc. by the executive via delegated legislation or determination of a court.[15] Making of binding laws for the State's territory by the legally recognised organs of the State falls under legislative jurisdiction. That may extend beyond the limits of States unless there were specific prohibitive rules under international law.[16] However, the tide of international law has since turned. Now, States may only exercise jurisdiction extraterritorially when they avail themselves of a recognised head of jurisdiction under international law.

Executive jurisdiction means implementing and enforcing the law passed by the legislature. Executive jurisdiction has the potential to meddle as it may and has to rely on coercive methods like arrest, search and seizure to ensure compliance to the law, rules or regulations[17] via the executive machinery like police or administration.[18]

Adjudicative jurisdiction refers to the jurisdiction of the State to subject, person entities, etc. and decide upon the matter in dispute whether in civil or criminal proceeding[19] via the courts, tribunals or other quasi-judicial bodies. Any authority or person capable of giving legally binding judgement in a matter aids the adjudicative machinery of the State.

---

[12] PATRICK CAPPS, MALCOLM EVANS, EVANS, STRATOS KONSTANDINDIS (ed.), INTRODUCTION IN ASSERTING JURISDICTION, xxii, (2003).

[13] Anthony Colangelo, *Constitutional Limits on Extraterritorial Jurisdiction: Terrorism and the Intersection of National and International Law*, 48 HARVARD INTERNATIONAL L.J., 121–201 (2007).

[14] Laker Airways Ltd. v Sabena, Belgian World Airlines, 731 F. 2d 909 (emphasising that "the prerogative of a nation to control and regulate activities within its boundaries is an essential, definitional element of sovereignty", and "the territoriality base of jurisdictional is universally recognised" and "is the most pervasive and basic principle underlying eh exercise by nations of prescriptive regulatory power").

[15] Section 401(a) of Restatement (Third) of U.S. Foreign Relations Law (hereinafter Restatement (Third)), *available at:* https://jura.urz.uni-heidelberg.de/mat/file_viewer.php?fid=10946 *(accessed on 23 March 2016).*

[16] S. S. Lotus (France v. Turkey) 1927 PCIJ (Ser. A), No. 10 at 19.

[17] ROBERT CRYER, HAKAN FRIMAN, DARRYL ROBINSON & ELIZABETH WIMSHURST, AN INTRODUCTION TO INTERNATIONAL CRIMINAL LAW AND PROCEDURE, 38 (2007).

[18] Section 401(c), *supra note* 15.

[19] *Id.,* Section 401(b).

It is clear that before a State invokes prescriptive jurisdiction and exercises the sequential executive or judicial jurisdiction, a link factor or a nexus should be established between the act in question and the assertion of jurisdiction of the State.[20] Earlier the link was established on territorial basis, but in today's scenario the linking point between the State and the crime is not only restricted to the territorial factor but includes different components, one of them being the community of interest as a whole.

3 Principles of Jurisdiction

The State's competence to claim jurisdiction over the criminal event occurring inside or outside the State territory is decided by the jurisdictional rules/principles. A jurisdictional rule acts as a compass to locate the authority which is capable of giving the final judgement in the matter before it. Jurisdictional rules act as a bridge between the sovereign/government and the governed.[21] They provide the nexus/link which confers the State to regulate a person or his/her activity. These jurisdiction principles are the territorial principle, the nationality principle, the protective principle and the universality principle.

3.1 Territoriality Principle

The territorial principle is the oldest and most primary basis of jurisdiction under the customary international law.[22] This principle is well established and is recognised by every nation. It means that a State has the right to regulate persons and activities within the territory.[23] Territoriality is an expression of sovereignty and thus

[20] BRAINERD CURRIE, SELECTED ESSAY IN THE CONFLICT OF LAW, 170 (1963).

[21] B.W.H, *Jurisdiction in Criminal Cases*, 21 MICHIGAN L.R. 792–795 (1923), In re Stupp, 11 Blatch (U.S.C.C.) 124 ("...the right of State to punish its own citizens for crimes committed abroad, even in places where it has not physical territorial jurisdiction, no quasi territorial jurisdiction and not treaty jurisdiction"); in In re Tivnan, 5 Best & S. 645–679 (Cockburn, C.J. said, "an offence may be cognizable, triable and justiciable in two places, e.g. a murder by British subject in foreign country. A British subject who commits murder in the United States of America may be punished in England land by our municipal law, which extend to its citizen in every part of the world").

[22] M. Cherif Bassiouni, *Theories of Jurisdiction and their Application in Extradition Law and Practice*, 5 CALIFORNIA WESTERN INTERNATIONAL L.J, 1–61 (1975); Henrik Horn, *International Jurisdiction over Standard- Essential Patents* (Research Institute of Industrial Economics, IFN Working Paper No. 1314, 2020), available at: https://www.ifn.se/media/z3tplrkc/wp1314.pdf (accessed on 4 January 2022).

[23] Uta Kohl, *Jurisdiction and the Internet Regulatory Competence over Online* Activity, 89 (2007) (stated that this maxim dates back at least to Ulricus Huber, *De conflict legume diversarum in*

well recognised under international treaty and customary law.[24] The backbone of national laws concerning criminal jurisdiction is the territoriality principle: States claim the right not only to enact but also to enforce the criminal norms with respect to any act that occurs on their territory.[25]

The importance of the territorial principle as a base of jurisdiction has been emphasised in various international cases such as the *Island of Palmas (Netherlands v. USA), Barcelona Traction, Light and Power Co, Ltd. and Arrest Warrant case (Democratic Republic of the Congo v. Belgium).*

The general principle of criminal jurisdiction is that the jurisdiction is determined by the locality of the offence irrespective of the nationality or other similar attributes for the offender[26] but only so long as such laws and rules should conform to a minimum standard and are administered fairly and impartially.[27] The exercise of territorial jurisdiction does not require that all of the acts or omissions constituting elements of an offence must occur in the territory of the State. For example, by means of the mails or modern electronic communications, a fraud can easily be committed by a person located in one country against residents of another country, who may be induced to send their money to yet another country.[28] In these cases, territorial jurisdiction may be exercised at the place where the offence was initiated and where it was executed.[29]

The territorial principle which is considered as jurisdictional starting point for claim of jurisdiction has gone to an extensive approach.[30] In 1935, an effort was made to codify international law of jurisdiction by the American Society of International Law (ASIL) and provided that there are two territorial principles. The first is when the crime commences outside the territory but concludes within it or has an effect in it, and the second is when the crime commences within the territory

---

diversis imperiss (1684), reiterated by JUSTICE STORY in THE APOLLON, 9 WHEAT 362–370 (1824)).

[24] Geoff Gilbert, *Crimes sans frontières: Jurisdictional Problems in English Law*, 63 BRITISH YEAR BOOK OF INTERNATIONAL LAW, 415–430 (1992), MICHAEL HIRST, JURISDICTION AND THE AMBIT OF THE CRIMINAL LAW, 1 (2003) at 192; Mills, *supra note* 4 at 190; MICHAL VAGIAS, TERRITORIAL JURISDICTION OF THE INTERNATIONAL CRIMINAL COURT, 13–14 (2014); Ryngaert, *supra note* 1 at 44.

[25] S. S. Lotus, *supra note* 16, paras 45 and 46.

[26] Mobarik Ali Ahmed v. State of Bombay, AIR 1957 SC 857.

[27] GREEN HAYWOOD HACKWORTH, INTERNATIONAL LAW, 84 (1941).

[28] Lotus Case, *supra note* 16 para 202–204 (the world court justified the Turkey action by applying the objective territorial principle.

[29] Stephan Wilake, *International Jurisdiction in Cyberspace: Which States may Regulate the Internet?*, available at: http://www.fclj.org/wp-content/uploads/1997/01/wilske.pdf (accessed on 23 November 2016).

[30] H.D. Wolswijk, *Locus Delicti and Criminal Jurisdiction*, XLVI NETHERLANDS INTERNATIONAL L.R., 361–382(1999).

but has an effect or is concluded outside it.[31,32] Anders Henrikson has taken the reference of 11 September 2001 terrorist attacks in the United States to explain these two principles:

> As the attacks were completed on US territory, the Americans had jurisdiction over the attacks on the basis of objective territoriality. But since a substantial part of the planning and preparation of the attacks occurred elsewhere, most notably in Afghanistan and Germany, other States could derive a claim of jurisdiction on the basis of subjective territoriality.[33]

Hence territorial principle may be identified in two forms:

(a) Subjective application of territorial principle
(b) Objective application of territorial principle

Subjective Application of Territorial Principle
The territorial concept is wider in application than that at first it appears. States have the jurisdiction over the crimes which just a component of the offence occurred in the territory beside the crimes committed within the territory.[34] "It is commonly accepted that regardless of where the criminal result or effect takes place, States are basically allowed to predicate jurisdiction over crimes, if one or more of unwarranted modes of conduct are performed within their territory. This is also called ***Locus of the Conduct.***"[35] The purpose of this principle is to suppress the criminal mind manifested in wrongful conduct for the protection of its community. For example, A, who from within the territorial limit of a State X, shoots and kills a person on foreign soil.[36] Here it is immaterial whether the crime is ultimately completed or consummated outside the territory, and it is just sufficient for State X to take action if the unlawful act/omission takes place within its territory.[37]

Objective Application of Territorial Principle
The State is allowed to predicate jurisdiction on the basis of the criminal result that takes place within its territory, even though the commencement or the preparation of the offence took place outside the territory. This is called ***Locus of the Result* or effect doctrine.** Professor Hyde wrote "the *setting in motion outside of a State*

[31] Surya Jyoti Gupta, *Civil and Criminal Jurisdiction in the Internet*, 39 INDIAN BAR REVIEW, 45-71 (2002).

[32] *Id.*

[33] ANDERS HENRIKSON, INTERANTIONAL LAW, 88 (2017).

[34] Wendell Berge, *Criminal Jurisdiction and the Territorial Principle*, 30 MICHIGAN L.R., 238–269 (1931).

[35] Robert Thee, *State Criminal Jurisdiction*, 9 MALAYA L.R., 38–95 (1967).

[36] *Id.* at 43.

[37] *Article 3. Territorial Jurisdiction*, 29 THE AMERICAN JOURNAL OF INTERNATIONAL LAW, 480–508 (1935), *available at: https://www.jstor.org/stable/2213639* (accessed on 26 March 2016).

which produces as a direct consequence an injurious effect therein, justifies the territorial sovereign in prosecuting the actor when he enters its domain".[38]

For example, a gun may be fired from State A, but the victim is struck dead in State B. Irrespective of the locus of conduct, State B should be permitted to take cognisance of the homicide.[39]

Transnational organised crimes like human trafficking or smuggling of contraband, narcotics or psychotropic are fundamentally continuing crimes, and all the affected States can base their jurisdiction by relying on the objective territorial principle.[40] Since the criminal act is not deemed to be ceased and may be continuing and produces effect in the territory of other State, the objective application of territorial jurisdiction seems legitimate due to "continuing act doctrine".[41] The objective territorial principle was also applied by Supreme Court of India in case of *Mobarik Ali Ahmed v. State of Bombay,*[42] wherein the accused who was a Pakistani National and while being in Pakistan obtained money by fraud from an Indian. He contended that neither he was citizen of India nor he has committed the offence on the territory of India; hence India had no jurisdiction over him. But the Supreme Court rejected his contention because the effect of the accused's action was in Bombay.

Judge Moore has recognised the effects of the act in the territory to invoke objective territorial jurisdiction and observed that:

> It appears to be now universally admitted that, where a crime is committed in the territorial jurisdiction of one State as the direct result of the act of a person at the time corporeally present in another State, international law, by reason of the principle of *constructive presence* of the offender at the place where his act took effect, does not forbid the prosecution of the offender by the former State, should be come within its territorial jurisdiction.[43]

After that the courts in the United States have used the subsidiary theory of **"Constructive presence of the** accused person"[44] for assuming jurisdiction on the basis of principle of locus of the result.

[38] I. HYDE, INTERNATIONAL LAW- CHIEFLY AS INTERPRETED AND APPLIED BY THE UNITED STATES, 798 (1945).

[39] Example quoted from Thee, *supra note* 35.

[40] Director of Public Prosecutions v. Doot UKHL [1973] 1 ALL ER 940.

[41] Ilias Bantekas, *Criminal Jurisdiction of States under International Law*, MAX PLANCK ENCYCLOPEDIAS OF INTERNATIONAL LAW, (2011), quoted Timberlane Lumber Co. v. Bank of America, 549 F.2d 597 (9th Cir. 1977).

[42] 1957 AIR 857.

[43] Lotus case, *supra* note 16, para 252.

[44] Simpson v. State 92 Ga. 41 (1983).

3.2 Nationality Principle

Every nation is nothing but a collection of individual human beings living within the territory of that nation. Nationality is the legal link connecting the nationals to its nations. The link is too strong and well established in international law, and on the basis of this link, the nationality principle empowers the States to exercise criminal jurisdiction on the national even for the crime which they have committed beyond the State's territory or on a foreign land.[45]

The nationality principle is an aspect of sovereignty and also authorises State's criminal jurisdiction over its nationals, even when the conduct may have occurred beyond territorial border.[46]

Aspects of Nationality Principle

Active Nationality Principle

A State has the right to extend the application of its laws to its national even in respect of events occurring entirely aboard. This type of jurisdiction is exercised by State against their nationals for the crimes committed abroad. It is deemed uncontested that a State can exercise jurisdiction on the basis of nationality of the accused, because it is believed that nationals are subject of the State and not a concern of international law.[47] Therefore, it is the jurisdiction on ground of the nationality of the perpetrator.[48]

Many treaties providing for the suppression of crimes having international repercussion recognise the jurisdiction of a State on the basis of the nationality principle.[49] The Harvard Draft Convention provided that the nationality concept should apply to the criminal offender who is a national when the crime is committed.[50] It means that the State authority will invoke the jurisdiction only if the culprit is a national at the time of commission of the offences. This also means that this principle should not apply to a person who becomes a national after committing a crime,

[45] Mills, *supra* note 4 at 196.

[46] Brownile, *supra* note 3 at 303.

[47] Ryngaert, *supra* note 1 at 99–100; Blackmer v. United States 421, 437 (1932) (held that " with respect to such an exercise of authority, there is no question of international law, but solely of the purport of the municipal law which established the duties of the citizen in relation to his own government"); Harvard Research, *Competence of Courts in Regard to Foreign States*, 26 AMERICAN JOURNAL OF INTERNATIONAL LAW (SUPPLEMENT) 451 (1932) at 531 ("It is believed, however, that limitation, however, that limitation on the exercise of active personality jurisdiction are matters which each State is free to determine for itself. Both the crimes abroad for which it will punish its nationals and circumstances under which it will punish its nationals and circumstances under which it will exercise jurisdiction are matters which international law leaves each State free to decide according to local needs and conditions".).

[48] Thee, *supra note* 35 at 52.

[49] https://www.amnesty.org/download/Documents/128000/ior530032001en.pdf (accessed on 21 March 2016).

[50] Harvard Research in International Law, *Jurisdiction with Respect to Crime,* AMERICAN LAW JOURNAL (1935).

again by a reason of the fact that he/she owed no allegiance at the time the wrong was done. Also, the exercise of jurisdiction on the basis of nationality principle should be based on a pre-existing specific or general criminal legislation so as to adhere to the principle of non-application of retrospective laws.[51] The legislative practices of various nations show several ways in which penal jurisdiction is assumed over nationals who commit crime outside the State of origin.[52]

Passive Personality Principle

This principle provides that the State may claim jurisdiction to try an individual for offences committed abroad which have affected or have the potential to affect nationals of the State; hence one can call it as jurisdiction by the victim's country of nationality.[53] Passive personality jurisdiction is the most controversial form of extra-territorial jurisdiction. The basis for this controversy was that it would be unfair to prosecute the foreign national for a crime committed on a foreign land against the national of that prosecuting State. Hence, it was suggested that it would encroach the sovereignty of the State on which territory the crime was committed.[54] Assertions by the States on the basis of passive nationality jurisdiction and consequent absence of international protest lend credence to its legality especially in regard to crimes like terrorism, hostage-taking and hijacking.[55] The treaties[56] now provide for passive personality jurisdiction in respect of terrorist acts and other matters of general international concern, and some States, such as the United States, which opposed it, now rely upon the principle in such contexts in their national legislation,[57] as noted by a Federal District Court in *US v. Yunis.*[58] Hence, this principle is now a consistent and

[51] Ilias Bantekas, *Criminal Jurisdiction of States under International Law*, MAX PLANCK ENCYCLOPAEDIAS OF INTERNATIONAL LAW, (2011).

[52] The concept of extra-territoriality finds its roots in Constitution of India, 1950; Criminal Procedure Code, 1973; Indian Penal Code, 1850 and Information Technology Act, 2000. For details refer to Chap. 2.

[53] Zerk, *supra note* 4; Geoffrey R. Watson, *Offenders Abroad: The Case for Nationality-Based Criminal Jurisdiction*, 17 YALE JOURNAL OF INTERNATIONAL LAW, 41–84 (1992).

[54] Geoffrey R. Watson, *The Passive Personality Principle*, 28 TEXAS INTERNATIONAL L.J., 2-46 (1993), quoted, Letter of Assistant Secretary of State Janet G. Mullin of 1989 (criticising passive personality jurisdiction); H.F. VAN PANHUYS, THE ROLE OF NATIONALITY IN INTERNATIONAL LAW, 132 (1959) (noting that passive personality jurisdiction raises similar issues in civil and criminal cases).

[55] Danielle Ireland- Piper, *Prosecutions of Extraterritorial Criminal Conduct and the Abuse of Rights of Doctrine* 9 UTRECHT L.R., 69-89 (2013), Ryangert, *supra note* 1, at 500.

[56] International Civil Aviation Organization (ICAO), *Convention on Civil Aviation ("Chicago Convention")*, 7 December 1944, (1994) 15 U.N.T.S. 295); International Civil Aviation Organization (ICAO), *Convention on Offences and Certain Acts Committed on Board Aircraft*, 14 September 1963; UN General Assembly, *Convention Against Torture and Other Cruel, Inhuman or Degrading Treatment or Punishment*, 10 December 1984 (Article 5(1)(c) of states are authorized but not obliged to establish criminal jurisdiction on the basis of the passive personality principle).

[57] DAVID HARRIS, CASES AND MATERIAL ON INTERNATIONAL LAW, 239 (7th ed. 2010).

[58] (1988) 82 I.L.R. 344. In this case, the defendant, a Lebanese national, and others hijacked a Jordanian airliner at Beirut Airport, with two US nationals and other passengers on board, ulti-

permanent feature of the vast majority of general international criminal law treaties.[59]

3.3 Protective Principle

There is a need for the States to develop methods for catching criminals beyond their borders, and this led to the rise in extraterritorial jurisdiction. The extraterritorial criminal jurisdiction based on the protective principle takes care of the offences committed abroad, if the crime threatens the "security, integrity or independence" of the State seeking to rely on protective principle.[60]

This principle gives jurisdiction to the State if the act of a person from outside the State territory is prejudicial or has the potential to harm the State's interest.[61] Any sovereign State would like the extra assurance that in the absence of an action from an alliance or other international organisation, it can bring to justice any person or entity acting from beyond the territory to cause harm to the State's sovereign right to security, peace and stability.[62]

---

mately blowing it up there. The defendant was arrested by FBI agents on board a yacht in international waters in the Mediterranean. He was convicted in US court of, inter alia, hostage-taking and air piracy and sentenced to 30 years of imprisonment. On the question of jurisdiction, it was held that the US courts had jurisdiction under the unambiguous wording of the Hostage Taking Act and Anti-Hijacking Act and that the terms of these statutes prevailed over any customary international law jurisdiction rules to the contrary. But the United States has invoked the principle to assert jurisdiction over a hijacker who seized an American hostage on foreign soil.

[59] The various treaties are Tokyo Convention on Offences aboard Aircraft of 1969 (Article 4), Convention against Torture and Other Cruel, Inhuman or Degrading Treatment and Punishment of 1984 (Article 5 (1)(c)) and other anti-terrorist's treaties.

[60] "Article 7- Protection-Security of the State." 29 THE AMERICAN JOURNAL OF INTERNATIONAL LAW, 543–561 (1935), *available at:* https://doi.org/10.2307/2213643 (accessed on 3 December 2019) (states that "The States assuming penal competence upon the protective principle include practically all States other than the United States and Great Britain. Nearly all of these States apply laws for the protection of their security, integrity, or independence of offences committed abroad either by nationals or aliens.").

[61] Manuel R. Garcia-Mora, *Criminal Jurisdiction over Foreigners for Treason and Offences Against the Safety of the State Committed Upon Foreign Territory*, 19 UNIVERSITY OF PITTSBURGH L.R., 567-568 (1958).

[62] Bruno Simma & Andreas T. Miller, *Exercise and Limits of Jurisdiction* in JAMES CRAWFORD & MARTTI KOSKENNIEMI (eds.), THE CAMBRIDGE COMPANION TO INTERNATIONAL LAW, (2012).

3.4 Universality Principle

Universal jurisdiction as the name suggests is a special kind of jurisdictional principle which does not require any link or connection between the State invoking jurisdiction and the act sought to be regulated or the offender brought to justice.[63] But the scope of invoking this principle is limited to a certain kind of offences or act which is seen as an abomination and danger to mankind. It refers to the right of the States to assert jurisdiction regardless of the nationality (of the victim or perpetrator) or the place of commission of the act.[64] Piracy, slavery, genocide and terrorism can be curbed by asserting universal jurisdiction.[65]

4 Assertion of Extraterritorial Jurisdiction

Due to the increase in the development of the transportation and communication, criminal activities are not restricted within one territorial limit, which means the elements of crime are committed or the result of a crime is sustained in more than one country or if the offence occurs wholly outside the State. Perhaps, a State can no longer afford sole reliance on the application of territorial principle for prosecuting the criminals and safeguarding its interest as with time it has become inadequate. Hence, States assert extending the jurisdiction beyond their borders over the crimes in which they have legitimate interest or have been affected by it and to bring the perpetrator to justice. Even if there is no clear indication in the statute with respect to extraterritorial application, the State, by relying on the rules of jurisdiction under international law, may result in extraterritorial application of the domestic law. But it requires that for the extraterritorial application of the statute, the conduct which occurred in more than one territory must be forbidden in each State, and States claiming jurisdiction must establish the prima facie nexus on the basis of territoriality, nationality, protection or universality. As discussed above, initially the extraterritorial jurisdiction was exercised by the States for specific crimes[66] and was limited to specific condition.[67] But it is also well established that presently States are

---

[63] Eugene Kontorovich, *A Positive Theory of Universal Jurisdiction*, 80 NOTRE DAME L.R., 4–25 (2004), *available at:* https://www.law.gmu.edu/assets/files/publications/working_papers/04-25.pdf (accessed on 27 December 2020).

[64] Zerk, *supra note* 4 at 20; L. REYDAMS, UNIVERSAL JURISDICTION, INTERNATIONAL AND MUNICIPAL LEGAL PERSPECTIVES, 5 (2003).

[65] Lotika Sarkar, *The Proper Law of Crime in International Law*, 11 THE INTERNATIONAL AND COMPARATIVE LAW QUARTERLY, 446–470 (1962).

[66] Hirst, *supra note* 24 at 45; Blakesley, *supra note* 2 at 1139 (he stated that "the most ancient offence of universal interest is probably piracy").

[67] *Ibid.*, at 201–203; Anne-Sophie Massa, *Jurisdiction in England and Wales and in the Netherlands: a comparative appraisal with a European touch,* in ANDRE KLIP, SUBSTANTIVE CRIMINAL LAW OF EUROPEAN UNION, 109-110 (2011) (he stated that in England and Wales, extraterrito-

more willing to exercise extraterritorial jurisdiction (based on protective, personality or universality principles).[68] Due to changing patterns of crimes, telecommunications, travels, globalisation, etc., the States have been compelled to expand the jurisdiction beyond their borders.[69]

Walden categorises extraterritorial concept into two groups: (1) a group which is reflecting an inward focus, for example, principles which safeguard national interests fall under this group, i.e. passive nationality and protective principle, and (2) a group which has external focus; it means active nationality and universality principles as their objective is to fight against certain crimes and to rely on international cooperation.[70] As long as extraterritorial application of jurisdiction by a State does not unduly infringe with the sovereignty of other State, they are deemed valid under international law.[71]

Extraterritorial Jurisdiction to Prescribe (Substantive Law Dimension)

The function of the criminal law is to identify the conduct which the State forbids and attaches punishments. In order to punish the individual for the crime committed, the State has to first establish the prescriptive jurisdiction.[72] Generally, the States are free to criminalise an act or conduct when exercising prescriptive or legislative jurisdiction, but it seems that the international community relies on a permissive principle or absence of prohibitive rule to grant legality to exercise prescriptive jurisdiction and, hence, has adopted a more restrictive approach.[73] Hence, law granting extraterritorial jurisdiction is not forbidden in the international law, rather it permits the States to regulate overseas conduct but establishes certain

rial jurisdiction mainly arises in two circumstances: (1) when a Statute is clear on the extraterritorial application and (2) only exercise extraterritorial jurisdiction when there is no obstacle or no request of extradition); Charles Doyle, *Extraterritorial Application of American Criminal Law*, 7 CONGRESSIONAL RESEARCH SERVICE, 94–166 (2010) at 21 (he states that States are applying their law beyond their border where there is some clear nexus between crime and State.).

[68] Watson, *supra note* 53 at 46; Hirst, *supra note* 24 at 55; Ryngaert, *supra note* 1 at 85 and 88.

[69] Hirst, *supra note* 24 at 59.

[70] IAN WALDEN, COMPUTER CRIMES AND DIGITAL INVESTIGATIONS, 304 (2007).

[71] Menno T Kmminga, *Extraterritoriality*, MAX PLANCK ENCYCLOPAEDIA OF PUBLIC INTERNATIONAL LAW, (2012).

[72] American Banana co. V. United Fruit Co., 213 U.S. 347, 35–57 (1909) (The general and almost universal rule is that the character of an act as lawful or unlawful must be determined wholly by the law of the country where the act is done).

[73] Lotus case, *supra* note 16 at 19, paras 46–47 (the State is free to exercise prescriptive jurisdiction, unless a prohibitive rule to the contrary could be identified); Cedric Ryngaert, *The Concept of Jurisdiction in International Law*, *available at*: https://unijuris.sites.uu.nl/wp-content/uploads/sites/9/2014/12/The-Concept-of-Jurisdiction-in-International-Law.pdf (accessed on 30 July 2018); Mills, *supra* note 4 (observes that "the idea of jurisdiction in international law as a matter of State discretion should no longer be starting point of thinking on the subject, but should be replaced by the idea of State jurisdiction as a mixture of discretionary, mandatory and prohibitive elements").

limits.[74] These limits are imposed to pay attention to the vital interest of the States[75] and to ensure consistency with the international law.[76]

Extraterritorial Jurisdiction to Enforce and Adjudicate (Procedural Dimension)

Under the public international law there is distinction between legislative jurisdiction, judicial jurisdiction and enforcement jurisdiction.[77] As the legislative jurisdiction which may be extended extraterritoriality, enforcement jurisdiction is strictly territorial. According to Justice Story, "every national possesses an exclusive sovereignty and jurisdiction within its own territory", and it would be conflicting with the equality and exclusiveness of sovereignty of States if one nation would be free to enforce the substantive law of the country in another State.[78] This understanding is widely recognised.[79]

One should note that under international law, the principle of territorial sovereignty and principle of equality prevail,[80] so it generally follows that the State cannot enforce law of their State on the foreign land, "except by virtue of a permissive

---

[74] Lotus case, *supra* note 16 at 19, para 45.

[75] The classification of interests of the State was made in 1935 by the Harvard Law School Study which divided them into five categories, which would be the bases for the State to assert the criminal jurisdiction: (1) territorial principle, (2) nationality principles, (3) the passive personality, (4) protective principle and (5) universal principle. In U.S. v. Aluminium Co. of American, 148 F. 2d 416 (2D Cir. 1945), the jurisdiction was justified on the basis of objective territoriality (Judge Hand stated that "it is settle law…that any State may impose liabilities, even upon person not within its allegiance, for conduct outside its borders that as consequences within its borders which the State reprehends; and these liabilities other State will ordinarily recognize").

[76] Murray v. Schonner Charming Betsy (Charming Besty), 6 U.S. (2 Cranch) 64, 118 (1804) (the Supreme Court placed limitations upon statutory interpretation 1804 that "an act of Congress ought never to be construed to violate the law of nations if any other possible construction remains"); Jeffrey A. Meyer, *Dual Illegality and Geoambigouous Law: A New Rule for Extraterritorial Application of U.S. Law*, 95 MINNESOTA L.R., 110–186 (2010) at 143 (it a customary international law and must be used for interpretation to avoid the interference with other nations).

[77] F.A. Mann, *The Doctrine of International Jurisdiction Revisited after Twenty Years*, 1 *RECUEIL DE COURS* (1984); Morten Peschardt Pedersen, *Territorial Jurisdiction in Article 1 of the European Convention of Human Rights*, 73 NORDIC JOURNAL OF INTERNATIONAL LAW, 279–305 (2004).

[78] JOSEPH BEALE, A TREATIES ON THE CONFLICT OF LAW, 311–312 (1935) ("since the power of a State is supreme within its own territory, no other State can exercise power there…. It follows generally that no Statute can force to affect any person, thing, or act, outside the territory of the State that passed it").

[79] Lotus Case, *supra* note 16; *Ex-Territorial Jurisdiction of Crime*, 1 ST. LOUIS L.R.,173–176 (!916), quoted Mr. Calhoun, Secretary of State to Mr Everett, M. S. Institute Great Britain XV, 211 (1844) (Mr. Cahlhoun, the Secretary of United State, said that the criminal jurisdiction of a nation is limited to its own dominions and to vessels under its flag on the high seas and that it cannot extended to act committed within the dominion of another without violating its sovereignty and independence).

[80] Mills, *supra* note 4 at 9 ("territorial character of enforcement jurisdiction is well established, and important reflection of the principle of non-intervention in the internal affairs of the States").

rule derived from international customs or from a convention".[81] Therefore the enforcement of jurisdiction is strictly local, i.e. limited to the territory of the State. If the State wants to exercise enforcement jurisdiction beyond its borders, then it has to invariably obtain the consent of the other State in which it intends to meddle as to exercise its enforcement.[82]

Pragmatically, the jurisdiction to adjudicate and enforce can be effectively exercised when the accused after committing the crime is found in the territory of the regulating State. Till then, the question of jurisdiction by such State over the foreigners does not arise in the absence of a permissive rule derived from a treaty, convention or international custom as such persons cannot be arrested or served with summon/notice or made to join the investigation.[83] Secondly, for adjudication, the physical presence of the accused is required in law; hence practically jurisdiction cannot be exercised extraterritorially by courts, except in the hypnotically rare case of court conducting its proceedings in some other country to ensure the presence of the accused.[84]

The position of different forms of jurisdiction is cleared by Cherif Bassiouni by asserting that the terms used to enforce and prescribe law are not often of equal scope. That is, "that a sovereign state, or an entity exercising some of the attributes of sovereign state or legal entity that has some sovereign attributes can enforce the prescription of another State, or international law, even though the enforcing power may not have prescribed what it enforces".[85]

---

[81] Lotus case, *supra* note 16 at 19, para 45; Attorney General of the Government of Israel v. Adolf Eichman, District Court of Jerusalem, Israel, Criminal Case no. 40/61 (1961) (Important instance in this relation is arrest of Adolf Eichmann by the Israeli in Argentina in 1960. He was captured in Argentina's soil with the permission of the Argentina government. It is a patent breach of Argentina's territorial sovereignty and unlawful exercise of Israeli's jurisdiction); Rynagert, *supra note* 1 at 7.

[82] D' ASPREMONT, FOR A DEFENCE OF SOVEREIGN CONSTITUTIONALISM, 310–314 (2010) (he argues that the State has to rely on the rules such as reasonableness and the principle of non-intervention; hence, it is not certain enough for the States to curtail unilateral exercises of jurisdiction).

[83] MAXSORNEN, MANUAL OF PUBLIC INTERNATIONAL LAW, 355 quoted in H.O. AGGARWAL, INTERNATIONAL LAW AND HUMAN RIGHTS, 223 (2013).

[84] Mills, *supra* note 4 at 10 ("states that ...criminal proceeding *in absentia,* because an exercise of prescriptive jurisdiction in the absence of possibility of enforcement jurisdiction may be considered futile").

[85] MACEDO STHEPTHEN, UNIVERSAL JURISDICTION: NATIONAL COURTS AND THE PROSECUTION OF SERIOUS CRIMES UNDER INTERNATIONAL LAW, 3 (2006).

5 Jurisdictional Conflicts

International Law permits extraterritorial jurisdiction. There are different forms of extraterritorial jurisdiction. The potential problems arise when two or more States establish the jurisdiction over the same act. There is formal equality among all the principles of jurisdiction and which pulls conflicts of jurisdiction with the interest of other State. These conflicts result in legal restraints or challenges in assertion of extraterritorial jurisdiction. Various constraints and challenges place significant limits on the State's assertion of extraterritorial jurisdiction.

The States still prefer territorial jurisdiction over extraterritorial jurisdiction. It may be so, being an undisputed basis of jurisdiction. The other factors include the principle of non-intervention, seeking evidence in another country for criminal investigations and recognition of legitimate interest of the affected State, as well as sometimes political consideration (extradition), which also work in favour of giving primacy to territorial jurisdiction.

Even if extraterritorial jurisdiction is recognised under international law, but each country will apply their own legal system, and every country has a different legal system. The strategic approach applied to the case involves selection of legal system on the immediate nexus between the harm done by the criminal and the State. This nexus is guided by various doctrines such as rule of jurisdictional reason, substantial connection, comity of nations, etc., which focus more on the rights of States and are ineffective in protecting the rights of individuals. And they are not sufficient to address the conflicts. Hence, the jurisdictional conflicts and targeting of perpetrator still remain which would damage future prospects for transitional justice.[86] After involvement of the UNSC in the Lockerbie case, it raises a possibility of future framework for resolving the jurisdictional issues. Perhaps, it would more political rather than a legal solution.

A particular danger arises from the *ne bis in idem* or double jeopardy rule against being repeatedly tried for the same offence. This is a general principle incorporated mostly in all criminal statutes of the States, but in most of the legal system, it is invoked once there has been a final decision. It means interlocutory judgements usually do not have that effect.[87]

There is a possibility of mishandling/lapses in investigation due to the non-availability of witnesses or other circumstantial evidences to substantiate the claim of a victim country when the offence has an extraterritorial reach. It would be more challenging when the two countries are not at good terms with each other.

---

[86] Mark Lattimer, Shabnam Mojtahedi & Lee Anna Tucker, *A Step Toward Justice: Current Accountability options for crimes under International Law committed in Syria*, CEASEFIRE-CENTRE FOR CIVILIAN RIGHTS (2014). *available at:* http://scholarship.law.cornell.edu/clr/vol50/iss1/2 (accessed 4 March 2017).

[87] L. Finaly, *Does the International Criminal Court Protect Against Double Jeopardy: An Analysis of Article 20 of Rome Statute,* 15 UC DAVIS JOURNAL OF INTERNATIONAL LAW & POLICY 221 (2009).

Another challenge associated with the extraterritorial jurisdiction includes the difficulty of complicated extradition arrangement. Extradition treaties require dual criminality, whereby offences are extraditable only if they are punishable under the laws of both countries in some manner listed in the treaty.[88] Some treaties provide for extradition for specified offences only, setting out a list or schedule of offences that are extraditable, typically specifying out the most serious crimes for which the penalty on conviction exceeds a certain threshold.[89] Hence such provision sometime does not solve the objective of extradition and also does not resolve the questions of how to prioritise competing jurisdictional claims.

It has been realised that mainly the conflict of jurisdiction over the extraterritorial offence revolves around the concept of sovereignty. When two or more sovereigns claim jurisdiction over the offence, then it leads to jurisdictional conflict. In such cases, there are two options with the State, i.e. denial or mutual respect. This upholds the equality and independence of sovereign State enshrined in Article 2 of the Charter of the United Nation.

This problem arises often when the two countries are not at good political or economic terms with each other. For example, in Pathankot terror attack case,[90] in spite of clinching evidence to relate the perpetrators with Pakistan and a consequential visit by the Pakistani agencies to the Pathankot Airbase, India failed to secure a prosecution for, let alone the conviction of the perpetrators.[91] Hence, political relations play an important role in securing the trial against the accused. But States show their willingness to cooperate with other States if they share similar political, cultural and economic world views.

It is also true that till date there is no clear answer with respect to the dispute relating to the exercise of extraterritorial jurisdiction. However, many scholars have advocated various approaches such as rule of reason, comity, substantial connection, etc. These approaches are based on mutual respect and cooperation, and the State with a stronger link with the alleged offence can exercise jurisdiction over the offence. These approaches may act as restraint on the multiple jurisdictions. These approaches are however unsatisfactory for various reasons like who will decide the strong and weak connection. Additionally, there is room for discretion. With no

---

[88] Argentina, Australia, Brazil, Finland, Germany, the Netherlands, Russia, Spain and Venezuela. Multilateral treaties also contain extradition requirements, which are similar in content to bilateral treaties but can be more complicated due to the increased number of States with an interest in the outcome of extradition requests.

[89] http://www.mea.gov.in/extradition-faq.htm (accessed on 7 April 2016).

[90] https://www.thehindu.com/news/national/Fresh-firing-at-Pathankot-air-base-Army-deploys-reinforcements-in-area/article60521192.ece (accessed on 12 April 2022).

[91] https://www.hindustantimes.com/india-news/centre-declares-pathankot-attack-handler-terrorist-101649787718602.html (accessed on 11 April 2022); Rajesh Parrihar representing India hits out at Pakistan at U.N., by saying that it is "regretful that victims of these dastardly attacks are yet to get justice, and the perpetrators, facilitators and financiers of these attacks continue to walk free, still enjoying State support and hospitality". *Available at:* https://www.thehindu.com/news/national/india-hits-out-at-pakistan-at-un-says-perpetrators-of-mumbai-pathankot-pulwama-terror-attacks-enjoying-state-support/article65051722.ece (12 April 2022).

obligation and inherent instinct to serve its interest, we cannot expect the competing States to reach a just and objective decision as to the jurisdiction. So this area is still underdeveloped, and competing claims of jurisdiction over the offences may be controversial.

6 Conclusion

International law strives for peaceful relations between States. The concept of sovereignty which helps in maintaining equality among States is enshrined in the United Nations Charter under the principle of non-interference and force against each other. The traditional jurisdictional rules of international law were developed on these above values and aim to lessen regulatory conflict and maintain the peaceful coexistence of States. But from late twentieth century, there has been a dramatic rise in criminal activities such as terrorism, child trafficking, etc., and hence and increased assertion of extraterritorial jurisdiction on different grounds—such as territoriality, nationality, protection and universality. An increase in the range of jurisdictional grounds in international law results in overlapping jurisdiction among States, which may also lead to jurisdictional conflict. These conflicts lead to challenges in collection of evidence, extradition of accused and violation of *ne bis in idem* and ultimately cause delay in justice to the victim as well as the accused.

As judges Higgins, Kooijams and Buergenthal noted in their Joint Separate Opinion in the *Arrest Warrant Case*:

> One of the challenges of present-day international law is to provide for stability of international relations and effective international intercourse while at the same time guaranteeing respect for human rights….[92]

There are number of approaches that serve to limit the conflict in the exercise of jurisdiction such as principle of non-intervention, comity, equity, rule of reason, etc., but some approaches are used in non-jurisdictional sense, some have definitional issue or some are based on negotiations and hence non-obligatory. Therefore, these approaches are not satisfactory to address the conflicts of jurisdiction.

It is not deniable that international law is dominated by international relations and politics. There have been many instances of competing jurisdictional claims that turned into internal or international politics. International cooperation is guided by political, economic and social affinity, which ideally should not be the case especially in respect of criminal conduct.

The following suggestion, though non-exhaustive, is being provided to avoid/resolve the conflicts in case of competing jurisdictional claims:

- Jurisdiction of a State is derived from the State sovereignty. Sovereignty is reflected in the principle of non-interference in the domestic affair and equality

[92] Arrest Warrant case (Joint Separate Opinion), *supra* note 12 at 64, para 5.

of States of international law. The jurisdiction is a manifestation of a State's penal power which gives right to the sovereign State to prosecute, try and punish the crimes occurring within the territorial limits. Also, States have an inherent right to protect the sovereignty from any interference or any danger to political independence. So territorial and protective principle can be given preference over other basis of jurisdiction.

- There is a need of multilateral treaty to deal with the extraterritorial criminal jurisdiction to determine the most efficient legal system among the competing claims.
  - Criteria for establishing the strong nexus to decide which State can prosecute and can apply their substantive law
  - Comprehensive rules and uniform procedure in procurement of evidences and admissibility of the same
  - Procedure to identify the jurisdictional conflicts and mechanism to resolve the same
  - Inclusion of *ne bis in idem*
  - Simplification of extradition process
- The international community has to maintain balance between the competing regimes of human rights with the customary concept of the immunity. The concept of immunity is derived from the concept of sovereignty. The issue of limitation of the immunity from criminal jurisdiction is a very heated, debateable and politically sensitive subject. The States are reluctant to forego immunity because they have a fear of infringement of sovereignty or maybe the concept of reciprocity encourages the State to include this into practice. It is also an admitted fact that "old doctrines die hard".[93] So far, it has been realised that *jus cogens* cannot displace the immunity *ratione personae* unless the State waives it. Moreover, the development with respect to exception and limitation on immunity is possible with the assurance of non-interference with the high-ranking serving officials. Secondly, national courts can play an active role in giving the shape of immunity. The case of *Pinochet (No. 3)* of the United Kingdom has become the important precedent for the non-availability of immunity *ratione materiae* in cases of international crimes. Though this is slow progress, the States have begun to realise that culture of absolute impunity no longer exists with the indictment of Taylor and *Pinochet.*
- The International Law Commission (ILC) can play an important role in shaping the attitude of States by providing guidance to States with respect to exception to immunity in respect of international crimes with the cooperation of the General Assembly.

Still, the State cooperation, mutual respect and balancing their jurisdictional interest with other States are surely the way to solve any conflict. Hence, the States need to change their attitude from right to duty not only towards other States but also towards individuals.

---

[93] Kateřina Uhlířová, *Head of State Immunity in International Law*, (2013) (Unpublished Ph.D Thesis, Masarykova univerzita Brno).

Chapter 9
Study on Value and Implementation Mechanism of African Constitutions

Mai Cheng

Abstract African constitutions show a strong value inclination, recognize the principles of the international community, position themselves as the basis of the social consensus, and indicate the direction of the development of the country. Out of the distrust against their political culture and the political qualities of their population, African constitutions pursue partially formal democratization. Some of them restrict the citizen's right to be elected based on property and education level. There are representatives appointed by the head of state in many African parliaments. Local autonomy is not fully protected, while political stability is paid much attention to. African constitutions adopt the theory of self-defense democracy, confer a strong position on the executive, and establish a strong central government. To fulfill the goals of the constitutions, the African constitutions highlight their binding force. Most constitutions establish constitutional review systems, providing citizens with formally convenient constitutional appeal channels. The constitutional review organs are also entitled jurisdiction over political disputes. Various special oversight institutes have also been established to implement the constitutions. Realities reveal, to turn the good wishes of institutional design into real-life constitutions, African countries still have a long way to go.

Keywords Africa · Implementation of constitution · Democratic politics · Constitutional consensus · System design

This article was previously published in Law Science—Selected Papers Volume 3, Issue 2 (2024).

M. Cheng (✉)
East China University of Political Science and Law, Shanghai, China

T. Du, X. Fei (eds.), *The BRICS Legal Cooperation and Perspectives*,
https://doi.org/10.1007/978-981-95-4356-4_9

1 Introduction

In comparison to the developed countries, African countries process shorter history and younger constitutions. After the end of the Cold War in the 1990s, most African countries embarked on democratization. A new wave of constitutional change occurred on the continent. Almost three decades later, after many trials and tribulations, their constitutions have been gradually stabilized. African countries share similar historical legacy and are facing many common development problems. These similarities not only render researchers the feasibility to analyze them as a somewhat homogeneous category but also lead these constitutions to similar value targets and hence implementation mechanisms. The latter similarities reveal themselves firstly from texts of their constitutions. In underdeveloped democracies lacking rule of law, it has been longly argued that constitutions of these countries remain on paper, being merely a constitution without constitutionalism,[1] therefore limiting the value of normative research based on the texts of the constitutions. However, the formal prescriptions of the constitutions still reflect, to a large degree, the value targets of the constitutors and their attitudes toward diverse constitutional issues. Moreover, many problems in implementation can trace their cause back in the institutional design. For certain constitutions apparently adhering to constitutionalist principle, their implementation process could yield in consequences contradicting constitutionalism. Practices of certain African countries have shown that the cause of this paradox could be traced back to their flawed constitutional design.[2] In light of these realities and features of African constitutionalism, based on the textual analysis of the African constitutions, this paper explored the value targets and their expected implementation mechanism.[3] Due to the limit of the length of this paper, this article focuses on the goals of the constitutions, democracy, political stability, and realization mechanism of the binding force of the constitutions.

Texts of African constitutions show a strong value inclination. They recognize the values and principles of the international community, position themselves as the basis of the social consensus, and indicate objectives of the development of the country. Out of a distrust against the political culture and political qualities of their population, many African constitutions pursue only a formal democratization. Some of them restrict the citizen's suffrage in terms of property and education level. Representativity of the parliament is limited, especially by the existence of appointed members. Local autonomy is not fully recognized and protected. In contrast, these constitutions pay much attention to the political stability. They adopt the theory of

[1] H.W.O Okoth-Ogendo, *Constitutions without Constitutionalism: Reflections on an African Political Paradox*, in *State and Constitutionalism: an African Debate on Democracy* 3–25 (I.G Shivji edl, 1991, SAPES 1991).

[2] For the case of Malawi, especially the flawed constitutional system design, see Kenneth R. Ross et al. eds, *Beyond Impunity: New Directions for Governance in Malawi*, UCT Press 2022.

[3] During the research process, all the texts of the African constitutions refer to the materials on the website of Constituteproject (https://www.constituteproject.org, January 12, 2022 last visited).

self-defense democracy, confer a strong position on the executive, and establish a strong central government. To realize the goals of the constitutions, African constitutions highlight their binding force. Most African constitutions have established a constitutional review process, providing citizens with formally convenient constitutional petition channels. The constitutional review organs are further entitled to adjudicate over political disputes. Various special oversight institutes have been established to promote the strict enforcement of the constitutions.

2 Value Inclination Trends

Analysis of the texts of African constitutions reveals a strong value inclination. The first evidence of this inclination is that African constitutions generally recognize the principles and norms enshrined in the various international documents. For example, under the context of a strong religious tradition of the African people, secular state principle accepted by the international community is adopted by most of these constitutions. Second, the African constitutions tend to define itself as the founding document of the whole country's consensus. For instance, these constitutions are generally binding on all aspects of social life, not only between citizens and state but also among citizens in their private lives. Third, the African constitutions tend to provide for a detailed list of civil duties, suggesting their plan to educate the citizens into a constitutionally expected image. Forth, in addition to this value inclination, the African constitutions indicate detailed objectives of the national development. The economic, social, and cultural rights of the citizens, i.e., the human rights of the second generation, are generally recognized. Many of these constitutions authorize affirmative actions. In summary, the African constitutions are indeed a comprehensive blueprint for development of the country, both for the nation, the society, and the individual.

2.1 Recognition of the Spirit and Value Principles of the International Community

2.1.1 Recognition of the Binding Force of International Documents

International documents are carrier of the spirit and value principles of the international community. Forty-four (81.5%) African constitutions refer in their preamble or text to the binding force of international documents to their constitutional order. Among the ten countries[4] without these references are the two countries of the oldest constitutions on the African continent, i.e., Botswana and Mauritius. The other

[4]These ten countries are Botswana, Mauritius, Eritrea, Nigeria, Guinea-Bissau, Sierra Leone, Lesotho, Tanzania, Liberia, and Zambia.

eight constitutions were enacted before 2000. It can be concluded that, after 2000, the binding force of international documents is explicitly recognized by all the new African constitutions. In the former 44 countries, the recognition of the binding force varies somewhat in their expression styles and mainly manifested in three ways.

The first way is mention of the international documents in the preamble of the constitutions. These preambles recognize the guidance of principles of international documents to the domestic constitutional and legal system of their respective countries. Among these countries, Article 65 of the Cameroonian constitution and preamble of the Moroccan constitution define the preamble as an integral part of the constitution, further strengthening the binding force of international documents. There are 21 such countries.[5]

The second way is recognition of their guidance in the main body of the constitution. In comparison to the first form of the articles in the preamble which tend to be abstract mention of certain principles and values, these second kind of articles tend be more detailed. There are 21 such countries as well.[6]

The third way is to confirm a direct legally binding force of the international documents in the main body of the constitution. This is certainly the most formal way. The first group of these constitutions stipulate that provisions of international documents ratified by the state possess the identical status with a domestic law, such as Article 93 of the Egyptian constitution.[7] The second group confers higher status to certain provisions of international documents, such as Article 20 the Tunisian constitution.[8] The third group integrates the basic principles of international law into their domestic legal systems, such as Article 2(5) of the Kenyan constitution.[9] The forth group incorporates specific provisions and rights of international law into their domestic legal order. For example, Article 19 of Rwandan constitution prescribes that "Every child has the right to specific mechanisms of protection by his or her family, other Rwandans and the State…as provided for by national and international law." There are 14 such countries altogether.[10]

[5] These 21 countries are Egypt, Benin, Burkina Faso, Togo, Congo, D.R. Congo, Djibouti, Guinea, Gabon, Cameroon, Comoros, Ivory Coast, Madagascar, Mali, Mauritania, Morocco, South Sudan, Niger, Senegal, Chad, and Central Africa.

[6] These 21 countries are Algeria, Ethiopia, Angola, Benin, Equatorial Guinea, Cape Verde, the Gambia, D.R.C, Guinea, Ghana, Zimbabwe, Libya, Malawi, Morocco, Mozambique, South Africa, Niger, Seychelles, Sao Tome and Principe, Swaziland, and Somalia.

[7] Article 93: International agreements and conventions: "The state is committed to the agreements, covenants, and international conventions of human rights that were ratified by Egypt. They have the force of law after publication in accordance with the specified circumstances." Egypt Constitution of 2014.

[8] Article 20: "International agreements approved and ratified by the Assembly of the Representatives of the People have a status superior to that of laws and inferior to that of the Constitution." Tunisia's Constitution of 2014.

[9] Article 2: "(5) The general rules of international law shall form part of the law of Kenya." The Constitution of Kenya, 2010.

[10] These 14 countries are Egypt, Ethiopia, Benin, Burundi, Kenya, Rwanda, Malawi, Namibia, South Africa, Senegal, Sudan, Somalia, Tunisia, and Uganda.

Sometimes, these three categories of constitutions overlap themselves. Some countries belong to two or even all three categories of these countries, such as the Beninese constitution which has adopted all these three types of prescriptions.

The Universal Declaration of Human Rights is the most favored international documents. Twenty-three constitutions referred to it. Followed is the African Charter on Human and Peoples' Rights, which is referred by 16 constitutions. The third favored international document is the Charter of the United Nations which is referred to by constitutions of ten countries.

2.1.2 Recognition of Secular State

As of now, three African countries, namely, Lesotho, Swaziland, and Morocco, maintain a constitutional monarchy. All other African countries have established a republic. All the African constitutions, including these three monarchies, establish a periodic election system for the parliament and head of state.

Considering the strong Islamic influence in North and West Africa, constitutions of 12 countries[11] in this region introduce preferential provisions on Islam, which do not exist in other parts of Africa.[12] These preferential treatments of Islam take various forms.

In nine of these countries, Islam is explicitly defined as the official religion of the state in the preamble or text of the constitution. These countries include Algeria, Egypt, Djibouti, Comoros, Libya, Mauritania, Morocco, Somalia, and Tunisia. Constitutions of Egypt (Article 24) and Somalia (Article 30) further establish the duties of citizens to accept compulsory Islamic religious education. Morocco forbids the change of the official status of Islam in any constitution amendment (Article 175). Gambia, Kenya, and Nigeria establish Islamic judicial system to implement Sharia. These three countries, however, do not prescribe the official status of Islam. In these constitutions, there are other provisions favoring Islam, such as requirement of the presidential candidate to be Muslim (Mauritania, Somalia, and Tunisia).

Nonetheless, in the previous discussion, the strong respect of the African constitutions for international documents has been revealed. The most referred documents are the Universal Declaration of Human Rights, the African Charter on Human and Peoples' Rights, and the Charter of the United Nations. Articles 2, 16, and 18 of the Universal Declaration of Human Rights provide for religious equality and freedom of religion, while Articles 2 and 8 of the African Charter on Human Rights and Peoples' Rights prohibit discrimination against citizens based on religious identity

---

[11] These 12 countries are Algeria, Egypt, Djibouti, Comoros, Libya, Mauritania, Morocco, Somalia, Tunisia, the Gambia, Kenya, and Nigeria.

[12] Preamble of the Zambian Constitution "DECLARE the Republic a Christian nation while upholding the right of every person to enjoy that person's freedom of conscience or religion." It is the only case that Christianity is mentioned in African constitutions. Distinct from the 12 constitutions with Islamic tendencies, this Zambian provision is far from privilege to Christianity.

and protect the freedom of conscience and religion. Articles 1, 13, and 55 of the Charter of the United Nations provide for equality between religions.

Among these 12 countries only constitutions of Libya and Nigeria do not accept the binding force of international documents explicitly. In the other ten constitutions, consequently, the requirements of international law and the constitutional provisions on Islam may conflict. Perhaps because of this potential conflict, these ten constitutions have some seemingly contradictory provisions. For example, apart from Mauritania, all the other nine countries recognize the religious equality and freedom. Even the constitutions of Libya and Nigeria provide protection for religious equality and freedom. Moreover, it is somewhat ironical to see that in the constitutions of Djibouti, Libya, and Morocco, the provisions on religious equality or religious freedom and those on the official status of Islam are in the same clause. A representative is Article 17 of Somalian constitution which after stipulating that "every person is free to practice his or her religion" immediately stipulates that "no religion other than Islam can be propagated in the Federal Republic of Somalia." In the three constitutions which establish Islamic law courts, Article 100.2.c of Gambia's constitution, Article 8 of the Kenyan constitution, and Article 10 of the Nigerian constitution stipulate that no state religion shall be established. Judging from these contradictions, it can be argued that these constitutions favoring Islam must take the universal principles of the modern constitution, especially the secular state, into consideration. Their official preference to Islam must make a compromise. This phenomenon may further attest the recognition of the African constitutions on the values of the international community.

2.2 *Defining the Constitution as Foundation of Social Consensus*

The classic constitutional thought, i.e., the liberal constitutionalism, holds that the constitution applies only to the vertical relationship between the individual citizens and their government. Its purpose is to protect citizens from the power abuse of the state. Constitution is a guarantee of civil rights against the governments. Based on these presumptions, the citizen's duty should not be included in the constitution. Instead, the obligations of citizens to society and government are expected to be regulated by criminal and administrative law. The relationship between citizens is left to the jurisdiction of civil law. Therefore, the constitution should have no horizontal effect upon the citizens. But it is crystally clear that the African constitutions do not accept this liberalistic point of view.

First, texts of 21 (38.9%) African constitutions[13] explicitly state that the constitution has universal binding force. Accordingly, the fundamental rights enshrined in the constitution can be applied among private entities. The authority of the

[13] These constitutions are those of Ethiopia, South Africa, Mozambique, Namibia, Lesotho, South Sudan, Rwanda, Eritrea, Swaziland, Zimbabwe, Liberia, Kenya, Uganda, the Gambia, Cape Verde, Malawi, Ghana, Somalia, the Republic of Congo, Zambia, and Nigeria.

constitution then penetrates all aspects of the society. Texts of 47 (87%) constitutions[14] provide for the duties of citizens to the state and the society. Some of these constitutional duties in some countries are really detailed. They range from military service, upholding national unity, taking basic education, protecting the public property or environment, to serving the society and so on. It can be concluded that most constitutions seek to educate citizens of their countries with constitutional provisions. There are 51[15] (94.4%) countries altogether in these two categories.

In terms of their constitutional function, the universal binding force and the civil duties are quite similar. Both expand the application field of the constitution. Classic constitutions tend to be treated as "guarantee of civil rights," being a limit to its application filed. Recognition of its universal binding force and constitutional duties, however, eliminates this limit. Extricating itself from the classic shackles, the constitution rises to the position as a guiding program for the whole society. Containing many prescriptions branded with stark value inclination, the constitution defines itself, explicitly or implicitly, as the founding document of the social consensus. That is exactly what is happening on the African continent.

Only constitutions of Botswana, Comoros, and Mauritius provide for neither the universal binding force nor the civil duties. Repeatedly, it is noteworthy that constitutions of Botswana and Mauritius are the two oldest on the African continent which represent more a classic liberalist constitution. Currently, Comoros is quite underdeveloped in terms of democracy and rule of law. Its constitution consists only 47 clauses. Being such a small and rough constitution, it might be concluded that the nonexistence of provisions on horizontal applicability and civil duties is more a result of slack enactment.

The wide existence of civil duties in the African constitutions might be related to their general reference the international documents. As discussed before, the African Charter on Human Rights and Peoples' Rights is the second favored international documents by the African constitutions. Its Chapter II, Part I (Articles 27–29)[16] of the Charter, explicitly provides for various duties of the citizen to other citizens, his/her family, community, and home country.

[14] The seven constitutions without these duties are those of Botswana, Comoros, Mauritius, Malawi, Liberia, Lesotho, and South Africa.

[15] The other three countries are Botswana, Comoros, and Mauritius.

[16] Art. 27–29, *African (Banjul) Charter on Human and Peoples' Rights.*

2.3 Developmental Aspirations

Further analysis shows that the African constitution intends to contribute to the national development. This fact is mainly attested by three categories of constitutional provisions: goals of national development, a detailed list of economic and social rights of citizens, and explicit mandate to the affirmative actions of the state.

Twenty-eight (51.9%) African constitutions[17] clearly define the national development goals. These goals frequently include the political, legal, economic, cultural, and even international objectives. Taking their role as the founding document of the social consensus into consideration, it might be argued that these constitutions have truly provided a comprehensive blueprint for the national and social development.

Forty-seven (87%) constitutions[18] provide a detailed list of the economic, social, and cultural rights of citizens, i.e., the second-generation rights whose realization depends on the positive action of the state. Underdevelopment of the African countries, however, constrains the resources available to the government. Under these circumstances, if these rights were awarded legally binding force upon the government, the government would be imposed an insupportable burden, which in turn would do harm to the authority and reputation of the constitution itself.

Out of this dilemma, in recognition of this second generation of rights, constitutions of Kenya, Zimbabwe, Eritrea, Burundi, and South Sudan declare clearly that the realization of these second-generation rights should take the availability of the resources into account. Besides, Article 91 of the Mozambican constitution stipulates that "... it shall be the duty of the State, in accordance with national economic development, to create the appropriate institutional, normative and infra-structural conditions" to realize the right to suitable home of the citizen. While providing a detailed list of the second-generation rights, Article 44 of the South Sudanese constitution prescribe that "Unless this Constitution otherwise provides or a duly enacted law guarantees, the rights and liberties described and the provisions contained in this Chapter are not by themselves enforceable in a court of law; however, the principles expressed herein are basic to governance and the State shall be guided by them, especially in making policies and laws." This provision might be the most vivid description of the true status of the second-generation rights in African constitutions.

To solve the problems in development of the country, 20 (37%) African constitutions[19] authorize the government to engage in affirmative actions, such as privileged

[17]These 28 constitutions are those of South Sudan, Egypt, Tanzania, Swaziland, Rwanda, Lesotho, Ghana, Sudan, Nigeria, Liberia, Sierra Leone, Eritrea, Zimbabwe, Zambia, Niger, the Gambia, Namibia, Mozambique, Ethiopia, Sao Tome and Principe, Kenya, Cape Verde, Equatorial Guinea, Morocco, Angola, South Africa, Guinea-Bissau, and Malawi.

[18]The seven other constitutions are those of Botswana, Djibouti, Cameroon, Comoros, Libya, Mauritius, and Mauritania.

[19]These constitutions are those of Zimbabwe, Angola, Swaziland, Malawi, Senegal, Ethiopia, Sudan, Uganda, Algeria, Kenya, Namibia, Niger, Ghana, South Sudan, Tanzania, Burundi, Morocco, Somalia, Egypt, and Rwanda.

treatment to the women, aged people, and minorities. In authorization of the affirmative actions, these constitutions attach importance to women's status, especially to their representativity in the state and public institutes. For example, Article 68.4 of the Malawi constitution stipulates that more than half of the members of the Senate shall be women; Article 61 of the Senegalese constitution stipulates that at least two-fifths of the Senators shall be women; and Article 109.3 of the South Sudanese constitution stipulates that the president shall ensure that at least 25% of the members of the Council of Ministers are women, etc. The historical and still existing discrimination against women is surely an important consideration behind all these affirmative actions.

Only constitutions of seven countries, i.e., Botswana, Mauritius, Djibouti, Cameroon, Comoros, Libya, and Mauritania, do not contain any of these three kinds of prescriptions in their main body. Among them, Botswana and Mauritius, as representatives of the classic constitutions, are naturally on the list. While the other five constitutions have none of these provisions in their main text, they all discuss detailly the development goals in their preamble. Consequently, it is safe to say that using the constitution to guide the development of the state is a universal practice on the African continent.

3 Democracy in Formality

As discussed before, the African constitutions generally recognize the principle of secular state. All African countries have parliament elected by people. In addition, 32 (59.3%) African constitutions[20] provide for referendum procedures, which make resolution to broad issues, ranging from ratification of international treaties, territorial changes to the organization of state power, and so on. In many countries, a referendum is initiated at discretion of certain state organs, such the president of Algeria, the National Assembly of Namibia. The Angolan constitution stipulates even more generously that one-fifth of MPs and a caucus in parliament can initiate a referendum, being a lower threshold than that of a normal legislative process. It appears to be a full trust and respect of the political qualities of the people and a firm determination to realize democratization of the country.

Further analysis reveals, nonetheless, a contradicting truth. Literally, African constitutions pursue more a formal democratization, far from allowing the average people a deciding say in the political life. In fact, the strong value inclination of the African constitutions has already exposed a deep constitutional distrust in the political qualities of the ordinary people. Out of this distrust, the political rights, the

[20] These 32 countries are the Republic of Congo, Chad, Tunisia, Algeria, Sao Tome and Principe, Namibia, Niger, Equatorial Guinea, Benin, Guinea-Bissau, Guinea, Senegal, Ghana, Burkina Faso, Cote d'Ivoire, Mali, Togo, Mauritania, Sierra Leone, Cameroon, Djibouti, Uganda, Sudan, the Democratic Republic of the Congo, Burundi, South Sudan, Gabon, Angola, Egypt, Mozambique, Cape Verde, and Rwanda.

forms of political participation, or even the composition of the parliament is subject to explicit constitutional restrictions. While the local autonomy is a cornerstone of modern democracies, the recognition and protection of local autonomy have been significantly neglected or even limited by many African constitutions.

3.1 The Colonial Languages as Official Language

Since language is carrier of education and culture, attitude toward a language reveals the respect level to the culture behind this language. An official language of a country is carrier of the political culture of this country. If the constitution of a country defines a nonlocal language to be its official language, it will inevitably reflect the constitutional distrust of the local political culture.

This distrust might do exist in many African countries. The ethnic compositions of African countries are generally complex. Most of the ethnic groups have their own languages of long history. Under this context, 49 (90.7%) African[21] constitutions define the official language or national language of the country. Many of them prescribe more than one official or national languages. These prescriptions reflect the importance that the African constitutions attach to the linguistic and cultural issues. When most African countries used to be colonized by European countries, 39 (72.2%) constitutions[22] define their respective former colonial language as their official language. Among these 39 countries, 22 constitutions[23] provide only the former colonial language as their official language, without mentioning the constitutional status of any local language.

There have been many explanations to this phenomenon. For example, someone might argue that because of the diversity of the ethnic composition and a historically rooted distrust among the ethnic groups, the choice of a foreign language is a good way to express the constitutional neutrality among linguistic issues. Another explanation might be that the colonial language has been using as the actual official language of many countries for a long time. The constitutional recognition of their status as official language is merely a constitutionalization of the status quo. Someone may even argue that to protect their monopoly on the political, economic, and social life of the country, the African elites prefer the colonial language that

[21]The fine other countries are Eritrea, Cape Verde, Guinea-Bissau, Ghana, and Sao Tome and Principe.

[22]These 39 countries are Chad, the Gambia, Sudan, Rwanda, Sierra Leone, Kenya, Tanzania, Botswana, South Sudan, Zimbabwe, Uganda, the Republic of Congo, Malawi, Nigeria, Niger, Mauritius, Swaziland, Liberia, Seychelles, Equatorial Guinea, Madagascar, Burkina Faso, Namibia, Lesotho, Togo, Cote d'Ivoire, Mali, Gabon, Angola, Central Africa, Mozambique, Zambia, Cameroon, Senegal, Comoros, the Democratic Republic of the Congo, Guinea, Benin, and Djibouti.

[23]These 22 countries are the Gambia, Sierra Leone, Botswana, South Sudan, the Republic of Congo, Malawi, Niger, Mauritius, Liberia, Equatorial Guinea, Burkina Faso, Namibia, Togo, Cote d'Ivoire, Mali, Gabon, Angola, Mozambique, Zambia, Cameroon, Guinea, and Benin.

most of the population are not able to use. As is revealed in the latter part of this paper, constitutions of the Gambia, Sierra Leone, Botswana, Malawi, and Mauritius require candidates for certain public offices to be able to read and write in English, and constitutions of Zambia and Senegal stipulate those candidates for certain public offices be literate of the official language, which is English and French, respectively. These provisions inevitably raise the educational threshold for political participation in the country's political life.

Whatever the consideration behind these provisions, definition of a foreign language as the official language inevitably reflects the constitutional distrust in the political culture of the country. It might be concluded that from a constitutional point of view, a local language is inadequate to fulfill the function as the media of political communication. When a local language fails to enter the formal political process, or at best is awarded a second-class status, the political culture behind it will be gradually marginalized in the formal political process. When these local cultures will still have great influence on average people, especially on the grassroots level, the competition between the "constitutional" and "local" culture may lead to the somewhat alienation of the constitutional culture, at least in the short term.

3.2 Restriction of Suffrage Based on Wealth or Educational Background

There are 22 (40.7%) African constitutions[24] setting wealth or education threshold on the suffrage, especially on the qualification to be candidates for certain public offices, such as president, minister, or parliamentarian. Wealth thresholds are mainly reflected in the ban against bankrupt citizen to run for office. Some constitutions further stipulate that becoming bankrupt, the parliamentarians lose their seats immediately, such as Article 77.1.i of the Sierra Leone constitution, Article 62 of the Botswana constitution, and Article 34 of the Mauritian constitution. Restrictions on educational levels are mainly manifested in the requirement for candidates to obtain certain educational qualifications or the ability to read and write in the official language of the country.

In early histories of Western constitutions, there were also those similar limitations. The purpose of these limitations was widely recognized to prevent the lower class of the society from participating in the political process. Although these African constitutions do not directly restrict the average citizen's right to vote, these restrictions on the right to be voted still have substantial impact on the principle of one man, one vote. In a healthy democracy, it can be expected that the political competition can filter out the irresponsible candidates, if bankruptcy or illiteracy

[24]These 22 countries are Kenya, Swaziland, Ghana, the Gambia, Sudan, Niger, Uganda, Sierra Leone, Tanzania, Nigeria, Zambia, South Sudan, Botswana, Somalia, Lesotho, Malawi, South Africa, Namibia, Mauritius, Senegal, Zimbabwe, and Egypt.

could be defined as criterion as irresponsibility. These constitutional restrictions reflect again the distrust of the African constitutions. They want no risk to rely solely on the political selection process. Nor did they believe that the voters are wise enough to choose the capable candidates, not to say the most capable ones. In these realties, it is a distrust of not only the common citizen's political qualifications but also the feasibility of fully democratic politics upon their home country.

Of these 22 countries are Botswana and Mauritius, the two pioneer countries in terms of democracy and rule of law in Africa. It might then be argued that this distrust has already existed since the independence of African countries, and after all these years, no essential change has taken place. Taking the strong value inclination, missions to foster a new kind of citizens and the substantial guidance to the development of the country into consideration, this constitutional distrust will be further enforced.

3.3 Limitations of Parliamentary Representativity

Currently, there are still 16[25] (29.6%) African constitutions that provide for parliamentary members appointed by the head of the state, namely, the president or the king (Swaziland). Defining these appointed members, these constitutions rarely provide concrete criteria for the appointment. Most of the time, vague terms are used, such as "eminent persons" (e.g., Article 80 of Burkina Faso constitution, Article 101 of Algeria constitution) and "enhance the representation" of the parliament (e.g., Article 68 of Zambia). These vague provisions give the head of state a considerable discretion to intervene in the composition and bargain process of the parliament. When the head of state in African countries often control the executive, existence of these appointed members will provide the executive an effective institutional channel to influence the parliament. The existence of these appointed members further reveals the relative weak position of the parliament against the executive. Parliament is the central platform for political participation. When the parliament itself cannot guarantee its independence and autonomy against other state organs, especially the executive, the democratic feature of the political process will be inevitably compromised.

[25]These 16 countries are the Gambia, Equatorial Guinea, Madagascar, Rwanda, Burkina Faso, Tanzania, Zambia, Botswana, South Sudan, Togo, Lesotho, Namibia, Cameroon, Egypt, Algeria, and Swaziland.

3.4 Neglect of Local Autonomy

In any country containing diverse ethnic groups, the organization and operation of local government and the relationship between the central and local governments are the key issues in maintaining the political stability of the country. Its constitution is expected to provide detailed provisions on these two issues. Accordingly, it is shocking to see that African constitutions are very brief, sometimes even crude, in their provisions on the rules of the local government. Literally, local autonomy receives little recognition from the constitution.

Currently, only three African constitutions, i.e., those of Ethiopia, Nigeria, and Somalia, explicitly define federalism as their fundamental principle of the vertical organization of the state. Nonetheless, there are 27[26] (50%) countries whose parliament consists of two chambers, namely, the first chamber representing the whole people and the second chamber representing diverse regional and social interests within the country. Constituency of the second chamber is usually the administration area of the second tier of the government. Members of the second are elected either directly by the electorate of the area or indirectly by the representative body of the region. In light of these election models, these second chambers serve to better reflect the diverse interests within the country. Sometimes, the function of the second chamber is to transmit the demands of not only the different regions but also different ethnic and social groups, such as the youth, women, and persons with disabilities. For instance, Article 61 of the Ethiopian constitution stipulates that "Each Nation, Nationality and People shall be represented in the House of the Federation by at least one member." These prescriptions paint the second chamber of more pluralistic colors while at the cost of less representativity of the regional interests on the central government level.

Half of the African countries have established a second chamber in the central parliament. This fact exposes the awareness of the African constitutions to respond to the diverse demands of the various ethnic groups within the country. If these constitutions were to respond to these demands seriously, it would be a reasonable expectation to find many protections on local autonomy in the constitutions. Relationship between the central and the local government would also be expected to be detailly regulated. The truth is, however, that the African constitutions contain few prescriptions on the organization of local governments, and constitutional protection for local autonomy rarely exists as well. In sharp contrast, some constitutions authorize explicitly the central government the power to intervene in the affairs of local governments.

---

[26]These 27 countries are Ethiopia, Burundi, Equatorial Guinea, Togo, the Republic of Congo, the Democratic Republic of the Congo, Gabon, Zimbabwe, Cameroon, Lesotho, Madagascar, Malawi, Mauritania, Morocco, Namibia, South Africa, Nigeria, Senegal, Somalia, Liberia, South Sudan, Burkina Faso, Algeria, Kenya, Rwanda, Swaziland, and Sudan.

First, among the 27 constitutions with a second chamber, 19[27] of them award the first chamber, i.e., the representative house, a dominant position over the second chamber which is mainly reflected in the prescriptions that when the two chambers have different opinions, the representative house can overcome the objection of the second chamber through a simple majority, conferring the latter to only on delaying role in the decision-making process of the representative house. Under these circumstances, if the constitutional review institution is yet to be taken into consideration, only 8 (14.8%) of the 54 African countries provide meaningful institutional protection for local governments, hindering the regional interests to be seriously pondered by the central government.

Second, African constitutions are prone to set an ambiguous delineation of powers between central and local governments. Only 14[28] (25.9%) of the African constitutions expressly handle the issue of allocation of legislative powers between the central and local governments. In these 14 countries, the constitutions of Nigeria, Comoros, South Africa, and Kenya stipulate that all residual power is vested in the central rather than the local government, further enhancing the dominant position of the central government. Ironically, Nigeria is one of the three African countries which explicitly recognize the constitutional principle of federalism. In the vertical state organization, the implementation of laws enacted by the central government, the distribution of financial resources among the central and local governments, and the self-organization of local governments are always the core issues. These core issues, however, receive little attention from the African constitutions. For example, confronting the widespread poverty and the relatively better financial situation of the central government in Africa, development of local governments depends largely on the financial support from the central government. Therefore, it is necessary that the central government be imposed constitutional duties to assist the local governments. However, only 13[29] (24.1%) of the African constitutions provide for these binding legal duties on the central government. These serious deficiencies of institutional design show inevitably the neglect of the African constitution makers to the protection of local autonomy.

[27] These 19 countries are Ethiopia, Burundi, Equatorial Guinea, Togo, the Republic of Congo, the Democratic Republic of the Congo, Gabon, Zimbabwe, Cameroon, Lesotho, Madagascar, Malawi, Mauritania, Morocco, Namibia, South Africa, Nigeria, Senegal, and Somalia.

[28] These 14 countries are Nigeria, Zimbabwe, Comoros, Ethiopia, South Africa, Ghana, the Democratic Republic of the Congo, Uganda, Kenya, Sudan, South Sudan, Sao Tome and Principe, Madagascar, and Tunisia.

[29] These 13 countries are Nigeria, Kenya, Ghana, Uganda, Sudan, Egypt, the Democratic Republic of the Congo, South Sudan, Malawi, Morocco, Tunisia, Comoros, and South Africa.

4 Promotion of Political Stability

As African constitutions show a strong value inclination together with a distrust of the local political culture, as they pursue more a formal democratization, it is more and more revealed that the true plan of the African constitutions is to realize the constitutional objectives steadily, relatively independent of the influence and participation of the local population. Further analysis exposes that political stability is an important goal of African constitutions. First, African constitutions have generally introduced the theory of self-defense democracy, such as prohibiting amendment to certain constitutional principles, giving citizens constitutional right to resist unconstitutional activities and organizations. Second, in sharp contrast to the somewhat restricted parliament, African constitutions are very generous in definition of the executive power and establish a powerful administration. Third, many African constitutions authorize the central government to intervene in the operation of local government under some circumstances. When the local autonomy has already been significantly neglected, these intervention powers further create strong central governments in Africa.

4.1 Self-Defense Democracy

After the Second World War, in reflection upon the disaster of the Nazi regime, the Basic Law of the Federal Republic of Germany first introduced the theory of self-defense democracy. It stipulates that certain articles and principles of the Basic Law should not be amended, and citizens, associations, and political parties should not jeopardize the basic order of "free democracy" established by the Basic Law, otherwise they will lose their corresponding constitutional rights. Article 20 of the Basic Law further provides that "All Germans shall have the right to resist any person seeking to abolish this constitutional order, if no other remedy is available."[30]

Since its first introduction, the self-defense democracy theory has exerted far-reaching influence on the development of modern constitutions. Endorsing value principles of the international community expressively, African constitutions have widely adopted this theory as well, further revealing their openness in design of the constitutions. Thirty-six[31] (66.7%) African constitutions contain provisions based on the theory self-defense democracy. These provisions include the prohibition of

[30] Two founding judgements on the self-defense democracy theory of German Federal Constitutional Court are BVerfGE 2,1-SRP Urteil, and BVerfGE 5, 85-KPD Urteil.

[31] These 36 countries are Djibouti, Algeria, Morocco, Liberia, Mozambique, Comoros, Benin, the Gambia, Senegal, Cape Verde, Chad, South Sudan, Sierra Leone, Burundi, Ghana, Tanzania, the Democratic Republic of the Congo, Niger, Rwanda, Burkina Faso, Madagascar, Sao Tome and Principe, Guinea, Egypt, Togo, Equatorial Guinea, Somalia, Namibia, the Central African Republic, Cote d'Ivoire, Mali, Mauritania, Guinea-Bissau, the Republic of Congo, Gabon, and Tunisia.

amending certain principles or provisions of the constitution, ban of unconstitutional political parties, and resistance right of the citizens, etc.

Among the prohibitions of amending certain constitutional principles and provisions, the most mentioned three issues are the polity, territorial integrity, and religion. The first one is the polity form of the state. Nineteen[32] African constitutions prohibit the amendment of state's polity. Among them, only the Moroccan constitution prohibits change to its monarchy, and all 18 other constitutions prohibit the change of its republic polity. Fifteen[33] constitutions prohibit amendment to its religious principles which can be further divided into two categories. Algeria, Morocco, Somalia, and Tunisia, these four countries prohibit change to the official and privileged status of Islam. The other 11 countries prohibit any change of the constitutional principle of secular state. Fourteen[34] constitutions prohibit any activities that will jeopardize the territorial integrity of the country. Facing these three kinds of prohibitions, it might be argued that the issues of polity, religion, and territorial integrity are of the primary significance in implementation of the African constitutions.

Other prohibitions to amendments of the constitution concern the fundamental rights, presidential tenure, and democracy principle in organizations of the political parties. Nine[35] African constitutions provide citizens the right to act against unconstitutional organizations and individuals. In five countries (Benin, the Gambia, South Sudan, Ghana, and Togo) it is even a constitutional duty of their citizens to fight against these unconstitutional organizations or individuals.

4.2 Strong Executive

In contrast to the relative short provisions on parliament, the African constitutions lay more emphasis on toward the executive, firstly exposed in their design of the horizontal organization of the central government. Thirty-six[36] (66.7%) African

[32] These 19 countries are Djibouti, Algeria, Benin, Cape Verde, Chad, Madagascar, Sao Tome and Principe, Equatorial Guinea, Cote d'Ivoire, Mali, Guinea-Bissau, the Republic of Congo, Senegal, Gabon, Morocco, the Democratic Republic of the Congo, Niger, Guinea, and Tunisia.

[33] These 15 countries are Algeria, Benin, Cape Verde, Chad, Sao Tome and Principe, Cote d'Ivoire, Mali, Guinea-Bissau, the Republic of Congo, Gabon, Morocco, Niger, Guinea, Tunisia, and Somalia.

[34] These 14 countries are Djibouti, Algeria, Comoros, Benin, Cape Verde, Chad, Burundi, Madagascar, Sao Tome and Principe, Equatorial Guinea, Cote d'Ivoire, Mali, Guinea-Bissau, and the Republic of Congo.

[35] These nine countries are Benin, the Gambia, South Sudan, Ghana, Tanzania, Burkina Faso, Togo, Mali, and the Republic of Congo.

[36] These 36 countries are Algeria, Angola, Benin, Botswana, Burkina Faso, Burundi, Equatorial Guinea, Cape Verde, the Gambia, the Republic of Congo, the Democratic Republic of the Congo, Djibouti, Guinea, Ghana, Gabon, Zimbabwe, Cameroon, Comoros, Cote d'Ivoire, Madagascar, Mali, Mauritius, Mauritania, Mozambique, Namibia, Niger, Sierra Leone, Senegal, Seychelles,

constitutions place chapter on the executive before that of the legislative, i.e., the parliament, awarding the executive the most important status in the state life.

Second, 41[37] (75.9%) African constitutions provide for a president elected directly. In addition, Article 70 of the Ethiopian constitution stipulates that the president is elected by a two-thirds majority of a joint session of the two chambers of the parliament. This supermajority rule creates undoubtedly a strong president as well. Eleven[38] of these 41 constitutions further stipulate that the president can appoint members of the government, including the prime minister (when there is) independently of the parliamentary control, while the parliament has no power to dismiss any government member or force the government to resign.

In addition to these 11 countries, while the constitutions of Togo, Rwanda, and Mali do provide for a parliamentary nonconfidence vote procedure against the government, this vote can only be successful with a two-third majority, which increases the difficulty in demanding the accountability of the government to the parliament. The Zambian constitution stipulates that the parliament can only dismiss appointment decision of the president twice, and by the third time, the president's decision will take effect automatically. There is no nonconfidence procedure in the Zambian constitution either. As a conclusion, one might say that constitutions of these four countries (Togo, Rwanda, Mali, and Zambia) also authorize the president independent position to appoint and remove the government members.

Besides the 41 countries with president directly elected, Swaziland is a monarchy. Its king is entitled to appoint the prime minister from the lower house of the parliament and selects other members of the government from among members of the two chambers of the parliament. During this appointment process, there is no need for the king to obtain consent of the parliament. The lower house of the parliament can only pass a nonconfidence resolution against the government by a two-thirds majority, forcing the government to resign.

Third, the strong executive is not only embodied in the independent appointment power of the president but also in its power independent of the parliamentary control. Twenty-three[39] African constitutions provide for these independent powers of the executive. The most common power is the independent legislative power of the

---

Sao Tome and Principe, Swaziland, Sudan, Tanzania, Zambia, Chad, and the Central African Republic.

[37]These 41 countries are Algeria, Egypt, Benin, Burkina Faso, Burundi, Equatorial Guinea, Togo, Cape Verde, the Gambia, the Republic of the Congo, the Democratic Republic of the Congo, Djibouti, Guinea, Ghana, Gabon, Zimbabwe, Cameroon, Comoros, Côte d'Ivoire, Kenya, Liberia, Madagascar, Malawi, Mali, Mauritania, Mozambique, Namibia, South Sudan, Niger, Nigeria, Sierra Leone, Senegal, Seychelles, Sao Tome and Principe, Sudan, Tanzania, Tunisia, Uganda, Zambia, Chad, and Rwanda.

[38]These 11 countries are Benin, Equatorial Guinea, the Gambia, the Republic of the Congo, Djibouti, Guinea, Zimbabwe, Comoros, Côte d'Ivoire, Malawi, and Mozambique.

[39]These 23 countries are Algeria, Benin, Burkina Faso, Burundi, Equatorial Guinea, Togo, Cape Verde, the Republic of Congo, Guinea, Gabon, Cameroon, Comoros, Cote d'Ivoire, Madagascar, Mali, Mauritania, Morocco, Niger, Senegal, Tunisia, Zambia, Chad, and the Central African Republic.

executive. For instance, Article 125 of Algerian constitution stipulates that "Matters other than those reserved to statutory legislation shall fall within the regulatory power of the President of the Republic." The second most common power is the budgetary power of the executive. In some of these 23 countries, if the parliament is not able to pass the money bill before the deadline prescribed by the constitution, the executive has the authority to issue money bill by its own. The third most common power is the emergency power. For example, Article 93 of the Algerian constitution stipulates that the president may issue a state of emergency order when the state is in certain critical conditions and that such a state of emergency is not subject to the prior or even after approval of the parliament. According to Article 101 of the Beninese constitution, the Council of Ministers may declare a state of siege or emergency. Only when it wants to extend the state of siege or emergency to more than 15 days will it require parliamentary approval, giving the executive the power to act independently within these 15 days. The fourth common power is the power to declare war independently. The constitutions of Algeria, Equatorial Guinea, Congo, Madagascar, Morocco, Niger, and Zambia award the executive this most horrible power.

4.3 Inclination Toward Strong Central Government

Previous discussion reveals the fact that African constitutions are quite slack in terms of the organization of local governments and protection of their autonomy. One example of this slack regulation is reflected in the distribution of financial resources. Thanks to international donation and their rich natural resources which always belong to the central government, the central governments of African countries possess the lion's share in the state income. Under these circumstances the central governments already enjoy a financially dominant position over the local governments. In light of these realities, however, few constitutional guarantees exist for the local governments to receive reliable resources to support its operation.

Further analysis shows that 13[40] (24.1%) of the African constitutions authorize the central government the power to take over the operation of local governments. The justifications for these interventions include the local governments' engagement in unconstitutional activities, violation of the law, dereliction of constitutional duties, jeopardizing the interests of other parts of the country, or falling into a political crisis being unable to maintain their own operation. When the need for intervention emerges, constitutions of eight countries (Ethiopia, Cameroon, Uganda, the Democratic Republic of the Congo, Niger, Mozambique, Namibia, Nigeria) require prior approval of the national parliament, and five constitutions (Guinea-Bissau, Cape Verde, Angola, Kenya, South Africa) stipulate that the executive can decide

[40]These 13 countries are Guinea-Bissau, Ethiopia, Cameroon, Cape Verde, Angola, Uganda, the Democratic Republic of the Congo, Kenya, Niger, Mozambique, Namibia, Nigeria, and South Africa.

alone whether to intervene. Whatever specific procedure defined, it can be argued that the local governments are in almost mere passive positions, basically lacking the opportunity to assert their own objections, at best the relief procedure afterwards. These provisions on strong central government reflect the universal lack of confidence of African constitutions in the local governments' ability to maintain their sound operation or stability.

5 The Binding Force of the Constitution

Strong value inclination, democracy only in formality, and high priority for political stability, all these attitudes reveal further and further a deep constitutional distrust of the political process. Its binding force is then a precondition for a successful regulation. To establish and entrench this binding force, most African constitutions have formally established a well-defined constitutional review system, entitling citizens an extensive and convenient access to constitutional relief. Additionally, African constitutions seem to expect themselves to be able to regulate the country's political life effectively. The constitutional review organs are authorized wide powers to adjudicate upon political disputes. Furthermore, many countries have established special constitutional oversight bodies to promote the implementation of the constitution and to foster a constitutional culture in the society.

5.1 Scope for Constitutional Review

The emphasis on the binding force of the constitution is first manifested in the fact that almost all African countries have established a constitutional review system. As of now, only two countries, Libya and Rwanda, do not establish a constitutional review system in their constitutions. Being a transitional constitution, the Libyan constitution contains only a provisional framework for the transitional government of the country. The future of a constitutional review system in Libya is yet to be decided. Therefore, Rwanda is the only country lacking a constitutional review system.

Among the 52 African countries which have established constitutional review system, only Guinea-Bissau and Ethiopia's constitutions provide that the central parliament is authorized to examine the constitutionality of law and government act. Hence, they establish a so-called legislative review model. Between them, the central parliament of Guinea-Bissau, the National Popular Assembly, is a unicameral institute. Being one of three African countries defining themselves as a federalist state, the Ethiopian national parliament contains two chambers, i.e., the House of Peoples' Representatives and the House of the Federation. The final constitutional review power lies in the House of the Federation. The Ethiopian constitution further establishes a Council of Constitutional Inquiry with 11 members. The president and vice president of the Federal Supreme Court are its ex officio counterparts. The president of the republic appoints six members of the Council under the recommendation of the House of Peoples' Representatives. The last three members are elected among members of the House of the Federation. The Council of Constitutional Inquiry has authority to investigate constitutional disputes by its own decision. When any federal or state law is contested as unconstitutional and such a dispute is submitted by any court or interested party, the Council should first consider the case and submit it further to the House of the Federation for a final decision. In light of these prescriptions, it can be declared that the Ethiopian legislative review model has also mixed certain elements of judicial review.

Thirty-one[41] (57.4%) African countries establish a special constitutional review organ whose titles are divided into two categories: Constitutional Council and Constitutional Court. The constitutions of nine[42] countries define their special constitutional review organ as the "Constitutional Council." Eight of these nine countries, except Mozambique, are former French colonies. Among the 22 states with constitutional courts are former colonies of France, Belgium, Spain, and Britain. Therefore, it is safe to say the constitutional court model has transcended the legal tradition of the diverse African countries, favored by most countries. It is noteworthy that the title does not necessarily determine the authority of the constitutional review organs. When the French Constitutional Council does not accept the direct petition of the citizens, the four African countries (Djibouti, Côte d'Ivoire, Chad, Mozambique) with Constitutional Council provide direct relief to citizens.

In the other 19 African countries without special constitutional review organs, their ordinary courts have the jurisdiction to review constitutional disputes. Taking all these arrangements into consideration, it is safe to say that African constitutions are serious in establishing a judicially enforceable constitution.

5.2 *Scope for Individual Constitutional Petition*

As discussed before, African constitutions are prone to define themselves as the founding document of the social consensus. For example, 21 African constitutions provide that the constitution can be applied directly among individual citizens. In fact, this direct applicability has opened a door for application of constitution in the proceedings of ordinary courts. Average citizens can support their demands with constitutional grounds.

---

[41] These 31 countries are Djibouti, Côte d'Ivoire, Chad, Algeria, Cameroon, Mauritania, Senegal, Mozambique, Burkina Faso, the Republic of Congo, Gabon, Zimbabwe, South Africa, Niger, Sudan, the Central African Republic, Angola, Benin, the Democratic Republic of the Congo, Morocco, Sao Tome and Principe, Somalia, Tunisia, Burundi, Mali, Madagascar, Equatorial Guinea, Guinea, Togo, Comoros, and Egypt.

[42] These nine countries are Djibouti, Côte d'Ivoire, Chad, Algeria, Cameroon, Mauritania, Senegal, Mozambique, and Burkina Faso.

In addition to this universal binding force, 43[43] African constitutions (79.6%) expressly authorize average citizens the right to initiate a constitutional review process, namely, a constitutional petition. Prescriptions on this process can be divided into three categories: (1) if the constitution adopts a decentralized review system that the ordinary courts have the power of constitutional review, the litigating parties in the ordinary proceedings obtain automatically the right to initiate a constitutional petition; (2) if the constitution establishes a model of centralized review system, the litigating parties in ordinary proceedings can dispute the constitutionality of a related law or government act and then require the trial court to submit a request for review to the constitutional review organ; (3) an average citizen may submit petition to the constitutional review organ directly. The latter two models can both exist in some countries.

Whatever the specific procedures, these provisions give the ordinary citizen a very convenient way of constitutional relief, at least formally. Given this formal convenience, it can be argued that African constitutions hope the citizen to be able to take full use of constitutional review system to protect their constitutional rights. The universal binding force of the constitution upon the political and social life of the country will then be established.

Only ten constitutions[44] provide neither their universal binding force nor a constitutional petition procedure for ordinary citizens. Although the Rwandan constitution provides for its universal binding force, it does not establish a constitutional review system of any form. It should be noticed that all these 11 countries are former French, Belgian, and Portuguese colonies. The constitutional review system in these European countries is also in the process of development and refinement. This legal tradition background might have an impact upon their former colonies.

However, among the 43 countries that do establish the constitutional petition procedure are countries from various colonially historical backgrounds. It might be demonstrated that the establishment of a constitutional petition procedure is a quite favored choice by many African constitutions.

5.3 *Constitutional Review and Political Disputes*

Although the constitutional petition procedure provides a formally convenient channel for the relief of the citizens, this channel gives the citizens more a possibility of obtaining relief than a real one. The realization of the relief relies largely on various factors which cannot be generated automatically by introduction of this petition procedure. Furthermore, it is a somewhat ironic fact that when this procedure does

[43] The 11 countries which have not introduced the citizen's petition procedure in their constitutions are Algeria, Cameroon, Mauritania, Senegal, Burkina Faso, Angola, Mali, Guinea-Bissau, Egypt, Libya, and Rwanda.

[44] These ten countries are Algeria, Egypt, Angola, Burkina Faso, Cameroon, Libya, Mali, Mauritania, Guinea-Bissau, and Senegal.

become increasingly active, the constitutional review organ will soon be overwhelmed by the working burden. They will have no choice but to take a variety of measures to screen and shunt appeals, narrowing the width of the relief channel. For instance, the German Federal Constitutional Court might be the most reputed constitutional court of the world. According to its own statistics, however, until the end of 2017, only 2.3% of the constitutional complaints (petition) have been successful.[45]

Facing these difficulties, it should be admitted that preservation and enhancement of a healthy democratic politics might be the best way to fulfill the various constitutional commitments to citizens. Promoting a healthy background, a constitutional democracy needs a competent authority to adjudicate over political disputes, based on the spirit and requirements of the constitution. Only then could it be guaranteed that the country's political life is moving toward the aim and objective of the constitution effectively. In terms of this effectiveness, the role of constitutional review organ as the political dispute adjudicator is more meaningful than that of the accepting organ of the citizen's constitutional petition. The same reflection existed in the establishment process of the German Federal Constitutional Court. In the first version of the Basic Law, the Federal Constitutional Court was given the power to judge over political dispute while lacking the power to rule over the constitutional complaints of the citizens. It might be argued that in the eyes of the constitutors of the Basic Law, the former power was more critical than the latter one.

In addition, as has been discussed before, the strong value inclination of African constitutions is embodied not only in their firm commitment to protect the constitutional rights of citizens but also in the detailed prescriptions on the development objectives of the country. With the aim to ensure that the political life of the country runs along the constitutional route, the African constitutions have a strong impetus to establish a constitution review system that can resolve political disputes in accordance with spirit and principles of the constitution.

Perhaps just based on these considerations, 38[46] (70.4%) African constitutions confer on their constitutional review organ the power to resolve political disputes, particularly in terms of constitutional relief to minorities in the political process, such as the minority group in the parliament. Moreover, many constitutional review organs have a broad jurisdiction over political disputes, especially in the francophone African countries. For instance, in these countries, the organizational laws

---

[45] "Federal Constitutional Court - Annual Statistics 2017", http://www.bundesverfassungsgericht.de/SharedDocs/Downloads/EN/Statistik/statistics_2017.pdf?__blob=publicationFile&v=4, 2018-05-10 last visited.

[46] These 38 countries are Algeria, Egypt, Angola, Benin, Burkina Faso, Burundi, Equatorial Guinea, Togo, Cape Verde, the Republic of Congo, the Democratic Republic of the Congo, Djibouti, Guinea, Guinea-Bissau, Gabon, Zimbabwe, Cameroon, Comoros, Cote d'Ivoire, Madagascar, Mali, Mauritania, Morocco, Mozambique, Namibia, South Africa, South Sudan, Niger, Senegal, Seychelles, Sao Tome and Principe, Sudan, Somalia, Tanzania, Tunisia, Zambia, Chad, and the Central African Republic.

and parliamentary rules of procedure must first be reviewed by the constitutional review organs on its constitutionality before promulgation.

Beside these 38 countries, Article 181 of the Egyptian constitution stipulates that any dispute over the jurisdiction of the local councils is settled by the governorate-level local council. Disputes over the jurisdiction of province-level local councils are handled by the General Assembly of the Legal Opinion and Legislation Departments of the State Council. Although it is far from a judicial procedure, it still could be treated as a mechanism of resolving political disputes.

However, it is noteworthy that these provisions pay much more attention to problems rising on the central government level. Local governments are seldom entitled the right to file a petition. Only 11[47] African constitutions recognize explicitly the local governments' right to appeal to the constitutional review organ when they find their rights were infringed. This fact might attest again the little weight laid by the African constitutions to the protection of local autonomy.

5.4 *Other Constitutional Oversight Bodies*

A shortcoming of the constitutional review system lies in that it can provide basically reliefs or resolutions afterwards. A fundamental aim of the African constitutions is to ensure the political life of the country to operate according to the principle and spirit of the constitution. A consequent expectation is that all parties involved in the political process consciously abide by and hold the constitution. Furthermore, most African constitutions show a strong value inclination and provide for civil duties to obey the constitution. All these facts might reveal a deeper constitutional purpose to foster a constitutional culture in the society.

Although via continual judgments with well-explained reasons, the constitutional review organ can educate the people on the spirits of the constitution. But this case-by-case education process is certainly very long. When most African countries are still underdeveloped countries, politically and economically, they cannot afford this high cost of sluggish improvement. As a result, a more active mechanism is needed to propel an efficient enforcement of the constitution, and hence a rapid transformation of the state and social life of the country into the expected model set in the constitution.

Perhaps just based on these considerations, 24[48] (44.4%) African constitutions further provide for special constitutional oversight bodies. These constitutions tend to authorize these organs the mandate to support democratic development, to

[47] These 11 countries are Egypt, the Democratic Republic of the Congo, Cameroon, Comoros, Madagascar, South Africa, South Sudan, Sao Tome and Principe, Sudan, Somalia, and Tanzania.

[48] These 24 countries are the Democratic Republic of the Congo, South Africa, Tanzania, Kenya, the Republic of Congo, Zimbabwe, Zambia, Malawi, Ghana, Mauritania, Madagascar, Uganda, Niger, Somalia, Burundi, the Gambia, Swaziland, Morocco, Togo, Guinea, South Sudan, Sudan, Rwanda, and Tunisia.

promote the implementation of the constitution, and to foster a constitutional culture. Given the significant influence of European constitutions on their African counterparts, institutions like the Ombudsman (or public protector in many African countries) might not be labeled as a design of African feature. The African characteristic lies more in the organs with special missions in enforcement of the constitution.

The most favored institute is the "Human Rights Commission," which was established by 19[49] countries. It might be revealed that African constitutions were aware of the realities that African countries still have a long way to go in terms protection and promotion of the human right. To distinguish it from the constitutional review organ which accepts the citizen's petition and makes binding judicial judgment, the human rights commissions normally do not have any power to make a legally binding decision. Its main role is to investigate cases violating human right, to issue corresponding reports, and to transmit factual reports of these cases to competent government authorities for appropriate relief. It might be concluded that the human right commission is more a political supervision institute rather than a legally administrative organ.[50] A full realization of the function of the human rights commission still depends on a healthy political and social culture respecting the promotion and protection of human rights.

Besides the human rights commission, in certain countries with history of severe racial conflicts or even genocide, their constitutions further establish institutions to promote unity and reconciliation of the country, such as Somalia (Truth and Reconciliation Commission), Burundi (the National Council for National Unity and Reconciliation, the National Observatory for the Prevention and the Eradication of Genocide, of War Crimes and of Crimes Against Humanity), and Rwanda (National Unity and Reconciliation Commission, National Commission for the Fight against Genocide).

6 Conclusion

Only a textual analysis of African constitutions has already provided us plenty of valuable clues. All these clues point to a combination of a high ambition and a sober assessment of the realities in the African constitutions.

[49] These 19 countries are South Africa, Tanzania, Kenya, the Republic of the Congo, Zimbabwe, Zambia, Malawi, Mauritania, Uganda, Niger, Somalia, Swaziland, Morocco, Togo, Guinea, South Sudan, Sudan, Rwanda, and Tunisia.

[50] For instance, as defined in Article 184 of the South Africa Constitution, the functions of South African Human Rights Commission are to promote respect for human rights and a culture of human rights, to promote the protection, development, and attainment of human rights, and to monitor and assess the observance of human rights in the Republic. Its activities mainly include to investigate and to report on the observance of human rights, to secure appropriate redress where human rights have been violated, to carry out research, and to educate. Concerning the second generation of rights, the relevant organs of state are required to provide annual report to the Commission toward the realization of these rights.

As has been shown, African constitutions are quite open-minded and internationally oriented, attested in their acceptance of the binding force of international documents and the adoption of the self-defense institutions. These efforts cast the African constitutions a modern appearance. Meanwhile, given the serious underdevelopment of their countries, African constitutions also show a deep distrust in the political qualities of the citizens and the political process of their countries. Just out of this sharp contrast between the ambition and realities, African constitutions sometimes show a contradictory strategy: while striving for a noble commitment to the political and social development of the country, they only allow a formal democratization of the political life and highlight the political stability at cost of other democratic values, say, the local autonomy.

Transformation of the beautiful words written into the real practices of the country relies on a successful implementation. This implementation depends heavily on a steady will and force adhering to the words and spirit of the constitution. This transformation is also a process of educating the citizens and reforming the political structure of the country. During this process, the African governments, especially the central government, will play a deciding role. Owing to the serious underdevelopment of the African countries, the financial resources of the African countries always fail the developing will of the country. Private sectors can seldomly be counted on to invest in the development. The governments, especially the central governments, possess the largest share of the financial resources of the country, let alone their monopoly of the coercion. Accordingly, the African constitutions always contain detailed social and economic rights and set specific goals for the development of the country. All these prescriptions are targeted naturally at the governments.

The government, however, is only an organizational shell of the political power. Under the African context, it is a question of more significance that which actors behave behind this shell. It is expected that these real actors are the social groups, classes, etc., which possess the most influence in the state and social life of the country. The will of the government to adhere to and to implement the constitution relies largely on the thought and attitude of these real masters of the country. Literally, the indifference of these actors of decisive influence toward the constitution and constitutionalism gives rise to the slackness of the government. The constitution itself, as in any country, cannot bring out these friendly will and attitudes automictically when they are enacted.

Consequently, besides the moral and ethnic arguments, impetus of real interests is needed to propel the relevant actors to adhere to the constitution. If the constitution is to be implemented faithfully, its institutional framework need to provide a platform on which interests of the relevant actors can be pursued. Benefitting from this framework, these key actors would contribute to entrenchment of the framework, and a positive feedback circle would then be created. In fact, existence of this positive feedback is the key to a successful implementation of a constitution. It is also where the severest difficulty lies.

Some African constitutions, such as that of the South Africa, were once blessed. During their enactment process and early history, they did an optimal compromise of all relevant parties, and a positive feedback circle did exist. But with the shifting of the social and political background, the former compromise could increasingly lose its attractiveness, at least to some relevant actors. Some actors might regard the once favorable institutional framework to be unacceptable and hence would deviate from it, gradually or abruptly. When this deviation occurs, constitutional review systems cannot always prevent it. The deviating motives come ultimately from the changed background. If the constitution could not cope with this change effectively, it is only a matter of time that the constitution will retreat back onto paper, being a constitution without constitutionalism again. Many failures of this kind have happened before, both in and outside Africa. There will be other occurrences in the future.

To prevent this failure, African constitutions have spared no effort to establish many precautious measures, such as highlight of the binding force of the constitution, introduction of the self-defense democracy theory, and establishment of various oversight institutes, etc. All these measures, however, are mere formal mechanisms. To a large extent, the expected political stability and strong central government in the African constitutions are yet to be realized in the practices of African politics. The coups d'etat in the last couple of years in central Africa are a vivid evidence of the failed design of these African constitutions.

The more important issue is how to establish a friendly background situation which could cultivate a solid respect for the arrangement of the constitution. The constitution itself is advised to possess the evolving ability to handle ever-emerging new challenges. A good answer to this question is far more important than that to how to enact a once ideal constitution. Few clues can be found from the beautiful words of the constitution or theories to the good answer. In this regard, a constitution is always a constitution on paper, which is no unique problem belonging to Africa.

MIX
Papier aus verantwortungsvollen Quellen
Paper from responsible sources
FSC® C105338

If you have any concerns about our products,
you can contact us on
ProductSafety@springernature.com

In case Publisher is established outside the EU,
the EU authorized representative is:
Springer Nature Customer Service Center GmbH
Europaplatz 3, 69115 Heidelberg, Germany

Printed by Libri Plureos GmbH
in Hamburg, Germany